Memory Politics and Transitional Justice

The interdisciplinary fields of Memory Studies and Transitional Justice have largely developed in parallel to one another despite both focusing on efforts of societies to confront and (re—)appropriate their past. While scholars working on memory have come mostly from historical, literary, sociological, or anthropological traditions, transitional justice has attracted primarily scholarship from political science and the law. This series bridges this divide: it promotes work that combines a deep understanding of the contexts that have allowed for injustice to occur with an analysis of how legacies of such injustice in political and historical memory influence contemporary projects of redress, acknowledgment, or new cycles of denial. The titles in the series are of interest not only to academics and students but also practitioners in the related fields.

The Memory Politics and Transitional Justice series promotes critical dialogue among different theoretical and methodological approaches and among scholarship on different regions. The editors welcome submissions from a variety of disciplines—including political science, history, sociology, anthropology, and cultural studies—that confront critical questions at the intersection of memory politics and transitional justice in national, comparative, and global perspective.

This series is indexed in Scopus.

Memory Politics and Transitional Justice Book Series (Palgrave)
Co-editors: Jasna Dragovic-Soso (Goldsmiths, University of London), Jelena Subotic (Georgia State University), Tsveta Petrova (Columbia University)

More information about this series at
http://www.palgrave.com/gp/series/14807

Hugo Rojas • Miriam Shaftoe

Human Rights and Transitional Justice in Chile

palgrave
macmillan

Hugo Rojas
Alberto Hurtado University
Santiago, Chile

Miriam Shaftoe
University of Ottawa
Ottawa, ON, Canada

ISSN 2731-3840 ISSN 2731-3859 (electronic)
Memory Politics and Transitional Justice
ISBN 978-3-030-81181-5 ISBN 978-3-030-81182-2 (eBook)
https://doi.org/10.1007/978-3-030-81182-2

Cover illustration. Photo courtesy of Luis Lobos Robles, 2019

This Palgrave Macmillan imprint is published by the registered company Springer Nature Switzerland AG.
The registered company address is: Gewerbestrasse 11, 6330 Cham, Switzerland

Preface

Chile peacefully regained its democracy in 1990, after 17 years of Augusto Pinochet's brutal military dictatorship. Thirty years of stability and seven democratic governments later, many Chileans were convinced that the legacy of the dictatorship had been dealt with and the country had overcome its history of human rights violations.

Presidents since Chile's return to democracy have committed to the declaration *Nunca Más:* Never again will the state commit human rights abuses against its people. Yet, on October 18, 2019, when massive social unrest erupted in Santiago, the government reacted with an almost instinctive return to repressive tendencies. In response to the protests, President Sebastián Piñera declared a state of emergency, imposed a curfew, and deployed the military on the streets within less than 24 hours. In the following weeks and months, Chileans were faced with a level of state violence that had not been seen since the years of the dictatorship. Between October 2019 and March 2020, 8827 citizens filed charges for human rights violations (Matus, 2020), including 388 cases of sexual violence and 413 cases of eye loss. In the first few months of protests, prosecutors investigated 466 state agents, of whom 90% are police. The government has faced criticism for its lack of transparency regarding the alleged abuses and for its slow investigation of claims of human rights violations.

How did we get here? The economic injustices at the core of the protest movement and the widespread state violence in response to the demonstrations are partly rooted in the institutional legacy of the dictatorship. The country's current neoliberal economic model and constitution were imposed under Pinochet and this has resulted in the privatization of social services like healthcare and education. This has generated significant inequality and economic precarity for many Chileans. Since the return to democracy, the governing elites have failed to respond to citizens' demands to reform the economic model and replace the Constitution. The growing sense of injustice, frustration, and political disillusionment within the population ultimately reached a boiling point when citizens took to the streets on 2019.

However, these recent events have also highlighted some of the progress that has been made over the years to create sustainable systems of human rights protection. Chilean civil society activists and human rights experts reacted swiftly during the crisis to prevent human rights violations from continuing and to demand accountability. The National Institute of Human Rights (INDH), an independent state-funded institution, has become a powerful human rights observer, promoter, and defender. Protesters were able to register and report state violence much more rapidly than in the past, and many of the abuses committed during the recent unrest are currently being investigated by the INDH, prosecutors, and courts. As of July 2020, the INDH had filed 2066 criminal complaints in the context of the social crisis, 77.5% of which correspond to acts of torture and inhuman or degrading treatment. Meanwhile, the government has filed legal actions against 3274 civilians in relation to the protests, for crimes such as public disorder (18.6%), fires (4.9%), and attacks on members of the police and armed forces (3.6%) (Weibel, 2020).

The concept of *Never Again* is taking on renewed force in Chile while new generations of human rights advocates recognize that accounts with the past have not been fully settled. The recent social insurrection and violence revealed to Chileans the fragility of their institutions, and the sustained protest movement has provided an opportunity to finally address some of the dictatorship's lasting institutional legacies and renew the social contract. As an escape valve against social pressure, on October 25, 2020, a plebiscite took place in which Chileans voted in favor of the creation of a new Constitution, to be developed through a constituent assembly whose members were elected in May 2021. This dynamic political context provides an important occasion to reflect on the lessons the Chilean experience of transitional justice offers about the process of transitioning from a violent dictatorship toward a fully realized democracy.

Thirty years after the return to democracy, this book seeks to look back and offer a comprehensive overview of the achievements and challenges of the Chilean transitional justice process. Chapter 1 provides an introductory overview of the concepts of human rights and transitional justice. Chapter 2 contextualizes the human rights violations in Chile during the dictatorship, by providing the necessary historical background from the 1960s to the present. The following chapters explain the initiatives that have been developed in Chile to uncover the truth about what happened during the dictatorship (Chap. 3), how the state and society have partially repaired the deep wounds of victims of state terrorism (Chap. 4), how Chilean society remembers and commemorates its stormy past (Chap. 5), and what progress has been made in the justice system to allow the punishment of some of those responsible (Chap. 6). Finally, in Chap. 7, we explore the guarantees of non-repetition that have been adopted.

Alberto Hurtado University
Santiago, Chile
Hugo Rojas

University of Ottawa
Ottawa, ON, Canada
Miriam Shaftoe

References

Matus, J. (2020, July 18). Fiscalía cifra en 8.827 las víctimas de violencia institucional en la crisis. *La Tercera*, p. 19.

Weibel, M. (2020, July 15). Balance penal del estallido: Fiscalía investiga a 466 agentes del Estado y gobierno acusa a 3.274 personas de cometer actos violentos. *Ciper Chile*, available at https://ciperchile.cl/2020/07/15/balance-penal-del-estallido-fiscalia-investiga-a-466-agentes-del-estado-y-gobierno-acusa-a-3-274-personas-de-cometer-actos-violentos/?fbclid=IwAR0w8pMGZp3F7AMPtTPdnBli1TPnnj0uQ4sWuE3sQDZ20XPHC3NzAT8sxAI

Acknowledgments

During the second semester of 2019, while discussing the previous drafts of the different chapters of this book on how Chilean society had been confronting the gross and systematic human rights violations committed during Pinochet's dictatorship, we were witness to Chile reliving an experience of state violence it had thought had been overcome. Our reflections about how the past is understood in the present were transformed. Our focus moved to what was happening in an extremely violent present and its undeniable links to the issues we had been discussing.

Conversations with our colleagues and friends have been deeply meaningful to the beginning of this book, and its pages reflect that it has been the result of a collaborative, interdisciplinary, and transnational effort. We particularly appreciate the contributions of Alan Angell, Macarena Bonhomme, Silvia Borzutzky, Simón Escoffier, María Angélica Garrido, Elizabeth Lira, Brian Loveman, Tomás Pascual, and Leigh A. Payne. We also thank Christine Cervenak, Denis Galligan, Solimar García, Pumla Gobodo-Madikizela, Valentina Infante, Jeff Kelly Lowenstein, María Belén Lagos, Mariana Lagos, Elena Maffioletti, Soledad Matus, Juan René Maureira, Florencia Olivares, Darío Páez, and Camila Villegas for the suggestions they made to the previous drafts.

We take this opportunity to thank the Millennium Institute on Violence and Democracy for funding this work (ANID, Millennium Science Initiative, ICS2019_025). We are also thankful of the stimulating discussions with academics and researchers of the Catholic University of Chile,

Alberto Hurtado University, the University of Oxford Latin American Centre, Wolfson College, and the University of Ottawa, and discussions with students from different nationalities that attended the course "Human Rights and Transitional Justice" at the Pontifical Catholic University of Chile Institute of Political Science (2019), and the program "Human Rights and Cultural Memory" at the University of California Education Abroad Program and Alberto Hurtado University (2019).

This book offers a panoramic vision of transitional justice in Chile that emanates from experiences directly in the field, from the perspectives of both policy-making and academic research. In the conversations between the authors, many discussions emerged from Hugo Rojas' academic trajectory and public commitment to the promotion of the rule of law and human rights in Chile. His experiences as an advisor to the first government of Michelle Bachelet and the Commission on Political Imprisonment and Torture contributed directly to the reflections that are shared in this manuscript. Preliminary versions of the different sections were discussed with friends and colleagues at the University of Notre Dame Center for Civil and Human Rights, the Foundation for Law, Justice and Society, University of the Free State, California Western School of Law, Adolfo Ibáñez University School of Government, University of Oxford (Department of Sociology, Latin American Centre, Oxford Transitional Justice Research, and Wolfson College), Loyola University Chicago School of Law, Simón Bolívar University, Columbia College Chicago, Latina and Latino Critical Legal Theory, Inter American University of Puerto Rico, Ibero-American University of Mexico, and Alberto Hurtado University.

A much shorter version of Chap. 1 of this text appears as a chapter with the title "El tránsito de la justicia transicional" in the book *Pasados Contemporáneos. Acercamientos interdisciplinarios a los derechos humanos y las memorias en Perú y América Latina*, edited by Lucero de Vivanco and María Teresa Johansson (Madrid & Frankfurt: Editorial Iberoamericana/Vervuert 2019). We thank the editors and the publisher of that volume for their permission to expand on those ideas. The editors of *California Western International Law Journal* gave their permission to reproduce some of the ideas presented in "Torture in Chile (1973–1990): Analysis of One Hundred Survivors' Testimonies". Chapter 2 constitutes an updated version of the historical chapter of Hugo Rojas' doctoral thesis entitled *Indifference to Past Human Rights Violations in Chile: The Impact on Transitional Justice Success (1990–2017)*, supervised by Leigh A. Payne and defended at the University of Oxford. This monograph was started in parallel to that doctoral thesis, but it required numerous conversations and prolonged additional research sessions that we held in Chile and online. The Palgrave Macmillan editors and anonymous reviewers not only trusted this project but also made valuable recommendations. We thank Luis Lobos Robles for permitting us to use one of his photos on our book cover. Finally, this book is dedicated to the people who generously collaborated in the different stages, and especially to our families and close friends.

Santiago and Ottawa, 2021

Praise for *Human Rights and Transitional Justice in Chile*

"Hugo Rojas and Miriam Shaftoe's analysis of the human rights abuses of the Pinochet dictatorship and the transitional justice policies that have been implemented in Chile, in the past thirty years, sheds light on both the successes and failures of these policies and their implications for Chilean politics and society. By connecting the evolution of human rights to the power of Chile's multiple political actors, the authors are able to provide an in-depth and detailed analysis of both the policies and the forces behind those policies. This book is essential to understand not only the human rights abuses of the Pinochet dictatorship and the policies that followed, but also the difficulties in achieving any substantial policy changes and success in a divided society."

—Silvia Borzutzky, Professor of Political Science at *Carnegie Mellon University*

Contents

1 Human Rights and Transitional Justice 1
1.1 The Essentials of Human Rights 2
1.2 The Elements of Transitional Justice 9
Bibliography 24

2 Chilean Recent History 29
2.1 Characteristics of Chilean Society Pre-Coup 30
2.2 Revolution in Liberty 33
2.3 Popular Unity 35
2.4 Pinochet's Dictatorship 39
2.5 Democratic Transition 47
Bibliography 58

3 Searching for the Truth 65
3.1 Hidden Truth: Censorship 66
3.2 What Is a TRC? 69
3.3 The Rettig Commission 71
3.4 The Mesa de Diálogo 76
3.5 The Valech Commission 77
3.6 Torture Victims' Testimonies 83
3.7 Conclusion 86
Bibliography 87

4 Reparations for the Victims 91
4.1 Laying the Foundations of a Comprehensive Reparations Framework 94
4.2 Evaluation of Chilean Reparations Policy 104
Bibliography 108

5 Memorializing and Commemorating 111
5.1 Collective Memory in Chile: Multiple Conflicting Narratives 113
5.2 Sites of Memory 117
5.3 Counter-Memory 125
5.4 Media, Culture, and Memory 127
5.5 Pedagogy of Memory 129
5.6 Conclusion 132
Bibliography 133

6 Investigating and Condemning the Perpetrators 137
6.1 Justice Under the Dictatorship 139
6.2 Early Transition 141
6.3 Pinochet in London 144
6.4 Key Human Rights Cases in Chile 148
6.5 Lessons from the Chilean Experience of Justice 150
Bibliography 152

7 "Never Again" and Guarantees of Non-repetition 155
7.1 Strengthening of Public Institutions 156
7.2 Reform of the Economic Model and the "Subsidiary State" 162
7.3 Dismantling of Armed Groups 164
7.4 Vetting 166
7.5 Toward a Culture of Respect of Human Rights 168
Bibliography 172

Final Remarks 175

Bibliography 183

Index 203

About the Authors

Hugo Rojas is Professor of Sociology of Law and Human Rights at Alberto Hurtado University School of Law and Researcher at the Millennium Institute on Violence and Democracy. M.Sc. in Law, Anthropology and Society from the London School of Economics, and D.Phil. in Sociology from the University of Oxford.

Miriam Shaftoe is Research Assistant at Alberto Hurtado University School of Law. She studied Social Sciences in Conflict Studies and Human Rights at the University of Ottawa.

Abbreviations

ANEF	National Association of Public Employees
AFDD	Group of Families of Disappeared Detainees
CGR	The Office of Comptroller General of the Republic
CIA	Central Intelligence Agency
CNI	National Information Center
CODEPU	Committee for the Defense of People's Rights
DC	Christian Democratic Party
DINA	National Intelligence Directorate
DINACOS	National Division of Social Communication
ECHR	European Court of Human Rights
ECLAC	Economic Commission for Latin America and the Caribbean
FASIC	Social Aid Foundation of Christian Churches
FPMR	Manuel Rodríguez Patriotic Front
FPMR-A	Autonomous Manuel Rodríguez Patriotic Front
FUNDASALVA	Anti-Drug Foundation of El Salvador
IACHR	Inter-American Commission on Human Rights
IACtHR	Inter-American Court of Human Rights
IC	Christian Left Party
ICC	International Criminal Court
ICCPR	International Covenant on Civil and Political Rights
ICESCR	International Covenant on Economic, Social and Cultural Rights
ICTJ	International Center for Transitional Justice
ILO	International Labour Organization
INDH	National Institute of Human Rights
IPPDH	Institute of Public Policy on Human Rights

MAPU	Unitary Popular Action Movement MAPU-Lautaro Lautaro Unitary Popular Action Movement
MIR	Movement of the Revolutionary Left
MMHR	Museum of Memory and Human Rights
OECD	Organization for Economic Co-operation and Development
OHCHR	Office of the United Nations High Commissioner for Human Rights
PC	Communist Party
PDI	Investigative Police
PRAIS	Programme of Reparations and Comprehensive Healthcare for Victims
PS	Socialist Party
TRC	Truth and Reconciliation Commission (Rettig Commission)
UDHR	Universal Declaration of Human Rights
UN	United Nations
UNESCO	United Nations Educational, Scientific and Cultural Organization
UP	Unidad Popular (Popular Unity)
US	United States of America
USSR	Union of Soviet Socialist Republics

List of Graphs

Graph 7.1	Questions on human rights in the 2013 Bicentennial Survey (*N:* 2014. Source: Rojas (2017), based on the Bicentennial Survey)	169
Graph 7.2	How to deal with the problem of Human Rights in Chile (%) (Source: Rojas (2011), based on UNDP et al. 2010)	170
Graph 7.3	Justice to the extent possible (%). (Source: CEP 1999)	170
Graph 7.4	How democratic is Chile? (on a scale from 1 to 10) (Source: Rojas (2011), based on the UNDP et al. 2008 and 2010 surveys)	171

CHAPTER 1

Human Rights and Transitional Justice

While societies have long grappled with how to navigate political transitions and recover from atrocities, the study of this topic as we know it today began to consolidate into an interdisciplinary field of academic study under the umbrella of "transitional justice" in the late 1980s and 1990s. Chile was among the Latin American, African, and post-Soviet bloc countries whose experiences navigating massive human rights violations and political transitions from violent authoritarian regimes at the end of the Cold War shaped the field of transitional justice (Teitel, 2003; Kritz, 1995). Dealing with the atrocities committed during the Pinochet dictatorship has been a long and contested process in Chile. As we will detail throughout this book, numerous transitional justice measures have been implemented in Chile, including significant achievements such as two separate truth commissions, a wide-ranging reparations program, the establishment of numerous sites of memory, persecution of perpetrators through the erosion of blanket amnesties, and the establishment of new human rights institutions. Yet the Chilean experience of transitional justice has also been marked by exclusions, and sometimes reversals in its course. Progress has been propelled by contestations and innovations from diverse local, national, and international actors, and human rights issues left unaddressed have periodically resurfaced with intensity. Due to this long, complex trajectory, the Chilean case is one of the most debated and discussed in transitional justice literature.

H. Rojas, M. Shaftoe, *Human Rights and Transitional Justice in Chile*, Memory Politics and Transitional Justice,
https://doi.org/10.1007/978-3-030-81182-2_1

In order to familiarize the unfamiliar reader and situate Chile's experience recovering from massive human rights abuses committed during a violent authoritarian regime, this chapter will seek to provide a brief discussion of the theoretical foundations and core theoretical debates surrounding the concepts of human rights and transitional justice.

1.1 The Essentials of Human Rights

The idea that all humans must be treated with dignity and respect has a universal resonance that has allowed it to spread widely, to such an extent that the concept of human rights has become omnipresent in today's day and age (Squella, 2019: 12). Human rights are the rights we have simply because we exist as human beings, and which are inherent to every person, regardless of race, sex, nationality, ethnicity, language, religion, or any other status (United Nations, 2021). These rights have now become a universally espoused and legally enforceable set of norms, values, and principles. Due to the work of local and international civil society activism as well as intergovernmental negotiations and cooperation, a system of international human rights protection has been developed to seek to ensure the respect and enforcement of these principles. Human rights have been incorporated into legal systems, both national, regional, and international, and have evolved and expanded significantly over the years, increasing in acceptance, complexity, and scope. In part, this broad acceptance of human rights across cultural and political boundaries is due to their flexibility and usefulness as political tools; while human rights rhetoric can be invoked by vulnerable actors in their struggle against oppression, it can also be operationalized by powerful actors seeking to maintain the status quo.

The influence and spread of human rights have made them an important, interdisciplinary subject of study. Human rights can be analyzed from at least three different but complementary dimensions:

1. The philosophical or axiological perspective analyzes the philosophical and moral foundations of human rights standards, as well as how these standards relate to values that are relevant to a society, for example, justice, equality, and liberty. This dimension seeks to answer questions such as: What is the basis of human rights? Why should we respect them? Which rights are human rights? Can human rights truly be universal?

2. The sociology of human rights focuses on the empirical dimension of human rights, analyzing what happens in real life in relation to the promotion, validity, protection, and defense of human rights in action and how they are understood and used in society. This dimension is focused on the question, how do human rights work?
3. The juridical, legal perspective analyzes the normative dimension of human rights, that is, the enshrining of human rights as set of norms in national and international legal systems. This dimension focuses on how best to guarantee the application and enforcement of human rights through the lens of the law.

In this section, we will have an overview of the origins, and the theoretical foundation of the concept of human rights, as well as the basics of the international system of human rights protection.

Origins of Human Rights

The notion of human rights has a winding and contingent history. In Western traditions, early conceptions of what we now understand as human rights emerged centuries ago in the ideas of theologians such as Saint Thomas of Aquinas and Francisco de Vitoria in the Middle Ages, who developed theological-legal theories arguing that every person was entitled to a set of God-given rights. These theories formed a normative-natural body called Natural Law (*Ius Naturale*). In the Modern Age, authors such as Hugo Grotius, Samuel Pufendorf, and John Locke argued that these natural rights to which every person was entitled could be understood and justified through reason, without belief in God and religious morals. Whether justified by God or by reason, the concept of natural law is based on the moral argument that all human beings have the same right to be treated with dignity. The core of this idea is what makes it so powerful and attractive: that we hold these rights as *human beings* rather than as citizens or by virtue of any other type of status.

The concept of inalienable natural rights went on to inspire some of the earliest projects to protect the civil and political rights of subjects and citizens, such as the English Bill of Rights (1688), the French Declaration of the Rights of the Man and the Citizen (1789), and the American Bill of Rights (1791). These early rights documents were focused on national protection of rights and were intrinsically tied to state sovereignty; rights movements in this era were "struggles over the form of the nation-state and the meaning of citizenship within it" (Moyn, 2010: 32). Yet, the idea that rights can actually *transcend* state sovereignty, which forms the basis of our current system of international human rights, is far more recent (Sikkink, 2017). The American Declaration of the Rights and Duties of Man (1948) and the Universal Declaration of Human Rights (1948) were the first international efforts to standardize and protect a broad set of human rights. These initiatives solidified our contemporary understanding of human rights as deserving of international promotion and protection if a state fails to protect them (Sikkink, 2017). While we often turn to domestic law and justice systems when we seek to enshrine and enforce our rights, the law is a regulatory system that can be coerced. There are numerous examples of regimes using the law to repress certain sectors of their population and deprive them of their fundamental rights, for instance, Apartheid in South Africa, Jim Crow Laws in the United States, or the Nazi regime. The strength of human rights thus lies in that they are moral claims to justice, which transcend legal rights, and can be claimed regardless of whether they are recognized within the national legal system (Nash, 2015: 5).

The origins of human rights have been a central aspect to the debate of cultural relativism, as the connections between Western philosophical tradition and modern notions of human rights have led some critical human rights scholars to cast doubt on the supposedly "universal" nature of human rights. Among these scholars, Mutua argues human rights are a Eurocentric, colonial project out of touch and incompatible with the cultural fabric of non-Western societies. He contends that current conceptions of rights retrench the Western savior complex and suggests the need for a new universal platform based on a more multicultural set of values (2001). Yet, other authors have argued that this vision of the origins of human rights underrepresents the diversity of non-Western political thought and erases the contributions of non-Western states in building the modern human rights project. Amartya Sen, for instance, emphasizes the importance of recognizing the diversity of political thought in all cultures and argues antecedents to modern concepts of rights and freedoms can be found in both Western and non-Western philosophical traditions (1997).

Historians of human rights have also challenged the view which presents the Universal Declaration of Human Rights (UDHR) as having been largely sponsored and promoted by the West. Susan Waltz demonstrates that the role of large Western states in developing the text has been over-exaggerated, as the US, USSR, and Britain in fact removed all but one mention of human rights in their initial proposal to the Charter Meeting of the United Nations. Simultaneously, substantial contributions to the UDHR by smaller and non-Western states, for instance, the instrumental role of India and the Dominican Republic in removing gender bias from the text of the UDHR, have been overlooked (2002). These debates around the origins of human rights center the importance of ensuring a sense of collective ownership over the concept of human rights.

Theoretical Foundations

Human rights communicate claims of moral force, and since their earliest conceptualizations, they have been used as a tool or device to challenge injustice and oppression. Human rights are value judgments, which assert what *ought* to be as a result of human choice (Macdonald, 1947). Human rights thus have no settled meaning and are shaped by human decisions and actions through law, precedent, and use. The basis and strength of human rights, therefore, lie in the fact that they are socially constructed ideas whose meaning is derived from the social and historical context in which they are discussed or invoked. In practice, this dynamic nature allows them to have a tangible effect in generating social change. Human rights can be simultaneously specific and local, and global and universal (Nash, 2015: 8): they are invoked at a grassroots level to address specific, local problems, and in doing so, they draw on international law and globally pervasive norms to support and reinforce their local calls for justice.

For example, torture survivors in Chile were excluded from truth and reparation policies for many years. Human rights activists and survivors organized grassroots campaigns, drawing attention to Chile's commitments under international treaties such as the right to fair and adequate compensation for victims in the Convention against Torture and Other Cruel, Inhuman or Degrading Treatment or Punishment—ratified by Chile in 1988. In doing so, activists succeeded in pressuring the government to create a broader human rights policy, including reparations for torture survivors and a second truth commission (Lira, 2006: 91). Thus, the power of human rights lies partly in their contradictions; they are simultaneously adaptable to local contexts, and universal under international law.

It is important to recognize that the discourse of human rights can also be operationalized by powerful actors to maintain and "stabilize a profoundly unjust, undemocratic, and, ultimately, illiberal global social order"

(Rensmann, 2017: 632). States have used the language of human rights to conceal the inequalities and discrimination in policies and to push illegitimate military interventions such as in the notorious American invasion of Iraq in 2003 (Kurth, 2005). Progressive scholars have pointed out the importance of engaging critically with social systems and structures that generate inequalities and injustices when theorizing about human rights, such as the exclusions generated through the concepts of state sovereignty and citizenship (Benhabib, 2004), or the injustices of hegemonic colonialism and globalization (Mendieta, 2007). Still others like Samuel Moyn explore the relationship between capitalism, inequality, and human rights, arguing that by advocating only for material sufficiency, human rights politics have failed to effectively confront the material injustices and inequalities generated by neoliberalism (2018). Ultimately, these perspectives advocate for a more critical understanding of how human rights work, and the context in which they are situated.

International System of Human Rights Protection

The basis of the international system of human rights protection is the International Bill of Rights, which includes the Universal Declaration of Human Rights (UDHR), the International Covenant on Civil and Political Rights (ICCPR), and the International Covenant on Economic, Social and Cultural Rights (ICESCR). These documents outline core principles affirming human rights as universal and inalienable, indivisible and interdependent. The principle of universality refers to the idea that human rights are held by every human, for the mere fact of being human, and are internationally recognized within a number of important treaties and conventions. Inalienability is the concept that human rights cannot be denied or withheld except under specific situations and according to due process. Indivisibility and interdependence refer to the idea that one set of human rights should not be prioritized over another, as they reinforce each other (UN, 2021).

International treaties are an essential part of the international system of human rights protection. There are three main sets of international human rights protected in international treaties: civil and political rights outlined in the ICCPR; economic, social, and cultural rights outlined in the ICESCR; and solidarity rights which encompass the right to self-determination, economic and social development, healthy environment, natural resources, and participation in cultural heritage (Vašák, 1977).

These rights are often distinguished by the negative versus positive duties they establish, individual vs. collective rights, and whether they impose national versus international liability (Domaradzki et al., 2019). Civil and political rights are often understood as negative rights, imposing obligations such as restrictions on behavior—for instance, the obligation of governments not to interfere with the citizens' right to freedom of association. Economic and social rights on the other hand are often understood as positive rights, which impose obligations to provide services—for instance, the obligation to fund schools to fulfill the right to education. Yet this distinction is not as clear as it may seem. For instance, civil and political rights require not only the respect of citizens' rights to participate in civil and political life, but they also depend on the existence of a functional justice system in order to be properly protected and fulfilled, which undeniably imposes positive obligations on the state to construct and maintain said system. Ultimately, both types of human rights and their corresponding international treaties impose duties on states to respect, protect, fulfill, and promote them (UN, 2021).

In order to enforce and uphold human rights, international human rights law relies on the interactions and interconnections between international, regional, and domestic institutions. Harold Koh calls this the "transnational legal process," which he argues involves three phases: institutional interaction with global norms of international law, interpretation of these norms at the domestic level, and finally internalization into domestic legal systems (Koh, 1999). The ratification of international treaties is an important part of this process. It brings with it a degree of international observation and criticism, for instance, under the Universal Periodic Review at the United Nations, or through the Optional Protocol to the Convention against Torture, in which states submit themselves to an assessment of their human rights situation and progress. This is meant to increase their accountability to meet these commitments. Pressure toward accountability also builds at the domestic level, as when international treaties are ratified, there is an expectation that states will amend their domestic law to enshrine these rights within their national legal system.

In Chile, for example, in the aftermath of the dictatorship, a set of 56 constitutional reforms were negotiated and approved the 1989 referendum (Spooner, 2011: 26; Fuentes, 2012: 50), which reinforced the importance and protection of human rights in the legal system. Article 19 of the 1980 Constitution is particularly important, as it establishes the catalogue of constitutional guarantees that include the right to life and the main freedoms that were violated during the dictatorship. Article 5 of the Constitution has allowed academic, legislative, and judicial arguments that international human rights treaties which Chile has ratified have the same hierarchy as the constitution.[1]

Much progress has been made over the years in promoting human rights standards. Yet, significant abuses continue to occur around the world and go unadressed, particularly if they are acts of violence committed by agents of the state. When these abuses occur, societies find themselves in the difficult position of having to deal with the human rights violations and violence they have experienced, while seeking to move toward a more just future. It is in response to this difficult situation that the interdisciplinary concept of transitional justice has emerged, seeking to establish how best to respond to human rights abuses, recognize the dignity of victims, and create the social institutions that will prevent them from occurring again (ICTJ, 2018). Transitional justice is intrinsically connected to the concept of human rights. It is a process intended to both address past human rights abuses and create a culture of respect for human rights in the present and future. Recovering from the legacy of massive human rights violations is no easy feat, and transitional justice processes aim to respond to and prioritize the specific, local needs of survivors and victims, while drawing on international human rights obligations and norms for support and guidance.

As the concept of transitional justice has become better established, many of its key principles, such as the right to know the truth regarding human rights violations and the right to compensation and reparations, are becoming norms and rights enshrined and recognized within the broader system of international humanitarian law and human rights treaties. Important developments have been produced and influenced by decisions made in international courts such as the Inter-American Court of

[1]Article 5 of the 1980 Constitution: "Sovereignty resides essentially in the nation, its exercise is carried out by the people through plebiscites and periodic elections, and also by the authorities that this Constitution establishes, no sector of the people, nor any individual can be attributed their exercise.

The exercise of sovereignty recognizes as a limitation respect for the sensitive rights that emanate from human nature, it is the duty of the State organs to respect and promote such rights, guaranteed by this Constitution, as well as by international treaties ratified by Chile and that are in force."

Human Rights (IACtHR), the European Court of Human Rights (ECHR), and the International Criminal Court (ICC). These decisions have further cemented key elements of the transitional justice agenda into the broader human rights framework.[2]

1.2 The Elements of Transitional Justice

Human rights violations have serious, long-lasting consequences. These consequences are especially difficult to reckon with when the abuses were systemic and long term. In the face of the monumental task of addressing the legacy of human rights violations, the concept of transitional justice can prove a useful tool. Transitional justice is a process implemented by societies in transition after an armed conflict, totalitarian regime, or dictatorship. It proposes a set of judicial and extrajudicial measures, such as public policies, to address the atrocities of the past (Lessa, 2013: 10–12), particularly in cases of human rights violations and state terrorism where the normal justice system has been eroded or will not be able to provide a sufficient response. According to Ruti Teitel, transitional justice is a "conception of justice associated with periods of political change, characterized by legal responses to confront the wrongdoing of repressive predecessor regimes" (Teitel, 2003: 69; Teitel, 2017: 31). The concept has gained momentum and importance within the international community as an important framework for navigating these difficult political contexts, and the UN now defines transitional justice as "the full range of processes and mechanisms associated with a society's attempts to come to terms with a legacy of large-scale past abuses, in order to ensure accountability, serve justice and achieve reconciliation" (UN Security Council, United Nations Security Council 2004: 4).

The political goals of post-conflict societies are often highly ambitious: the preservation of peace, reconciliation and social cohesion, and promotion of democracy and the rule of law. These ambitions are difficult to

[2] For example, IACtHR, *Case Barrios Altos v. Peru*. Merits. Judgment of March 14, 2001; IACtHR, *Case of Almonacid Arellano* et al. *v. Chile*. Judgment of September 26, 2006; IACtHR, *Case of La Cantuta v. Peru*. Merits, Reparation and Costs, Judgment of November 29, 2006; IACtHR, *Case Claude Reyes* et al. *v. Chile*. Merits, Reparations and Costs, Judgement of September 19, 2006; ECHR, *Case of El-Masri v. The Former Yugoslav Republic of Macedonia*, Judgment of December 13, 2012; ECHR, *Case of Janowiec and Others v. Russia*, Judgment of October 21, 2013; and ECHR, *O'Keeffe v. Ireland*, Judgment of January 28, 2014, among other relevant cases.

meet initially. As Alexandra Barahona de Brito et al. (2001: 1) warn, "varying degrees of political, social and institutional constraints affect the solutions adopted or limit opportunities to deal with the past." In order to manage these obstacles, public authorities, political leaders, and civil society use transitional justice mechanisms such as truth commissions, criminal trials, amnesties, pardons, and reparations, among other measures. These mechanisms can generally be classified into five key categories: truth, reparations, memory (symbolic reparations), justice, and guarantees of non-repetition or reform. Consequently, the concept of transitional justice refers to political transitions and specific public policies and initiatives adopted in the circumstances of large-scale human rights violations to respond to the injustices committed and prevent that they be committed again.

Transitional justice has become the subject of an interdisciplinary and systematic academic study within the social sciences since the term in the early 1990s. While societies have long grappled with how to navigate political transitions and recover from atrocities, the study of this topic as we know it today began with the crimes against humanity committed during World War II and was further consolidated with the emergence of Latin American and post-Soviet bloc countries from dictatorships at the end of the Cold War (Teitel, 2000: 31–36; Kritz, 1995). The varied experiences in transitional justice have become the subject of systematic academic study, as researchers in this field seek to understand how societies in transition face their violent past, while at the same time consolidating democracy and the rule of law, ultimately aiming to forge a new era of political coexistence.

Early models of transitional justice were narrower in scope, often seeking to address the most affected victims through more time-limited mechanisms; however, the field has broadened to account for the long-lasting legacies of political violence and seek to understand the long-term societal effects of various mechanisms (Collins, 2017: 56). Some have argued that transitional justice must go further to address long-term underlying structural injustices (Gready & Robins, 2019) and gender justice (Buckley-Zistel & Stanley, 2011) or include development agendas (De Greiff & Duthie, 2009). These widening notions of the field have led to significant debates about how and to what extent transitional justice can effect change on systemic structures of violence and inequality, which we will touch on later on in this chapter.

The expression "transition," implicit in the notion transitional justice, is also a source of many debates. Experts and practitioners often disagree about what brings about the end of a "transition," and what makes it successful. Is the transition over when perpetrators have been held accountable? Or when societies have achieved some form of recognition, reconciliation, or political coexistence? In the Chilean case, what exactly marks the end of the transition is difficult to agree on, and as such, many argue that transitional justice must be understood as a *process* rather than a goal. From this perspective, even when the outcome is uncertain, the act of engaging in the process has value (McAdams, 2011). Given that there is no consensus as to what brings about the end of a transitional justice process, the end of the process can be understood as being when a society perceives it to be over. The focus on the idea of "transition" sometimes puts excessive emphasis on the occurrence of a political transition. What is relevant is how the country "transits"—using an expression coined by Teitel (2003)—or advances along the path toward taking charge of the traumatic events of its past, seeking to restore peaceful coexistence, and reconstructing its social fabric.

Tricia Olsen, Leigh A. Payne, and Andrew Reiter argue that the academic debate in transitional justice can be divided into four main theoretical approaches: maximalist, minimalist, moderate, and holistic (2010a, 2010b, 2010c).

The maximalist approach argues that perpetrators must be held accountable to the highest degree possible through human rights trials and retributive justice. Proponents of this approach would argue that social reconciliation does not need to be understood as an alternative to justice, and holding the perpetrators of the most serious crimes accountable can in fact help conflicting sectors of society reconcile. Retributive justice acts as a form of deterrence for future perpetrators, combats impunity, and is essential to reinstate the rule of law (Akhavan, 1998). The reinforcing of the rule of law is the prerequisite to the creation of a just social order, where people see themselves as holders of rights, free to organize themselves and express dissent, and where there is no space for impunity for those responsible for human rights violations. Maximalists also highlight states' legal obligation to prosecute perpetrators of past atrocities under international law (Orentlicher, 1991; Roht-Arriaza, 1990).

In direct contrast, proponents of the minimalist approach advocate for the use of amnesties, arguing that the pursuit of accountability can be too dangerous and that amnesties can foster the stability needed in fraught political transitions to achieve democracy. Minimalists argue that states do not always have the capacity to undertake criminal trials and prosecute the perpetrators when segments of the authoritarian apparatus of the state continue to hold significant power to derail the fragile efforts of democratization and backslide into conflict or authoritarianism (Stedman, 1997). This approach is marked by pragmatism in the face of political constraints for the sake of peace and social reconciliation (Snyder & Vinjamuri, 2003). Minimalists thus suggest that amnesties can provide political stability which can create the conditions needed to strengthen democracy in the long run and thus eventually prevent further human rights violations in the future.

The moderate approach situates itself between these two poles and argues for the use of non-judicial measures as an alternative approach to accountability, centered on the dignity of victims while still combating the impunity of perpetrators (Kritz, 1995; Teitel, 2000). This approach suggests truth commissions are uniquely suited to respond to the need for both accountability and political stability. Moderates recognize the limits on the possibility of accountability through trials in the context of a conflicted democratic transition and suggest transitional justice approaches be tailored using the truth mechanisms that best allow them to ensure accountability for perpetrators and dignity for victims (Zalaquett, 1990; Nino, 1996).

Finally, the holistic approach, which has been adopted by the International Center for Transitional Justice (ICTJ), advocates for the use of a combination of various mechanisms, arguing that any one mechanism is likely to be insufficient on its own. Pablo de Greiff, the Special Rapporteur on the promotion of truth, justice, reparation, and guarantees of non-repetition at the United Nations, holds that the elements of transitional justice are "interrelated action areas that can mutually reinforce each other in the process of correcting the aftermath of abuse and massive human rights violations" (2012: 21). Numerous investigative teams and organizations specialized in transitional justice have argued the importance of taking an approach that integrates the various elements of transitional justice (UN, 2010: 6; Macdonald, 2013). The holistic approach argues that each society has a different experience of conflict and oppression and must therefore tailor their solutions accordingly.

Current investigations about transitional justice processes have worked to systematically analyze and generalize, based on empirical evidence, the impact of the different mechanisms that are being used by regimes in transition to confront the past, with the hopes of establishing guidelines and recommendations for success. These investigations center on measuring and comparing the social impact of the various types of mechanisms, such as truth commissions, criminal trials, amnesties, and pardons. Their results have shown that countries which combined a number of devices and mechanisms such as truth commissions, criminal prosecutions, memorialization, and institutional reforms, which address a combination of the distinct components that constitute the *corpus* of transitional justice, have made significant advances, with certain combinations being more successful than others (Ramji-Nogales, 2010; Lie et al., 2007; Olsen et al., 2010b, 2010c; Skaar et al., 2016; Kim & Sikkink, 2012–2013).

The success of a transitional justice process depends on achieving certain intermediate and long-term goals. In the intermediate term, the state must work on officially recognizing the victims and building trust. In this context, it is crucial to recognize victims in their status as rights holders, because it allows for an understanding of the magnitude of the suffering they experienced by having their human rights violated, as well as recognizing the importance of their participation in the process of repairing the harm done. This makes it possible to implement reparation measures which mitigate the suffering they experienced, restore their rights, and confirm their status as persons authorized to exercise them. As to the building of trust, this requires that the state and all of its agencies comply with the norms that rule society and its institutions. Trusting implies sharing rules and values that are binding for all those who make up society. States who have broken their people's trust must therefore prove that they will respect and submit to the laws and values of society. The long-term goal of transitional justice processes is to create a sustainable culture of respect for human rights, through the promotion of reconciliation and the rebuilding of a healthy and cohesive society, and through the promotion of the rule of law to achieve a just social order.

Transitional justice does not have one-size-fits-all formulas or recommendations to deal with a tormented past, because while there are common trends, each society in transition has a different experience of repression. In this book, we will advance the argument that it is essential that a society answers the following five questions when engaging in a process of transitional justice: (1) What mechanisms should be used to find reliable information about the nature and extent of human rights violations or crimes against humanity? (2) What measures, public policies, or mechanisms should the state adopt to repair the damage caused to victims and their families during the years of repression? (3) How should the horrors of the past be remembered socially and how should victims be commemorated? (4) What measures should be taken to investigate crimes committed, combat impunity, and hold accountable those responsible for the human rights violations? (5) How can the chances be reduced of human rights violations being repeated in the future? As societies in transition grapple with these complex questions, survivors, victims, and their families must be supported and included in all aspects of the process. Their participation is essential to the success of any effort to address the human rights violations of the past and move forward. This section will provide a brief description of each of the five interdependent components that answer these questions and constitute the core of transitional justice: truth, justice, reparation, memory, and non-repetition.

Truth

While victims and their families may be interested in obtaining economic compensation for the harm caused in their lives, in general what they want most is to know the truth about what took place. This could occur through criminal trials that establish a faithful account of the circumstances of death or disappearance of their loved ones and lead to the condemnation of those responsible. This is often complicated by the fact that those who order or commit the human rights violations nearly always seek to prevent the truth about the repressive acts they committed from coming out (Hau et al., 2019: 222).

To avoid leaving registers or proof of the crimes, high-ranking officials often verbally order the destruction of archives, documents, and other materials that could be useful for the clarification of the circumstances related to the human rights violations. One of the most horrible measures taken, in some cases, to erase all trace of crimes is clandestine elimination, or the disappearance of the bodies of victims. This inhumane practice impedes the process of mourning for the families whose loved ones have been executed and continues to cause pain over time. Without the body of the detained and disappeared, it is impossible to perform the funeral rights and fully acknowledge the death of a loved one. The search for the bodies of the disappeared is not only an objective of the families affected, but also an ongoing drama that affects the whole population (García, 2011: 113). Society, families of victims, and survivors all have a right to know the truth about what happened, and for this truth to be officially recognized

(Gómez, 2006: 37–8). The state thus has an obligation to fulfill society's right to the truth, and there are several ways it can go about doing this.

The right to the truth has become a norm of common law, which means it cannot be modified by a subsequent state or international norm. Juan Méndez explains that the right to the truth is an "obligation (which falls on the state) to reveal to victims and society everything that can be confidently known about the circumstances of the crimes, including the identity of the perpetrators and investigators" (Park, 2010: 24). Many argue that knowing the truth, which is achieved by determining the facts around the perpetration of the crimes, can restore dignity to the victim whose human rights were violated and can help ensure that these awful acts are never repeated (Orentlicher, 2005: 23). An integral understanding of what happened contributes to a deeper awareness of the causes of the conflicts in the context of which human rights violations occurred. The search for truth can help secure justice—by fighting against impunity—promote the social and psychological reconstruction of a society, and encourage reconciliation as well as being a first step toward preventing the occurrence of the abuses again in the future (Mendelof, 2004: 356).

A mechanism used widely in the last 30 years to investigate the traumatic past is the truth commission. Official truth commissions are charged with elucidating the truth and providing official reports about human rights violations. The report published by a truth commission serves to publicly recognize the abuses of the past; helping to eliminate the veil of denial and silence that often descends when societies seek to forget widespread human rights abuses (Hayner, 2011: 55). The attributes and legal mandates of said commissions have been very diverse, which makes both their findings and their political effects difficult to compare from one country to another.

Criminal prosecution of the human rights abuses also contributes to the establishment of the truth. The justice system is destined to establish the facts and determine the identity of the wrongdoers, and as such, in theory, it can satisfy the obligation to investigate and uncover the truth. National inquiries and civil society efforts such as investigative journalism and academic research can also help further the search for the truth. Both in the cases of extrajudicial killings and forced disappearances, the investigation must go on until the whereabouts of the victim are determined, and the circumstances surrounding their death or disappearance are elucidated.

Reparations

In an ideal world, the abuse, harm, and losses suffered by the victims would be repaired and reversed completely. Unfortunately, it is impossible to fully compensate and atone for the types of profound losses caused by human rights violations. Nonetheless, there are a variety of public policies destined to compensate victims of human rights violations with public funds. Reparations can take both material and symbolic form and work best when the two types are combined. Symbolic reparations, such as memorials or official apologies, work to repair the moral wrong done to victims by officially acknowledging and taking responsibility for human rights abuses, while material reparations aim to provide economic compensation for the damage caused. Some of the measures worth noting are pecuniary compensation, restoration of confiscated property, reallocation of lost jobs due to purges or persecution in public administration, restoration of citizenship (when a regime has taken it away), mental health and health services, free counseling, scholarships, and other welfare benefits of the state.

These measures are palliative and can never repair completely the far-reaching impacts of human rights abuses. Part of their value is that, through reparations, the state is officially recognizing victims and committing through public policies to repair, to the extent possible, the damage caused. The difficult part of reparations policies is not merely implementing them but creating policies which victims *perceive* as compensatory for the harms caused. Victims want to see at the very least that society has tried to repair the damage done. It is therefore crucial that victims and civil society play a role in the design of reparations programs.

In the context of systematic human rights violations, reparations policies often consist of several different laws which aim to compensate specific victims. The scope of the reparations must as much as possible seek to cover all the damages suffered by the victims, which in many cases includes physical and psychological trauma. In Chile, reparations measures are varied, including monthly pensions as financial compensation as well as other measures such as healthcare benefits and post-secondary scholarships for the children of torture survivors, to seek to combat the impacts of generational trauma.

In the terms used by the Inter-American Court of Human Rights, reparation of the damage caused implies restoring the previous situation to the greatest extent possible, and in those cases in which this cannot be done (which often happens in the context of transitional justice), the reparation should include fair compensation, or pecuniary compensation, to which the positive measures of the state must be added to ensure that such damaging events are not repeated (e.g., *Trujillo Oroza Case*, *Bámaca Velásquez Case*, *Loayza Tamayo Case*, and *Paniagua Morales Case*, inter alia). The concept of reparations has been expanded in recent years to go beyond simply restoring the previous situation and instead seeks to improve the present situation by addressing the underlying causes which may have led to the outbreak of conflict and repression in the first place. Antonio Cançado Trindade, judge on the International Court of Justice, has argued that the central aspect of reparations is considering the victim's perspective. According to him, reparations programs must keep in mind the importance of restoring the dignity of victims and treating them with the respect owed to a human being, something which has often been stripped from them in their experience of violence, and which reparations symbolically seek to amend (IACtHR, 1997: 17).

Memory

After a period of polarization and conflict, societies, just like individuals, must rebuild their understanding of the past in the present. The diverse and sometimes conflicting collective memories that exist within a political community can be investigated in order to answer to the questions how, when, why, and which events are remembered. In divided societies, conflicting memories are likely to coexist in such a way that the group does not share collective memories, but rather they are constant sources of tension and dispute. As argued by Elizabeth Jelin, memory of traumatic events can be a controversial topic which can reignite political conflict between different sectors of a society (2002: Ch. 3). Memory makes sense of the past but can also be a source of mobilization in the present. While memorialization can be polarizing, in our opinion, memory can contribute to preventing that such atrocities be committed again and provide symbolic reparations to victims.

Remembering human rights violations contributes to the political project of *Nunca Más*, or *Never Again*, by preserving the experiences and lessons learned from the horrors of the past. A significant political and public policy challenge consists of promoting a shared interpretive or narrative framework for the past in societies in transition, where conflicting interpretations of the past exist (Jelin, 2002: Ch. 4). Society not only has the right to know what took place, but also to *remember* what took place. This topic is especially sensitive for victims, survivors, and their families, since the collective narrative of memory affects the way others value and recognize them as human beings. Survivors and their families are often those who advocate the strongest to preserve sites of human rights violations as places of memory.

Museology and memorial sites are methods of memorializing, and they are necessary mechanisms for the intergenerational transmission of traumatic past memory. This intergenerational element is why memorialization initiatives cannot be left in the hands of civil society and memory entrepreneurs alone. The state must also finance commemorative initiatives and carefully consider their contents. However, even ensuring state involvement is not a fail-safe way to preserve the past, because as the political control of the state changes, memorialization and commemoration can reemerge as a political issue many years later. For example, the recent resurfacing in the United States of political controversy about monuments to heroes of the Confederacy (Confederate States of America), who were also defending the right to own slaves, is a clear example of how conflicts over memory do not disappear, even centuries after the fact. The past can be resurrected as munition for present-day politics.

Justice

The search for justice is a tense and complicated affair in many societies in transition. Justice can take many forms and can be approached from many different perspectives. For some, retributive justice is the ideal scenario; for others, selective amnesties, or restorative justice approaches are more effective. These approaches favor rectifying and compensating for the harm caused by the crime rather than the punishment of those responsible, and suggest alternate forms of accountability mechanisms, such as truth commissions or distributive justice in the form of reparations. The particular context of the society in question must be taken into account when these various justice approaches are being considered. In the corresponding chapter related to this element of transitional justice, we will focus on retributive justice, understood as criminal charges and investigation by the courts, ultimately seeking the criminal conviction and restriction of freedom of the perpetrators. Alternate approaches to justice tend to consider truth commissions and reparations, which we will cover in their own separate chapters.

Some scholars of transitional justice consider judicial investigation and judgment of the perpetrators to be of utmost importance in order to avoid human rights violations falling into oblivion, and perpetrators escaping with impunity. Those responsible tend to use various legal tactics to evade justice, such as self-amnesties, the prescription of crimes, and the application of statutes of limitations, among others. There is consensus in the international community that these attempts to avoid liability must be addressed, and the jurisprudence of the international courts has been clear in this regard: amnesties or statute of limitations cannot be invoked in cases of genocide, torture, and crimes against humanity (e.g., IACtHR, 2001, 2006).

In transitional justice contexts, it can be difficult for the crimes to be investigated and the accused be condemned by national courts or by courts with international jurisdiction. During the years of transition when perpetrators often continue to hold significant political power, the justice system can easily be manipulated, and perpetrators often seek to ensure situations of impunity for themselves. For example, in the first years of the Chilean transition, perpetrators were confident they would be able to remain unpunished thanks to the authoritarian enclaves that persisted in the political system. According to Juan Guzmán, former judge of the Santiago Appeals Court, "Despite the return to democracy, they were convinced of having achieved impunity. The system had remained completely controlled by the military before handing over the power to civilians. The amnesty law, unofficial agreements with the *Concertación* parties: everything was planned so that they would never be disturbed" (2005: 135).

Faced with these kinds of scenarios, it may be necessary for societies in transition to introduce changes to the judiciary, the legal culture, the constitution, and other sources of law in order to strengthen the rule of law. Retroactive application of these changes can, however, pose questions about the legitimacy and legality of ex post facto criminal law, a topic which aroused much attention in the Chilean judicial debates during the military dictatorship and the return to democracy in 1990. This important norm in criminal law establishes that one cannot be convicted of a crime if it was not illegal at the time it was committed (*nullum crimen, nulla poena sine lege penali, praevia, stricta et scripta*).

All things considered, for the satisfaction of the right to justice, states must move forward with timely, meticulous, independent, and impartial investigations of human rights abuses. In the words of the Inter-American Commission of Human Rights (IAHRC), "the right to access to justice must guarantee, within a reasonable term, the right to justice of the victims' families; that everything necessary will be done to know the truth about what took place and sanction those responsible" (2007: 115). In other words, part of the right to justice is the punishment of those responsible in proportion to the magnitude of the crimes they committed. This does not rule out the possibility of restorative justice approaches, or other alternate justice mechanisms; however, these initiatives must be developed in consultation with survivors, victims, and their families and must prioritize accountability.

Allowing perpetrators of serious human rights abuses to go free opens space for impunity, which in turn complicates the process of advancing the rest of the elements that constitute transitional justice and the objectives that it pursues. States must therefore adopt all the necessary mechanisms to facilitate the access to justice for victims and their families. Any other course of action places international responsibility on the state, as this denial of justice constitutes inhuman treatment of the victims and their families.

Non-repetition

The ultimate goal of a transitional justice process is to create the conditions that will prevent the repetition of human rights abuses and ensure their protection. This involves first recognizing the status of victims who suffered the consequences of the conflict, as only through recognition of the horrors they faced can the victims begin to have faith in the state again, which contributes to strengthening the new institutions. Taking steps to avoid the reiteration of violations of human rights helps build trust in state institutions and ultimately rebuilds the social fabric that has been broken as a consequence of the past conflict. The commitment to non-repetition can promote political reconciliation, prevent the emergence of new armed actors, and contribute to legitimizing the rule of law (Uprimny, 2006: 50). The Inter-American Court of Human Rights (2003, 2009) has invoked this guarantee as part of a right to integral reparations, while the Universal System maintains that non-repetition implies creating preventive mechanisms and supporting the fulfillment of the other obligations. In other words, "the states must undertake institutional reforms and other measures necessary to ensure respect for the rule of law, promote and maintain a culture of respect for human rights, and restore or establish public confidence in government institutions" (Joinet, 1997: 35). As with all of the other elements discussed, the establishment of reforms must be preceded by consultations, which permit the participation of the victims and of civil society as a whole.

Some of the commitments to non-repetition included in institutional reforms in contexts of transitional justice processes are related to (i) unrestricted subjection of public institutions to the law; (ii) repeal of laws that favor impunity or that facilitate human rights violations; (iii) civil control of security and armed forces including intelligence services, as well as the dismantling of parastatal armed forces; (iv) reintegration of children who have participated in armed conflict in society; and (v) human rights and international humanitarian law education. When implementing policies related to the guarantee of non-repetition, short-, medium-, and long-term measures must all be kept in mind, for instance, actions like reparations programs for victims, and institutional reforms intended to prevent human rights abuses in the long term.

Non-repetition is not limited to the context of transitional justice. The search for structural reforms and consequent strengthening of the rule of law must be thought of as preventive mechanisms, which will endure beyond the context of a transitional justice process and become part of the normal functioning of the state and society. Preventative measures must therefore be built in as part of permanent state policy that differentiates this element from the search for truth, justice, reparations, and memory, as these are theoretically more restricted to the process of transition. An example of a permanent preventative mechanism would be the National Institute of Human Rights in Chile, created in 2010. This government agency issues a report on the state of human rights in Chile every year, as well implementing educational campaigns and training, and providing a means through which citizens can file human rights complaints. Efforts to assure non-repetition must continue to be adopted and modified in an unending process as the national context of each state progresses.

The international community has made significant progress in setting standards for transitional justice processes. These standards are linked to the international obligations that emanate from international treaties and conventions. A good example of how standards of transitional justice have been established over time is the right to the truth. This norm was first incorporated in article 32 of the First Optional Protocol of 1979 of the Geneva Conventions of 1949 and establishes the right of victims and their families to know what happened in contexts of internal or external conflicts. Many victims, families, and human rights activists drew on this norm to seek to hold their governments accountable, which gave way to the emergence of the concept of the right to truth. Practically 30 years later, it was expressly incorporated in the International Convention for the Protection of All Persons from Enforced Disappearance. This and other norms impose obligations on states, which over the years become standards of compliance with respect to distinct elements of transitional justice. The consecration of the five elements of transitional justice within international treaties illustrates universal recognition of the importance of this framework for societies seeking to overcome their difficult past.

Yet, as transitional justice standards and mechanisms have increasingly been enshrined into international human rights frameworks, the field has also faced some important limitations and drawn significant criticism over the years, as many have questioned how well these processes have truly worked. Namely, transitional justice is criticized for promoting surface level solutions, which do not adequately address the underlying causes of the conflicts and human rights violations they seek to address (Gready & Robins, 2019). Long-standing and entrenched issues such as economic inequalities and violations of economic, cultural, and social rights are often overlooked or else not adequately addressed in transitional justice frameworks, and the approach has also been criticized for being too focused on state-based "top-down" solutions which do not directly address the needs and demands of communities on the ground (Roht-Arriaza, 2019). Other criticisms have focused on the failure of transitional justice mechanisms to adequately address gender-based discrimination and violence (Buckley-Zistel & Stanley, 2011; Dhawan, 2011), or the legacies of colonialism (Yusuf, 2018; Maddison & Shepherd, 2014).

These criticisms are weighty and have led scholars to advocate for an expansion of the concept of transitional justice to incorporate or focus more on these underlying inequalities, injustices, and exclusions (Miller, 2008; Nagy, 2008). Transitional justice mechanisms have traditionally focused on repairing, to the extent possible, the damage caused by violations of civil and political rights and crimes against the integrity of the person (e.g., violations of the right to life). However, the scope of transitional justice processes has widened as mechanisms focus on addressing not only the direct harms caused by human rights abuses, but also the underlying causes that lead to massive human rights violations. These deeper causes are often identified as long-term violations of economic, social, and cultural rights, such as situations of economic inequality and social exclusion (Aciru et al., 2016: 244). The broadened scope of the transitional justice agenda centers the importance of human rights policies not only in dealing with the horrors of the past but in creating a more just future. Others have argued that these limitations are too profoundly entrenched in the foundations of transitional justice, and have proposed an alternative theoretical framework, transformative justice, which is defined by Paul Gready and Simon Robins as "transformative change that emphasizes local agency and resources, the prioritization of process rather than preconceived outcomes, and the challenging of unequal and intersecting power relationships and structures of exclusion at both local and global levels" (2019: 32). This alternate framework seeks to reform, shift, and change the approach typically used in transitional justice to focus more closely on participation and locally driven responses rather than top-down approaches.

These concerns about the limitations of transitional justice merit deep consideration in the Chilean context, because many of the demands and frustrations of protesters in the most recent outbreak of social unrest in Chile are closely tied to the failures of the transitional justice process to address underlying issues such as economic injustice, the exclusion of the Mapuche people, and the limited inclusion of gender-based issues. This brings up important questions about how much we can expect from transitional justice processes, and how effective they are in addressing structural and systemic forms of violence and inequality. As the field of transitional justice grapples with these questions of how best to address the root causes of conflict and injustice, the recent experiences of social unrest and constitutional reform add new relevance to the Chilean case. In the following chapters, we will seek to offer a comprehensive overview of the transitional justice measures implemented in Chile in each of the five elements overviewed above: truth, memory, justice, reparations, and guarantees of non-repetition. Our goal is to offer a synthesis of the Chilean experience and its achievements and failures, so as to inform and support future reflection and study of transitional justice.

While much has been done over the past 30 years to address the brutal legacy of the dictatorship, there has been insufficient institutional reform within the armed forces to create a culture of respect of human rights, and other institutional legacies of the dictatorship like the 1980 Constitution and neoliberal economic model have also been left unaddressed. Much of the progress made in transitional justice in Chile has been driven by survivors and victims' families, and greater state engagement and a broader culture of human rights in Chilean society as a whole are necessary to close some of the pending gaps. The social unrest and state violence that erupted in the fall of 2019 highlight the importance of engaging with the whole, complex legacy of the past, when seeking to build a more just future.

Bibliography

Aciru, M., Parmentier, S., Saeed, H., & Rauschenbach, M. (2016). Human Rights in Situations of Transitional Justice. In E. Fishwick, M. Marmo, & L. Weber (Eds.), *The Routledge International Handbook of Criminology and Human Rights* (pp. 261–272). Routledge.

Akhavan, P. (1998). Justice in the Hague, Peace in the Former Yugoslavia? A Commentary on the United Nations War Crimes Tribunal. *Human Rights Quarterly, 20*(4), 737–816.

Barahona de Brito, A., González-Enríquez, C., & Aguilar, P. (2001). *The Politics of Memory: Transitional Justice in Democratizing Societies.* Oxford University Press.

Benhabib, S. (2004). *The Rights of Others: Aliens, Residents, and Citizens.* Cambridge University Press.

Buckley-Zistel, S., & Stanley, R. (2011). *Gender in Transitional Justice.* Palgrave Macmillan.

Collins, C. (2017). Truth-Justice-Reparations Interaction Effects in Transitional Justice Practice: The Case of the 'Valech Commission' in Chile. *Journal of Latin American Studies, 49*(1), 55–82.

De Grieff, P., & Duthie, R. (Eds.). (2009). *Transitional Justice and Development: Making Connections.* Social Science Research Council.

Dhawan, N. (2011). Transitions to Justice. In S. Buckley-Zistel & R. Stanley (Eds.), *Gender in Transitional Justice* (pp. 264–282). Palgrave Macmillan.

Domaradzki, S., Khvostova, M., & Pupovac, D. (2019). Karel Vasak's Generations of Rights and the Contemporary Human Rights Discourse. *Human Rights Review, 20*(4), 423–443.

Fuentes, C. (2012). *El Pacto: Poder, Constitución y Prácticas Políticas en Chile (1990–2010).* Ediciones Universidad Diego Portales.

García, A. (2011). *La muerte lenta de los desaparecidos en Chile.* Editorial Cuarto Propio.

Gómez, F. (2006). El derecho de las víctimas a la reparación por violaciones graves y sistemáticas de los derechos humanos. In F. Gómez (Ed.), *El derecho a la memoria* (pp. 23–75). Instituto de Derechos Humanos Pedro Arrupe de la Universidad de Deusto.

Gready, P., & Robins, S. (Eds.). (2019). *From Transitional to Transformative Justice.* Cambridge University Press.

Guzmán, J. (2005). *En el Borde del Mundo: Memorias del Juez que Procesó a Pinochet.* Editorial Anagrama.

Hau, B., Lessa, F., & Rojas, H. (2019). Registration of State Violence as Judicial Evidence in Human Rights Trials. In O. Bernasconi (Ed.), *Political Violence Resistance in Latin America: Documenting Atrocity* (pp. 197–228). Palgrave Macmillan.

Hayner, P. (2011). *Unspeakable Truths: Transitional Justice and the Challenge of Truth Commissions* (2nd ed.). Routledge.

Inter-American Court of Human Rights (IACtHR). (1997). *Case Loayza Tamayo v. Peru*, Judgment of September 17, 1997.

Inter-American Court of Human Rights (IACtHR). (2001). *Case Barrios Altos v. Peru*. Merits, Judgment of March 14, 2001.

Inter-American Court of Human Rights (IACtHR). (2003). *Case of Bulacio v. Argentina*. Judgment of September 18, 2003.

Inter-American Court of Human Rights (IACtHR). (2006). *Case of Almonacid Arellano et al. v. Chile*, Judgment of September 26, 2006.

Inter-American Court of Human Rights (IACtHR). (2009). *Case of the "Las Dos Erres" Massacre v. Guatemala*. Preliminary Objection, Merits, Reparations, and Costs, Judgment of November 24, 2009.

International Center for Transitional Justice (ICTJ). (2018). *What Is Transitional Justice?* available at https://www.ictj.org/about/transitional-justice

Jelin, E. (2002). *Los Trabajos de la Memoria*. Siglo XXI.

Joinet, L. (1997). *The Administration of Justice and the Human Rights of Detainees. Question of the Impunity of Perpetrators of Human Rights Violations (Civil and Political)*. Commission on Human Rights, Sub-Commission on Prevention of Discrimination and Protection of Minorities, 49th Session, available at https://undocs.org/E/CN.4/Sub.2/1997/20/Rev.1

Kim, H. J., & Sikkink, K. (2012). How Do Human Rights Prosecutions Improve Human Rights After Transition? *Interdisciplinary Journal of Human Rights Law, 7*(1), 69–90.

Koh, H. (1999). How Is International Human Rights Law Enforced? *Indiana Law Journal, 74*(4), 1397–1418.

Kritz, N. (1995). *Transitional Justice: How Emerging Democracies Reckon with Former Regimes*. United States Institute of Peace.

Kurth, J. (2005). Humanitarian Intervention After the War in Iraq: Legal Ideals Vs. Military Realities. *Orbis, 50*, 87–101.

Lessa, F. (2013). *Memory and Transitional Justice in Argentina and Uruguay: Against Impunity*. Palgrave Macmillan.

Lie, T., Binningsbø, H., & Gates, S. (2007). *Post-Conflict Justice and Sustainable Peace* (Policy Research Working Paper No. 4191). World Bank.

Lira, E. (2006). The Reparations Policy for Human Rights Violations in Chile. In P. de Greiff (Ed.), *The Handbook of Reparations* (pp. 55–99). Oxford University Press.

Macdonald, M. (1947). Natural Rights. *Proceedings of the Aristotelian Society, 47*, 225–250.

Macdonald, A. (2013). *Local Understandings and Experiences of Transitional Justice: A Review of the Evidence* (JSRP Paper No. 6). The Justice and Security Research Programme, London School of Economics, available at http://eprints.lse.ac.uk/56354/1/JSRP_Paper6_Local_understandings_and_experiences_of_transitional_justice_Macdonald_2013.pdf

Maddison, S., & Shepherd, L. (2014). Peacebuilding and the Postcolonial Politics of Transitional Justice. *Peacebuilding, 2*(3), 253–269.

McAdams, A. (2011). Transitional Justice: The Issue that Won't Go Away. *International Journal of Transitional Justice, 5*(2), 304–312.

Mendelof, D. (2004). Truth-Seeking, Truth-Telling, and Postconflict Peacebuilding: Curb the Enthusiasm? *International Studies Review, 6*(3), 355–380.

Mendieta, E. (2007). *Global Fragments: Latinamericanisms, Globalizations, and Critical Theory.* State University of New York Press.

Miller, Z. (2008). Effects of Invisibility: In Search of the 'Economic' in Transitional Justice. *The International Journal of Transitional Justice, 2*, 266–291.

Moyn, S. (2010). *The Last Utopia: Human Rights in History.* Belknap Press of Harvard University Press.

Moyn, S. (2018). *Not Enough: Human Rights in an Unequal World.* Available at ProQuest Ebook Central, https://ebookcentral.proquest.com

Mutua, M. (2001). Savages, Victims, and Saviors: The Metaphor of Human Rights. *Harvard International Law Journal, 42*(1), 201–245.

Nagy, R. (2008). Transitional Justice as Global Project: Critical Reflections. *Third World Quarterly, 29*(2), 275–289.

Nash, K. (2015). *Political Sociology of Human rights.* Cambridge University Press.

Nino, C. (1996). *Radical Evil on Trial.* Yale University Press.

Olsen, T., Payne, L., & Reiter, A. (2010a). *Transitional Justice in Balance: Comparing Processes, Weighing Efficacy.* United States Institute of Peace.

Olsen, T., Payne, L., & Reiter, A. (2010b). The Justice Balance: When Transitional Justice Improves Human Rights and Democracy. *Human Rights Quarterly, 32*(4), 980–1007.

Olsen, T., Payne, L., & Reiter, A. (2010c). Transitional Justice in the World, 1970–2007: Insights from a New Dataset. *Journal of Peace Research, 47*(6), 803–809.

Orentlicher, D. F. (1991). *Report of the Independent Expert to Update the Set of Principles to Combat Impunity.* UN Economic and Social Council.

Park, G. (2010). Truth as Justice: Legal and Extralegal Development of the Right to Truth. *Harvard International Review, 31*(4), 24–27.

Ramji-Nogales, J. (2010). Designing Bespoke Transitional Justice: A Pluralist Process Approach. *Michigan Journal of International Law, 32*(1), 1–72.

Rensmann, L. (2017). Critical Theory of Human Rights. In M. Thompson (Ed.), *The Palgrave Handbook of Critical Theory* (Political Philosophy and Public Purpose) (p. 632). Palgrave Macmillan.

Roht-Arriaza, N. (1990). State Responsibility to Investigate and Prosecute Grave Human Rights Violations in International Law. *California Law Review, 78*(2), 449–513.

Roht-Arriaza, N. (2019). Measures of Non-Repetition in Transitional Justice: The Missing Link? In P. Gready & S. Robins (Eds.), *From Transitional to Transformative Justice* (pp. 105–130). Cambridge University Press.

Sen, A. (1997). Human Rights and Asian Values: What Kee Kuan Yew and Le Peng Don't Understand About Asia. *The New Republic, 217*(2–3), 33–40.

Sikkink, K. (2017). *Evidence for Hope: Making Human Rights Work in the 21st Century.* Princeton University Press.

Skaar, E., García-Godos, J., & Collins, C. (Eds.). (2016). *Transitional Justice in Latin America: The Uneven Road from Impunity Towards Accountability.* Routledge.

Snyder, J., & Vinjamuri, L. (2003). Trials and Errors: Principle and Pragmatism in Strategies of International Justice. *International Security, 28*(3), 5–44.

Spooner, M. H. (2011). *The General's Slow Retreat: Chile After Pinochet.* University of California Press.

Squella, A. (2019). *Derechos Humanos.* Editorial UV de la Universidad de Valparaíso.

Stedman, S. (1997). Spoiler Problems in Peace Processes. *International Security, 22*(2), 5–53.

Teitel, R. (2000). *Transitional Justice.* Oxford University Press.

Teitel, R. (2003). Transitional Justice Genealogy. *Harvard Human Rights Journal, 16*, 69–94.

Teitel, R. (2017). Genealogía de la justicia transicional. In R. Jimeno (Ed.), *Justicia Transicional: Historia y Actualidad* (pp. 31–67). Thomson Reuters/ Ed. Aranzadi.

United Nations. (1948). *Universal Declaration of Human Rights*, available at https://www.un.org/en/about-us/universal-declaration-of-human-rights.

United Nations. (2010). *Guidance Note of the Secretary General: United Nations Approach to Transitional Justice*, available at https://www.un.org/ruleoflaw/files/TJ_Guidance_Note_March_2010FINAL.pdf

United Nations. (2021). *What Are Human Rights?* available at https://www.ohchr.org/en/issues/pages/whatarehumanrights.aspx

United Nations Security Council. (2004). The Rule of Law and Transitional Justice in Conflict and Post-Conflict Societies. Report of the Secretary-General. UN Doc. S/2004/616.

Uprimny, R. (2006). *¿Justicia transicional sin transición?: Verdad, justicia y reparación para Colombia* (p. 1). Centro de Estudios de Derecho, Justicia y Sociedad.

Vašák, K. (1977). Human Rights: A Thirty-Year Struggle: The Sustained Efforts to Give Force of Law to the Universal Declaration of Human Rights. *UNESCO Courier, 11*, 29–32.

Waltz, S. (2002). Reclaiming and Rebuilding the History of the Universal Declaration of Human Rights. *Third World Quarterly, 23*(3), 437–448.

Yusuf, H. (2018). Colonialism and the Dilemmas of Transitional Justice in Nigeria. *International Journal on Transitional Justice, 12*, 257–276.

Zalaquett, J. (1990). Confronting Human Rights Violations Committed by Former Governments: Applicable Principles and Political Constraints. *Hamline Law Review, 13*(3), 623–660.

CHAPTER 2

Chilean Recent History

In the last half century, Chile has experienced a rollercoaster of political regimes: the Revolution in Liberty (1964–1970), the Chilean Road to Socialism (1970–1973), the Military Dictatorship (1973–1990), and the Transition to Democracy (1990–present). The dramatic shifts between these radically different political experiments have profoundly marked several generations of Chileans, who have had to navigate and adapt to these dramatic changes in political and economic institutions (Albertus & Menaldo, 2018: Ch. 7).

The social reforms implemented by President Frei Montalva between 1964 and 1970 were too radical for some, and not radical enough for others. Consequently, the 1970 presidential election saw Salvador Allende inherit a polarized society. While Allende's bold socialist project won the support of peasants, workers, and progressive groups, these same reforms provoked outrage from conservative sectors and opponents of social justice, who actively made efforts to destabilize the economy and his government. A plot between the conservative elite, high-ranking officers of the armed forces and the White House ultimately led to the military coup in 1973 (Haslam, 2005; González, 2013; Harmer, 2013, Ch. 7). The following 17 years of dictatorship under General Augusto Pinochet had a huge impact on Chilean society and institutions. The military sought to re-found the nation by imposing a new political-economic model and purging political dissidents through brutal acts of repression and human

H. Rojas, M. Shaftoe, *Human Rights and Transitional Justice in Chile*, Memory Politics and Transitional Justice,
https://doi.org/10.1007/978-3-030-81182-2_2

rights abuses against anyone associated with the political left. Meanwhile, Pinochet's political supporters argued that the repression and restriction of liberties were a necessary part of the fight against "subversive elements" of society, justified also by the necessity to implement economic and social policies that would modernize Chile.

This constant rearranging of the political landscape has defined the way Chileans understand their past and has shaped the context of Chile's process of transitional justice. It is not easy to understand the subjectivities of Chilean adults because it is a society which continues to be characterized by deep political and ideological divisions (Huneeus, 2003). The process of transitioning to democracy began in 1990, and the seven civilian governments since then have faced the challenge of reckoning with the dictatorship's violent past, and its lasting institutional impacts in a society which continues to be profoundly divided.

2.1 Characteristics of Chilean Society Pre-Coup

In its first 200 years as an independent country, Chile enjoyed substantial political stability. The republic survived several periods of conflict in the nineteenth century, including four civil wars (1830–1831, 1850–1851, 1857, and 1891), and political turbulence in the twentieth century (1924–1925 and 1931–1932). However, the military coup in 1973 marked the beginning of a profound rupture with Chile's democratic tradition. The Pinochet dictatorship was the longest and most intense period of political violence in Chilean history. In order to understand how the coup came about, as well as the impact of the military regime, an overview of the key characteristics of Chilean society before 1973 is necessary:

Agrarian Society. The colonial hacienda system persisted in such a way that late into the twentieth century Chilean society was still, in some ways, a traditional agrarian society (Bengoa, 1988; Bellisario, 2006). Agricultural land ownership reproduced a system of hierarchical, servile, pre-capitalist social relations. In the 1930s, amidst political efforts to industrialize Chile, landowners managed to resist reforms and defend their economic interests. For several decades, landlords successfully delayed land reform and prevented unionization laws that favored peasants. This resulted in, even though American and British investments in the nitrate and copper industries played a significant role in the Chilean economy during the twentieth century, social structures of domination continuing to be closely related to land. As late as 1960, 80 percent of agricultural land corresponded to large estates (*fundos*, *haciendas*, or *latifundios*) owned by 2.1 percent of the population (Bellisario, 2006: 179). This concentration of power in the hands of landowners explains why the agrarian reform policies implemented under Presidents Frei Montalva and Allende had such a polarizing effect in the lead up to the coup in 1973 (Orellana, 2002: 67–70).

Unequal Society. Wealth and the means of production in Chile were heavily concentrated in the hands of a small number of economic groups or "clans" (Lagos, 1961), comprised of landlords as well as bankers and urban manufacturers. The proletarianization of labor-rent tenants (*inquilinos*), their family members, and salaried workers generated internal migration from rural to urban areas, where workers lived in impoverished conditions and barely subsisted on their meager paychecks. Most Chileans lived in poverty, with the poverty rate at 58.6 percent in 1951 (Ahumada, 1958). Meanwhile, oligarc FPar1 hs, businessmen, and landlords controlled the lives of workers and their families, who did not have enough resources to satisfy basic needs. In addition, the indigenous populations in northern and southern Chile were socially and economically marginalized. The social policies of Frei Montalva (1964–1970) and Allende (1970–1973) sought to address these high levels of inequality. The increasing political influence of the masses in the late 1960s, as well as the impending loss of economic power of the former ruling classes, fostered a growing sense of discontent among the elite, and an increasingly intense atmosphere of polarization.

State-Centrism. Before 1973, the state played a central role in the Chilean economy. After the world economic crisis of the 1930s, Chile adopted an economic strategy known as import substitution industrialization (*desarrollo hacia adentro*), which depended on state-led policies (Kay, 2000: 126). This developmental state model persisted for the next four decades, gaining further momentum in the 1950s and 1960s from the theories of development formulated by the Economic Commission for Latin America and the Caribbean (ECLA, then ECLAC). In addition, the state was the major employer of the middle class in public services, state-owned companies, public schools, infrastructure, armed forces, police, etc. However, the project of economic modernization via industrialization did not achieve the expected results, and Chile ultimately had low levels of manufacturing efficiency and technological development. After the coup, the military regime began to experiment with new economic models, and, ultimately, state-centrism was abandoned in favor of neoliberal economic policies (Atria et al., 2013: 24).

Mobilized Society. From the 1960s, until the military coup, as part of a greater trend throughout Latin America, protesters, union organizers, and radical political parties began to mobilize and demand improvement of their living conditions, hoping to put an end to decades of marginalization and social exclusion. The governments of Frei Montalva and Allende sought to address the social demands of underprivileged sectors through policies aiming to improve public education and public health services. Social and political mobilization of workers and peasants challenged the old order, provoking reactive counter-protests from the political and economic elites, defending their wealth, income, and privileged positions in society. Between 1970 and 1973, Chileans lived through the climax of the polarization of the class struggle. The outcome of the resulting political turmoil was deeply violent. As Alfredo Jocelyn-Holt points out, this was the most convulsive period in Chilean history: "Nothing before compares to the last thirty years. Neither density, drama, surprise endings, needless to say euphoria and chaos, dizziness and tears, fear and paralysis, anger and despair, or currently, complacency and self-flagellation, forgetfulness and apathy" (1998: 255).

Culture of Impunity. Chilean society has been divided by numerous political conflicts during the nineteenth and twentieth centuries. While policy compromises and constitutional reforms were sometimes used, Chile has a long history of using state repression, pardons, and amnesty laws to resolve political and ideological conflicts. According to Elizabeth Lira and Brian Loveman, the rule of law and impartiality of the criminal justice system were permanently subordinated to the search for political stability and governability (2014). In other words, since independence, Chilean institutions have always favored stability over directly confronting wrongdoing and crimes committed during political conflict. Generations of Chileans grew accustomed to this reality and had no expectation that justice would be served after a political conflict (Lira & Loveman, 2014). This pervasive culture of impunity allowed the military coup leaders to assume they would not be held accountable for their actions, and the prioritization of stability over justice persisted well after the dictatorship and into the political transition of the 1990s.

Legalistic or Formalistic Society. The Chilean legal culture was characterized by a pre-eminence of the written law. This meant that lawyers were highly respected and played a leading role in public debates, and that legal actors regarded the sources of written law as exceedingly important. This excessive respect for written law is evident in that for 140 years only two constitutions were in force in the country: the 1833 and the 1925 Constitutions. Furthermore, state repression has mostly been carried out in accordance with the legal system; the public authority used sources of law to validate their repressive actions. The elite that governed Chile gave special priority to public order and security, often at the expense of citizens' constitutional guarantees. Courts thus became the "everyday arena for the outcome and containment of political and ideological conflicts in a country so polarized" (Lira & Loveman, 2014: 275). In general, the lack of independence of judges prevented them from questioning the decisions of the executive branch. Pinochet took advantage of the legalistic nature of Chilean society to enshrine many of the institutional changes of his regime into law, for instance, through the creation of a new constitution in 1980. This made it difficult to reverse many of the dictatorship's policies even years after the transition to democracy.

2.2 Revolution in Liberty

The 1959 Cuban revolution sent a shockwave throughout Latin America, inspiring some and striking fear into others (Westad, 2018: 369). Against the backdrop of the Cold War, the goal of the US administration was to prevent more socialist parties from reaching power or emulating the Cuban phenomenon (Haslam, 2005: 12). In 1961, the Kennedy administration thus announced a new Latin American policy: the "Alliance for Progress." This policy took a positivist, developmental approach, seeking to prevent other revolutionary outbreaks in the region by providing economic aid to support policies and reforms that would improve the standard of living of impoverished populations (Casals, 2014: 94). It was in the context of this program that the CIA financed the campaign of reformist and moderate Christian Democrat Eduardo Frei Montalva in the 1964 presidential election. However, in addition to spending US$2.6 million on Frei's campaign, the CIA funded an anti-communist propaganda campaign known as the "campaign of terror" (Casals, 2014) with US$3 million to prevent Socialist Salvador Allende from winning (Kornbluh, 2004; Gustafson, 2007). Frei campaigned on the promise of a "Revolution in Liberty," combining a political program of economic modernization with social-Christian-inspired populism (Angell, 2009). In the end, with 56 percent of the votes, Frei won not only the election but also considerable support in the National Congress.

The Frei Montalva government sought to revitalize the economy through land reform, *chilenización* (partial nationalization) of copper mining, and housing construction, among other measures led by the state. Through these and other sweeping reforms, the Christian Democrats sought to decrease economic inequalities and increase productivity. They introduced important legal reforms regarding property rights, eminent domain, and agricultural land tenure. These reforms angered landowners and the political right. At the time, there was consensus between the political party leaders of the center and left on the need to implement an agrarian reform that would end the high levels of concentration of land ownership.

As such, in July 1967 Frei's government was able to enact Law No. 16,640, according to which all *fundos* and *latifundios* of more than 80 basic irrigated hectares were subject to expropriation if the agricultural land was underutilized or inefficiently farmed.[1] Landowners were only able to retain up to 80 hectares (*reserva*). Land reform inevitably introduced significant changes to the agrarian social structure, as it allowed peasants and less privileged sectors of society to own land and begin to form an agrarian middle class (Crispi, 1982: 481; Góngora, 1988: 129). The process of redistribution was as follows: first the inefficient large estate was expropriated, and then cooperative farms known as *asentamientos* were created (where the farmland was worked in common, but with small private plots for each family). Later, in theory, once the land was more productive, it would be redistributed among peasants. As compensation, the landlord received state bonds payable in the future. Alongside the agrarian reform, the Christian Democratic government adopted new labor and unionization legislation that promoted an expansion of the unionized labor force in industry and agriculture. This legislation and government support for labor mobilization greatly disrupted traditional labor relations, especially in the agricultural sector.

Another significant economic reform implemented by the Christian Democrat administration was the chilenización of large copper mines, such as El Teniente, Chuquicamata, and El Salvador (Magasich 2020a, 2020b: 73–9). In the 1960s, copper represented 60 percent of Chile's exports, and American companies Anaconda and Kennecott owned 85

[1] "Basic irrigated hectares" was a table of equivalencies applied to the agrarian reform, meant to adjust for farm size and economic potential in comparison with irrigated farms in the central valley.

percent of the copper industry (Sands, 1982: 54). After protracted negotiations, the Chilean state purchased 51 percent of the largest copper mines. Two additional relevant social reforms were implemented during Frei's government: the educational reform brought an increase of 46 percent in the total enrolment of students between 1964 and 1970—from 1.6 million to 2.2 million primary and secondary students—and about 250,000 houses were built and given mostly to the poor. While Frei's government had support from the urban middle classes, peasants, and the Catholic Church, its greatest ally was the White House; the financial support provided by the United States through the Alliance for Progress, as well as tax revenues, made it possible to fund major state-led initiatives (Winn, 2013: 40–41).

Collectively, the reforms implemented during the years of the "Revolution in Liberty" benefitted sectors of society who until then had had limited possibilities for education, housing, and economic progress. Nevertheless, these initiatives were not enough to convince the electorate. In the 1964 election, conservatives had voted for the Christian Democrats as the lesser of two evils, despite disagreeing with Frei's reformist policies (Riquelme, 2014: 8). The Christian Democrats had positioned themselves as an alternative to both liberal, capitalist individualism, and orthodox Marxism (Casals, 2014: 8). *El Pueblo* (the people) were waking up to the idea that radical change was possible, and so, despite the progress made by the Christian Democrats and their promises to accelerate the pace of the reforms, voters did not favor them in the 1970 presidential election. Alan Angell effectively summarizes the situation of the Christian Democratic Party in 1970 as follows: "For some the transformation was too slow, for others too fast" (1971: 87). In an increasingly polarized society, the middle ground was less attractive than the extremes. Salvador Allende triumphed in his fourth attempt at the presidency, supported by the Communist Party and the other leftist parties that formed the Unidad Popular (Popular Unity) coalition.

2.3 Popular Unity

On November 3rd, 1970, Socialist Senator Salvador Allende became the first freely elected Marxist president in the world's history. In the midst of the Cold War, Allende's victory immediately drew the attention and dismay of the Nixon Administration (Magasich, 2020a, 2020b: 48). The novelty of the Popular Unity (UP) coalition's approach was the so-called

Chilean road to Socialism: establishing a socialist government through democratic means, without violence or revolution, and within the bounds of the law (Westad, 2018: 376). Some authors and politicians have called this revolution without sacrifices and sought within the rules of the democratic game "revolution with empanadas and red wine" (Orellana, 2002: 77; Winn, 2013: 45). But this would not be an easy task as, unlike Frei, Allende did not have the support of the majority in Congress. He narrowly defeated both the conservative right-wing and the reformist Christian Democrat candidates, receiving 36.6 percent of the 2.9 million valid votes. Despite the political difficulties that the UP faced in passing legislation, nearly half of Chilean voters were in favor of accelerating the process of social transformation and reform, which is evident in the fact that the UP Coalition parties reached 49 percent in the 1971 local elections, and 44 percent in the 1973 parliamentary elections.

The UP government sought to drastically change the social, political, and economic structures of domination in Chilean society through the implementation of a sweeping political program of nationalizations, with the goal of developing a socialist economy and reducing the high levels of economic inequality. On July 11, 1971, a constitutional reform and a new law (No. 17,450) aimed at nationalizing the large mining sector were unanimously approved. This meant that the most important copper mines in the country became state owned. American investors were not fully compensated in the takeover, as the Chilean government considered they had been compensated for years in unpaid taxes. The Nixon administration predictably responded with outrage at these attacks against the United States' strategic and economic interests. Allende then began the process of nationalizing the private banks by buying shares, and, by the end of 1971, the state controlled 90 percent of the banking sector (Winn, 2013: 55). In addition to these new reforms, the UP government also radicalized the agrarian reform begun under the previous administration, by speeding up expropriation processes and proposing the formation of new forms of peasants' organizations.

The agrarian reforms implemented under Frei and Allende transformed property relations in the agrarian sector and dismantled the old *hacienda* social structure. During their respective governments, 59 percent of Chile's agricultural land was expropriated (5809 estates, nearly 10 million hectares) (Crispi, 1982: 483; Grupo de Investigaciones Agrarias, 1979; Bellisario, 2006: 199), benefiting nearly 61,000 peasant households and

15,000 single men who worked directly on the new land units or small-sized family farms (Bellisario, 2007). The final major objective of the UP was the development of a social sector of the economy, which required the nationalization of 90 strategic companies, such as electricity distributors and cement producers (each with more than one million dollars capital). The state intervened in most of these industries using decree-laws (*decretos leyes*), which were legal loopholes (*resquicios legales*) that originated in the 1930s, in order to force the owners to sell to the state (Novoa, 1992; Sepúlveda, A, 2020: 56).

Through these actions, Allende's government sought to develop a socialist economy by controlling the mining, financial, and other relevant industrial sectors (Schlotterbeck, 2018: 2). A state-centrist planning approach was adopted to coordinate the decision-making process throughout the country. On the one hand, these broad reforms infuriated bankers, landlords, the Chilean elite, and business owners, while on the other they garnered the UP significant support from many sectors the agricultural and industrial working classes.

Public authorities of the UP were empowered by the idea of creating a new, more equal society by transforming socio-economic structural conditions, and the project of developing a socialist economy had the support of the most vulnerable, neglected, and marginalized sectors of Chilean society. After so many years of abuse and hopelessness, it was the first time that many of them felt dignified and represented. Allende's government worked to improve and increase social services, which allowed many people who would not otherwise have had the resources to access a higher education: 70,795 students were registered in the eight universities throughout the country in 1970, and three years later that number more than doubled to 146,451 (Brunner, 1986).

These changes sparked anger and fear in the traditional elite, transnational corporations, right-wing political parties, conservative press, and the White House. These groups not only opposed the UP's program of change, but actively contributed to the destabilization of the economy and the exacerbation of tensions (Kornbluh, 2003; United States Senate, 1975). They were behind a number of efforts to undermine Allende's government including a 76-day strike at El Teniente copper mine, which produced more than US$300 million per year (Ruiz-Tagle, 1973: 217); the track owners' strike of 27 days in 1972 and 1973, which the CIA financed with more than US$2 million; and 253 violent attacks and acts of terrorism in 1973 from both left- and right-wing extremist groups.[2]

These destabilization efforts included sponsored street violence and misinformation campaigns, such as that of El Mercurio newspaper, which received US$4,165,000 from the CIA to misinform the population and cause fear, and they exacerbated supply problems and galloping inflation (Agüero, 2008; Skoknic, 2013). The results of these tactics scared urban and middle classes into political action; women from the upper classes protested in the streets with their pots and pans (*cacerolazos*). Faced with this difficult atmosphere, President Allende sought a political solution by including certain senior members of the armed forces in the cabinet, but negotiations with the leaders of the Christian Democratic Party were unsuccessful. At the end of 1972, Allende personally visited the Soviet Union to request economic and military support but returned to Chile with only US$20 million (Fermandois, 2013: 461–462; Lagos, 2013: 246).

In the 1973 congressional elections, the opposition had hoped to obtain the necessary seats in parliament to impeach and remove President Allende, but they fell short. Interestingly, despite the volatile political atmosphere that existed in the country, and the importance of this particular election, 18.25 percent of registered adult voters chose not to vote, demonstrating that even at a time of high political tension there was a sector of citizens relatively indifferent to public issues, or at least unmotivated to vote in an important election.

On August 22, 1973, the Chamber of Deputies declared that the UP government had violated the 1925 Constitution. Feeling besieged, Allende chose to play his last card: to call a referendum for the population to state whether the government had the support of the electorate (González, 2013: 325). But the same day that Allende had scheduled to address the country, the military coup took place. On September 11, 1973, Chileans could only watch on in shock and horror as state forces bombed La Moneda presidential palace; events which would bring about the death of President Allende. That fateful day in 1973 forever marked the lives of 10 million Chileans, and the generations to come.

All of this took place even though more than 40 percent of voters supported the democratically elected government. The right-wing and most of the Christian Democrats thought that the armed forces were going to reestablish order and convene new elections within a reasonable timeframe.

[2] Left-wing groups such as the Movimiento de Izquierda Revolucionaria (MIR) and right-wing groups such as Frente Nacionalista Patria y Libertad and Comando Rolando Matus.

This opinion was shared by former President Frei—then President of the Senate—who rather naively thought that the military would call him promptly to preside over the country. For the left, September 11, 1973, marked the end of an organized and profoundly aspirational political process that sought to create a more equal society. The coup disrupted a long-lasting democratic and republican tradition in Chile and launched the country into a long period of violence and repression.

2.4 Pinochet's Dictatorship

After Frei's "Revolution in Liberty" and Allende's "Chilean Road to Socialism," the 1973 military coup and subsequent 17 years of dictatorship were essentially a counter-revolution, led by the armed forces and right-wing civilians. The project of this counter-revolution was the refounding of Chile, with the goal of permanently transforming its institutions and culture. This transformation involved four main steps: neutralizing the opposition and eradicating all forms of dissent (Echeverría, 2008: 84), dismantling glimpses of the welfare state promoted in the previous governments, replacing it with the neoliberal economic model, and implementing a new constitution that would permanently enshrine these changes in the country's most important institutions.

The process began with the repression and elimination of all opposition to the regime. The armed forces, the police, and the secret police controlled society. Congress was immediately dissolved, and political parties were banned (Winn, 2013: 126). The armed forces and the secret police services strongly suppressed the popular movement and the social and political leaders who for a decade had managed to introduce reforms and structural transformations in Chilean society. Two parallel social realities began to develop under the dictatorship: for some, the Pinochet years were defined by fear, persecution, tragedy, and state terrorism, for others—mainly those who reaped the benefits of the institutional and economic changes introduced by the military regime—the repression was a justifiable and necessary stage in the supposed re-foundation of modern Chile (Pino-Ojeda, 2011: 15).

To justify the state terrorism against members of the opposition and the political left, the armed forces spared no time or resources in creating an official narrative and interpretation of what was happening in the country. Immediately after the coup, the regime used the media to spread a discourse of fear, declaring that the country was in the first stages of a potential civil war. This was done through a fake news campaign exposing Plan Z, an alleged plot by left-wing extremists to overthrow the government, kill the civilian and military elite, and seize their property in a violent communist revolution. According to Steve Stern and Peter Winn, "the false Plan Z was a typical disinformation campaign. It facilitated the formation of a climate of war and indifference toward, the repression…in that sense, Pinochet was the savior of the nation" (2014: 206). This propaganda tool ensured that supporters of the dictatorship perceived the armed forces as having prevented a civil war between Chileans, and as having saved Chile from becoming a second Cuba in Latin America. This supposed climate of war was used to justify severe repression of left-wing politicians and citizens, especially throughout the first five years of the dictatorship.

The armed forces and their secret police services, first the National Intelligence Directorate (DINA, 1974–1977) and then the National Information Centre (CNI, 1977–1990) (Salazar, 2011; Salazar, 2012), "widely and systematically kidnapped, tortured, and subsequently and secretly murdered (and hid the bodies of) opponents as an instrument of state terror" (Sanabria, 2007: 363). Leaders and members of the parties that formed the UP—Socialist Party (PS), Communist Party (PC), Christian Left Party (IC), Unitary Popular Action Movement (MAPU), and other smaller political parties—as well as the Revolutionary Left Movement (MIR) were violently persecuted, leaving the dictatorship's political opposition eviscerated by fear and repression.

The military not only targeted those who expressed direct opposition to the dictatorship but also sought to frighten the whole of society into submission (Lira & Castillo, 1991). They controlled civilians in all aspects of life, generating an atmosphere of fear throughout the country (Ochoa & Maillard, 2011: 21). The defense of human rights was almost impossible, and most of the habeas corpus writs (*recursos de amparo*) were rejected by courts. In 1978, the dictatorship approved a self-amnesty decree-law that prevented most attempts at criminal investigations against state agents in the following years.[3] Without the possibility of defending themselves, the Chilean people were left to the whims of the secret police and armed forces.

The repression carried out under the Pinochet regime was organized and systematic. As Silvia Borzutzky points out, the repression "was the

[3] See Decree-Law No. 2191, Amnesty Law (19 April 1978).

result of a well-planned and structured process coordinated at the highest level of government by two men [Augusto Pinochet and Manuel Contreras] determined to eradicate Marxists and Marxism from the face of Chile" (2017: 20). The extent of the human rights abuses that occurred during this period has since been officially investigated through a series of national truth commissions (O'Shaughnessy, 2000: 69). These concluded that 3216 people were executed or are still missing (Collins et al., 2013: 46; Collins 2013: 88), 40,018 people have been recognized as victims of political imprisonment or torture, 12,000 people sought asylum in embassies, 1132 torture centers have been identified throughout the country (Presidential Advisory Commission for the Qualification of Disappeared Detainees, Political Executed, and Victims of Political Imprisonment and Torture Report, 2011), 200,000 people lived abroad in exile (Wright & Oñate, 2007; Stern, 2009: 24), and only a quarter of them have returned to the country. Even outside the country Chileans were not safe from state terrorism because of the so-called Operation Condor (Echeverría, 2008: 114)—a secret police alliance between Argentina, Bolivia, Brazil, Chile, Paraguay, and Uruguay, in which the neighboring authoritarian regimes, with financial support from the United States, collaborated in persecuting those seeking political exile (Winn, 2013: 12; Lessa, 2019). These figures show the magnitude of state terrorism. One of the most widespread practices under the dictatorship was torture; however, due to social stigma, many torture victims' testimonies have only come to light recently. These testimonies reveal shocking levels of sadism and cruelty by state agents, attacks on the dignity of the victims, and inhumane conditions of detention (e.g., Kunstmann & Torres, 2008; Valdés, 1996[1974]; Cassidy, 2002[1977]; Montealegre, 2003; Policzer, 2009: Ch. 5; Becker, 2011; Casassus, 2013). The wounds from this long period of state violence and repression run deep in Chilean society, and the traumatic consequences of torture, as well as the continued search for the bodies of disappeared detainees, continue to haunt victims and their families. These crimes were denounced to the Inter-American Commission of Human Rights, the International Labour Organization, and human rights advocacy groups such as Amnesty International and Human Rights Watch.

Among the civilian population, many people knew of the dictatorship's repression. While some civilian groups took action to try and help victims of state terror, such as the interfaith group Peace Committee, and later the Vicariate of Solidarity led by Cardinal Raúl Silva Henríquez (Aranda, 2004: 86), much of the population remained silent. Many civilians identified, reported, and actively collaborated in the arrest and torture of others, while others ignored or even agreed with the actions of the state against alleged "subversives." The conformity of many sectors of the population to the action of the dictatorship can partially be attributed to fear, but indifference and self-interest also played a role. The military regime could not have lasted for 17 years without a significant amount of civilian complicity.

Civilian complicity and support for the dictatorship is nowhere more evident than in the implementation of the neoliberal model in Chile. Upon seizing power in 1973, the coup leaders made their intentions clear: to re-establish social and economic order and undo the excessive "statism" of the UP government. The military did not have a concrete economic plan, however (Gárate, 2013: 5), and instead sought economic expertise elsewhere. They found it in the "Chicago Boys," a group of Chilean economists who had studied under Milton Friedman and Arnold Harberger at the University of Chicago (Valdés, 1995). The Chicago Boys' neoliberal economic program consequently became a cornerstone of the regime's project of transforming the country from its very foundations. As David Harvey points out in *A Brief History of Neoliberalism*, Chile was the first neoliberal experiment ever implemented in the world (2007: 7).

Throughout the course of the dictatorship, the armed forces set about liberalizing the Chilean economy and establishing the foundations of a free market economy based on private capitalism. The precarious welfare state was taken apart: most state-owned companies were privatized, with labor and employment laws, as well as the education, health, and pension systems all being modified according to neoliberal postulates. During the first years of the dictatorship, agrarian reform was reversed, and trade union activities were restricted. Three-fifths of the expropriated land was granted back to former landowners, auctioned off in the private market, or given to public or non-profit organizations. Nearly 29,000 peasant families lost their newly acquired land, and only two-fifths of the expropriated land remained in the hands of peasant families (Crispi, 1982: 487; Bellisario, 2006: 199). As the beginning of what would become a long trend of repression of labor organizations, the government tried to depoliticize and co-opt trade unions, attempting to create a restricted, new form of syndicalism in Chile.

However, the neoliberal doctrine began to solidify in 1975 with the implementation of the National Economic Recovery Program. This program had three goals: reduce inflation, balance the public budget with a severe austerity program, and introduce free market initiatives. Tariffs were lowered, interest rates were freed, price distortions were eliminated, and foreign investments were encouraged by tax stability and the repatriation of profits. The severe austerity measures, known as the "shock treatment," had a profound impact on the middle-class, industry workers, and small businesses. Chile experienced a deep recession, and by 1976 unemployment had risen by nearly 20 percent and real salaries had fallen to about 40 percent of what they had been in 1970, while inflation had not lowered significantly (Gárate, 2013: 26).

The second generation of structural reforms, known as "The Seven Modernizations," was initiated in 1979. In this new phase, the aim of the Chicago Boys was that the state interfere as little as possible in the economy. As such, the mediating role of the state in labor disputes disappeared, and over 100 state-owned companies were privatized. The new set of reforms included privatization of the pension system, "municipalization" of the educational system, privatization of healthcare, decentralization and modernization of the public administration, agrarian modernization, transformation of the judiciary, and deregulation of labor and employment relations (Foxley, 1982: 83–87; Silva, 1991: 395). The reform of labor legislation (*Plan Laboral*) in particular drew the ire of many workers. It deregulated the labor market, limited the right to strike, and decreased the representative power of trade unions.[4]

On several occasions, trade union leaders denounced the dictatorship to the International Labour Organization (ILO) for violating freedom of association and human rights, forcing the government to respond but also to consider the recommendations made by the ILO (Lira & Rojas, 2009). Along with these reforms, a process of ideological and bureaucratic clearance was conducted in universities and public services, and those who spoke out against or were known to disagree with the regime were laid off. These measures severely affected the incomes of thousands of Chilean families (Brunner, 1986: 141). The neoliberal changes made by the regime, a key pillar of the "counter-revolution" of the armed forces and the elite, would not have been possible in a democracy, where competing views and models for the future of Chile would have required any reform to undergo substantial debate, discussion, and compromise. Furthermore, the brutal repression of the dictatorship prevented the population from protesting against the decisions of the military leaders.

[4] See Decree Law No. 2200, Labour Code (June 15, 1978); Decree Law No. 2756, Trade Unions Law (July 3, 1979); Decree Law No. 2758, Collective Bargaining Law (July 6, 1979).

In order to permanently enshrine these changes within the state's institutions, the armed forces imposed a new social contract: the 1980 Constitution. The 1925 Constitution was abolished and the new one approved in a dubious referendum without sufficient electoral guarantees (Angell, 2009: 238; Fuentes, 2013). The new constitution established the structures of the institutions of the Chilean state, providing stability and legitimacy to the Military Junta and its decisions. It strongly protected the right to private property, favored the subsidiary role of the state, declared that the armed forces were the guarantors of the institutional order, prohibited the existence of Marxist political parties—in the infamous Article 8, which would be derogated nine years later—and set authoritarian enclaves and the timetable for the transition to democracy.

Even the civil and political rights guaranteed under the new constitution did not protect civilians, as the Chilean people continued living under a state of constitutional exception for several years. There was no freedom of the press, and the media were permanently controlled and censored (Sorensen, 2011: 400). The 1980 Constitution continues to be in force today, although it has been modified various times. Some elements of the armed forces' "counter-revolutionary" project continue to be protected by the constitution and its associated organic laws (*leyes orgánicas constitucionales*), which preserve many elements of the regime's ideology, as well as many of the Pinochet-era reforms, namely, those regarding the healthcare, education, and pension systems. Despite having been partially modified, these policies have survived 30 years of transitional governments and have contributed to increasing the wealth gap in Chile.

Soon after the approval of the 1980 Constitution, Chile experienced its worst economic crisis since the Great Depression. In the short term, the von Hayek-Friedman-Harberger neoliberal economic reforms made by the Catholic University's Chicago Boys did not achieve the expected results (Sanhueza, 1999; Winn, 2013: 131). The main causes of the crisis were not only international economic factors but also errors in the domestic economic policy (Hojman, 1996: 77). In 1982–1983, the GDP fell by -14.5 percent (Huneeus, 2000: 508). With eight banks bankrupted, interventions were made in the financial sector: free-floating exchange rates replaced the US dollar fixed exchange rate, the unemployment rate exceeded 23 percent—the highest in the last 55 years, and, reaching 32 percent if emergency and precarious employment programmes are included (Contreras & Ffrench-Davis, 2012)—the real wages decreased, and Chile's external debt rose to 17 billion dollars (one of the highest debts per capita in the world). All this resulted in economic instability that led to an increase of poverty and a sense of insecurity within Chilean society.

The severe economic crisis triggered a series of national protests in rejection of the dictatorship. From May 11, 1983, copper workers, trade unions, university students, human rights movements, grassroots organizations, and political leaders called for a set of national protests on the streets of the major cities (Passmore, 2017: 7). As they did not have authorization, the police, the military, and CNI agents repressed protesters, conducted raids, and systematically violated the human rights of opponents of the dictatorship. In response to the recession, Pinochet appointed a new technocratic economic team to make drastic adjustments, including trade liberalization, financial deregulation, privatization of state enterprises at low prices, recapitalization of firms and banks, etc. The economy began to recover in 1984, and after 1985, the international community highlighted Chile's sustained economic growth, even labelling it "the Chilean Miracle" (Drake, 2004: ix.).

The economic crisis and subsequent popular protests marked an awakening of Chilean society, confronting this supposed "silent revolution" carried out during the dictatorship (Winn, 2013: 131). Despite the ban declared by the Junta immediately after the 1973 coup, from 1983 onward, political parties began to reorganize their activities. New political magazines and newspapers were created opposing the regime and circulated underground. However, there was division among opponents of Pinochet around how to end the dictatorship. The center-left decided to follow the path to transition laid out in the 1980 Constitution, which called for a referendum in 1988 to decide whether Pinochet would remain another eight years or whether presidential elections would be held, while the extreme left such as the Manuel Rodríguez Patriotic Front (FPMR), MIR, and MAPU-Lautaro, opted for the more radical means of armed resistance.

During the mid-1980s, the center-left constructed an alternative, dissident political project (Tironi, 2013); mainly Christian Democrats and Socialists were united in the Alianza Democrática (Democratic Alliance). This partnership later became the Coalition of Parties for the No Vote (known as Concertación), who worked together on the No campaign in the 1988 referendum. Meanwhile, the FPMR attempted to organize undercover sabotage operations and clandestinely smuggle weapons into the country. On September 7, 1986, the FPMR carried out an ambush in the hills on the outskirts of Santiago with the intention of assassinating Pinochet (Peña, 2007). The dictator survived the attack, but 5 of his bodyguards were killed and 11 were injured.

After the attack on Pinochet took place, the repression intensified and the extreme left was brutally persecuted (Tricot, 2015). There were several exceptionally violent crimes during this period of civil resistance which shocked the population, such as the Slaughtered Case (*Caso Degollados*) in 1985, the Case of the Burnt (*Caso Quemados*) in 1986, the murder of Tucapel Jiménez, President of the National Association of Public Employees (ANEF) in 1982, and the murders of 12 members of the FPMR at the hands of state agents in the so-called Albania Operation in 1987, among other cases. While the number of dead and missing was lower than in the first phase of the dictatorship, the levels of political imprisonment and torture remained considerable. For example, the Truth and Reconciliation Report (1991) recognized a total of 345 cases of death or disappearance between 1983 and 1990. The 1980s were thus marked by a combination of underground resistance on the one hand, and repression and fear on the other.

According to the constitution, in 1988 voters would have the opportunity to choose between another 8 years of Pinochet's rule (the Yes option), or free presidential elections within a year after the referendum (the No option). The leaders of Concertación believed it would be possible to defeat Pinochet according to the rules that he had set in 1980 and called on the population to register on the electoral rolls. In 1987 the Political Parties Law was enacted, and electoral registers were opened. In April of that same year, Pope John Paul II visited Chile for 6 days. In his speech to young people in the National Stadium, he asked them not to fall into apathy about what appeared to be impossible. Chileans needed to hear words of hope and peace, and this is exactly what the Pope's narrative gave them—hope. This message of hope inspired the social scientists and electoral experts of the Concertación to design the televised marketing campaign for the No campaign in 1988 (Otano, 2006: Ch. 4; Tironi, 2013: Ch. 22).

The armed forces designed and implemented a political campaign of fear and false information, warning Chileans that the triumph of the *No* option would imply returning to the chaos of the UP. Censorship, control of the media, and restrictions to freedom of expression continued to govern the country. In response to this message of fear, and chaos, the No campaign created an inventive television campaign full of hope whose symbolism and theme song have become iconic of the end of the dictatorship. Political leaders of the left spoke out and criticized the regime openly; in the first live televised interview with Ricardo Lagos of the Partido por la Democracia, he courageously challenged General Pinochet on camera, addressing the dictator directly on live TV. Lagos invited the undecided to trust in the project of Concertación, and his bravery in speaking out encouraged the population to hope and trust that change was possible (Lagos, 2013: 615–631). The *No* campaign was not only a turning point, but an epic feat that inspired adults to register in the electoral rolls and vote in favor of holding democratic elections (Tironi, 2013).

Society was strongly polarized leading up to the referendum between supporters and opponents of Pinochet. On the date of the referendum, October 5, 1988, there was a very high voter turnout as "almost 82 percent of eligible Chileans cast valid votes in the 1989 legislative elections" (Carlin, 2006: 636). The anti-dictatorial political project triumphed in the referendum called by the Junta de Gobierno: the No campaign won, with 56 percent of the valid votes. The fact that 44 percent of voters still supported Pinochet in 1988 can be partly attributed to the *Yes* campaign's message of fear and chaos, which persuaded some undecided voters to stick to what they knew rather than risk the unknown. Fifteen years of dictatorship, censorship, and political propaganda in favor of Pinochet, likely also influenced many voters (Tironi, 2013: Ch. 21).

Nevertheless, the win of the *No* campaign was a historic moment which marked the beginning of a complex process of transition. The subsequent democratic governments had to contend with the continued presence of Pinochet in government for many years. The armed forces' project of refounding of the country was intended to last forever. As such, the psychological and institutional impacts of the dictatorship's legacy have proved difficult to undo.

2.5 Democratic Transition

After nearly 17 years of dictatorship, re-democratizing society and public institutions has not been a simple task for the democratically elected authorities. In 1989, after the win of the No campaign, the Democratic Alliance and the armed forces negotiated Chile's pacted transition, determining the conditions of the return to democracy. This pact included constitutional reforms that aimed to remove the most evident authoritarian elements of the 1980 Constitution and shift the balance of power toward civilians. The reforms reaffirmed the state's obligation to protect human rights and removed certain presidential powers such as the power to exile citizens or to dissolve parliament (Escudero, 2018: 120).

However, many authoritarian features of the 1980 Constitution such as institutions and processes designed to preserve the institutional and political-economic models imposed under the dictatorship remained (Garretón, 1989). As a result, the transfer of government from military to civilian hands in 1990 did not equate to a full transfer of power. The "transition" of the Chilean transitional justice process is therefore difficult to define, as the legacy of the dictatorship has been dismantled slowly overtime. Since the end of Pinochet's rule, there have been seven democratically elected governments: Patricio Aylwin (1990–1994), Eduardo Frei Ruiz-Tagle (1994–2000), Ricardo Lagos (2000–2006), Michelle Bachelet (2006–2010), Sebastián Piñera (2010–2014), Michelle Bachelet (2014–2018), and Sebastián Piñera (2018–2022).

On March 11, 1990, General Pinochet handed over the presidential sash to Christian Democrat Patricio Aylwin, the newly elected president of Chile, in what marked the official political transition to democracy. The core theme of Patricio Aylwin's government was political reconciliation (Loveman & Lira, 2000: Ch. 9). In the first years of his government, reconciliation seemed to go hand in hand with addressing past human rights abuses. One of Aylwin's most significant transitional justice actions was the creation of the Truth and Reconciliation Commission, also known as the Rettig Commission, a few months after getting into office. The Rettig Commission investigated the most serious crimes of the dictatorship: executions of political prisoners and disappeared detainees. Other types of human rights abuses, including crimes of torture, were excluded from the investigation. The report strongly condemned various different state institutions for their involvement or collaboration in committing human rights abuses. It also included various recommendations for reparations for victims of the dictatorship, including the reparations program implemented under Aylwin's government.[5]

When the Commission's report was released on March 1991, President Aylwin addressed the country and tearfully apologized to the victims and their relatives on behalf of the state, calling on the military to make gestures of recognition as well. However, the armed forces, the judiciary, and right-wing parties flatly rejected the findings and declared that the report did not offer an objective and complete interpretation of what had

[5] *See* Chap. 4: Reparations for the Victims.

happened in the country since the late 1960s. Steve Stern and Peter Winn refer to this reaction as the wall of "military silence" (2014: 214). In March and early April 1991, soon after the release of the report, four homicides were committed by the extreme revolutionary group FPMR against known Pinochet supporters: a CNI doctor who had assisted in acts of torture in the military regiment in Rancagua, his wife, a prefect of the investigative police (PDI), and Santiago senator Jaime Guzmán, a well-known *pinochetista* and the mind behind the 1980 Constitution (Spooner, 2011: 50). These violent events overshadowed the report, and social tensions began to reemerge (Angell, 2009: 256).

In the first years of the transition, the threat of a return to authoritarianism and violence was very present. The fragile state of Chilean democracy was especially evident in two military demonstrations, on December 19, 1990, and May 28, 1993, respectively, which Pinochet used as a show of power to frighten the new government and the population. The authoritarian enclaves in the 1980 Constitution made constitutional and political reform extremely difficult: the armed forces and right-wing parties were overrepresented in both chambers of the National Congress due of the presence of nine appointed senators and the effects of the binominal electoral system.[6] Pinochet and his allies had designated the appointed senators, and under this electoral system, the opposition only needed 34 percent of the valid votes in each electoral district to win half of the elected parliamentary seats.

Due to the high quorums required in Congress, the right-wing opposition had an impressive veto power. Consequently, pro-dictatorship and pinochetista factions worked to prevent the Concertación coalition from controlling legislation and constitutional reform. In fact, Pinochet himself remained present in government first as Commander in Chief of the Army until March 11, 1998, and then as senator for life (*senador vitalicio*). In Aylwin's own words, his government acted and made changes to the extent possible, i.e., as far as the de facto powers allowed.[7] The leaders of

[6] The appointed senators were eliminated in the constitutional reform of 2005. The binominal electoral system was replaced in 2015 by a proportional model (Law No. 20.840, May 5, 2015).

[7] The expression "justice to the extent possible" was coined by Patricio Aylwin on December 31, 1990, when explaining how much justice could be accomplished in human rights cases. The expression *poderes fácticos* (de facto powers) was made by Andrés Allamand when referring to the armed forces, the business elite, and El Mercurio (Drake & Jaksic, 1999: 28).

Concertación had to negotiate political agreements with the right-wing parties to address all strategic or politically sensitive issues, including past human rights violations, and thus they approached the issue with pragmatism and moderation (Hidalgo, 2011: 66).

The pursuit of justice was difficult, as the former dictator threatened that if one of his men was touched it would mean the end of the rule of law (Agnic, 2006: 40), and because the main way to prevent a return to authoritarianism was to govern through consensus. The influence and antagonism of the armed forces and pinochetista factions meant that the Concertación had to be creative in order to allow the course of transitional justice to continue. For instance, to prevent the closure of human rights cases, Aylwin asked the Supreme Court to reinterpret the Amnesty Law, allowing judges to continue investigating human rights violations even if eventually they would be required to apply the amnesty decree. As the judicial culture had been complicit with the dictatorship, from the beginning of the transition, it was possible to warn that the judicial battles for the cases of human rights violations would be complex.

Many politicians were afraid to address human rights issues because of their politically charged nature, worrying that the conflicts and hatreds of the past could return, which would in turn jeopardize democratic governability (Hite, 2000). For this reason, the Truth and Reconciliation Commission was lauded by many as resolving the "human rights problem." President Aylwin suddenly announced in 1991 that the transition was over. As such, the concept of social reconciliation replaced the notion of human rights that had been a key element in the narrative of the Concertación in the 1988 referendum.

Instead of promoting an honest and complete confrontation of the past in order to be able to move forward, the desire for peace and consensus imposed an unacknowledged culture of silence and oblivion with regard to human rights violations, even while many of the human rights violations perpetrated by the regime had not yet been investigated or brought to light, especially the widespread use of torture. Alex Wilde refers to the transition's public life as the "conspiracy of consensus," an aversion to discussing and debating among the political elite, in favor of consensus-building. This conspiracy of consensus permeated the whole of Chilean society, which was dominated by a profound fear of conflict or of a new military coup (Wilde, 1999: 476). In retrospect, the leaders of Concertación may have exercised an excess of political prudence because the constant search for consensus had tremendous political and cultural costs: the demobilization of society, acceptance of the veto power of the right-wing and the armed forces, and renouncing the introduction of significant changes in the economic-political model. As Gómez-Barris points out, "reconciliation as a form of concealment operated through patriarchal pacts of transition, forcing closure over what had yet to be revealed" (2009: 25).

The conspiracy of consensus reached new heights when Christian Democrat Eduardo Frei Ruiz-Tagle was elected president for the period of 1994–2000. President Frei was elected on the promise of "modernization." His aim was to consolidate economic growth, further internationalize the economy, reduce poverty, and reform the educational system. However, his human rights policy was virtually non-existent, and there were even explicit declarations by members of his administration that human rights would not be a "fundamental theme" of his government (Borzutzky, 2017: 92). According to Collins, "the dead and disappeared in Chile vanished from the eyes of many people who were not directly linked to this cause, so naturally other concerns took their place" (2014: 148). In terms of "modernization," on the other hand, the growth of the economy between 1990 and 1998 was remarkable, with a growth rate that averaged more than 7 percent per year (Jadresic & Zahler, 2000: 3). In 1990 38.6 percent of the population lived in poverty, and that figure was reduced to 21.7 percent in 1998 (Larrañaga & Rodríguez, 2014: 17). The search for high rates of economic growth required the development of an entrepreneurial culture in the country, where innovation and self-confidence were overvalued. Chilean society began to display signs of arrogance. The culture of silence and oblivion that had begun to emerge surrounding human rights violations solidified into a culture of blatant indifference.

During the dictatorship, those who were indifferent simply remained silent, but in the 1990s the indifferent people began to openly say that they were not interested in the country's affairs. Chilean tennis player Marcelo Ríos, who was number 1 in the world in 1998, coined the expression *no estoy ni ahí* (I could not care less), epitomizing the common social attitude of indifference. The public's sense of discomfort with politicians and political activity was manifested in the phrase *no estoy ni ahí con la política* (I could not care less about politics): in this competitive, consumerist, and individualistic society, the only things that matter are my own efforts and plans. *No estoy ni ahí* became the mainstream motto of the 1990s. The growing disinterest in politics was evident in regular public opinion surveys, particularly within the younger generations. In 1993, 19 percent of citizens did not answer or did not know when asked about their political self-identification on a spectrum from right to left. That figure rose to 56 percent in 1998 (Joignant, 2002: 93). As Lechner remarks, "old solidarities [were] displaced by a negative individualism" and social ties were weakened (1998: 238). In this technocratic market logic, public affairs were gradually displaced from the political arena, and private life was privileged as never before (Atria et al., 2013: 12–13).

Citizens were frustrated with the limited achievements during the transition, and they held the leaders of the *Concertación* partially responsible because of their political caution. There was disappointment among the *Concertación* electorate regarding broken promises made in the 1988 referendum and ensuing electoral campaigns: a new constitution was not passed, the population had limited access to the truth about the human rights abuses, and the vast majority of the perpetrators were eluding prosecution and punishment for human rights violations. Steve Stern and Peter Winn summarize the dilemma in which society found itself at that time in the following terms:

> In a society of divided memory and devoid of significant initiatives, the feeling of frustration and abandonment was powerful for civil society activists. Measures taken against oblivion could occur in a very restricted level but seemed stuck in a dead end—the indifference, ambivalence, the impasse—in the whole political body. (2014: 225–226)

Then, an unforeseen event occurred. The arrest of Pinochet in London on October 16, 1998, changed the course of the Chilean transition (Rojas, 2001; Blanco, 2010: 114), reigniting a strong desire for justice and once again sparking public interest in human rights issues. In response to the public outcry, Frei's government began the *Mesa de Diálogo* (The Dialogue Roundtable) between August 1999 and June 2000. This initiative brought together human rights activists, lawyers, academics, religious leaders, and representatives of the armed forces, with the main objective of locating the corpses of the disappeared detainees or obtaining information to clarify their fate. While the results of the Mesa de Diálogo were inconclusive and disappointing for human rights organizations, it was the first time the armed forces had accepted responsibility for any of the abuses under the Pinochet regime.

Moreover, it put the issue of human rights on the political agenda: in January 2000, Ricardo Lagos was elected president on the promise that he would seek to complete the transition to democracy and settle accounts with the past. Two months later, after 503 days under house arrest, Pinochet was declared unfit to stand trial by the British government and returned to Chile on March 3rd, 2000. However, the trials abroad created momentum and desire for Pinochet to be tried at home, and upon his return to Chile, he faced judicial investigation not only for the commission of human rights violations but also for the commission of tax fraud (known as the Riggs Case). After eight years of legal battles, he died on December 10, 2006, managing to avoid conviction for the atrocities in which he participated (Amorós, 2019: 755).

The tension brought about by Pinochet's detention in London triggered unexpected scenarios not only for public authorities but for ordinary citizens as well. Issues that had been silenced for years began to receive public attention. In particular, the issue of the use of torture during the dictatorship emerged as a pending issue that had yet to be addressed. To commemorate 30 years of the coup, there was an "explosion of memory" in September 2003. Citizens spoke out about their experiences. Intellectuals and some center-left politicians had already begun to criticize the democratic transition and the slow pace of transitional justice (Moulian, 1997; de la Parra, 1997; Cortés Terzi, 2000; Lechner, 1998). In response to these demands, President Lagos proposed a new policy on human rights *No Hay Mañana Sin Ayer* (There is no tomorrow without yesterday, 2003), which included new reparation measures and proposed the creation of a second truth commission. The Commission on Torture and Political Imprisonment released the official identification of victims in 2004, and then supplemented these results in 2005 and 2011, finally bringing to light and acknowledging the experiences of more than 40,000 torture victims who had been silenced until then.

Lagos hoped to complete the transition to democracy, and as part of this ambition, he realized the importance of putting an end to the constitution's authoritarian enclaves. Lagos opened a discussion with political parties to explore the possibility of replacing Pinochet's Constitution. Lacking sufficient votes in Congress to approve a new Constitution, he could only adopt a text which partially amended the 1980 Constitution, successfully eliminating appointed senators, allowing the president to remove and replace the commander in chief, and reducing the power of the National Security Council, among other reforms. While he succeeded in reforming several of the most problematic pending elements of the 1980 constitution, Lagos recognized that the transition was not going to be complete if other key undemocratic features of the constitution remained untouched, namely, the binominal electoral system (SQC, 2012).

The binominal electoral system was established in the 1980 Constitution and contributed to causing an increase in voter disenchantment with Chilean politics, as many voters felt their voices were not being heard in parliament. The design of the electoral system allowed the two main coalitions to be overrepresented in Congress. This system also prevented the governments of the *Concertación* from implementing significant reforms, particularly in the early years of the transition, as it overrepresented the opposing coalition. The constitution also established that voting was mandatory for registered citizens throughout their lives (Navia, 2004).

Yet, as the transition progressed, the number of adults who enrolled in the electoral registers gradually decreased. Many young people ceased to register to vote in political elections. For instance, in the 1988 plebiscite, 90 percent of those aged 18 or older went to the polls, but that figure had decreased to 64 percent in the 2009 elections (Contreras & Navia, 2013). Partly due to the system, and partly due to lack of will, the inability of politicians to enact significant change created an increasing sense of disillusionment among potential voters. The system was eventually changed in 2015. This increase in voter disenchantment highlights the paradox of the Chilean transition; it emerged from social political mass mobilizations against the Pinochet dictatorship in the 1980s, but the transition itself has been marked by an elitist "governability" model wherein political parties demobilized and disengaged civil society (Delamaza, 2016: 109), worried that civil society actions would provoke military action. This has ultimately resulted in political parties, of the left in particular, being deeply out of touch with the needs and demands of their electorate.

In 2006, Socialist Michelle Bachelet became the first woman popularly elected head of state in Chile. Bachelet built on Lagos' momentum to continue addressing human rights issues. Under her administration, the mandate of the Commission on Torture and Political Imprisonment was extended through the Presidential Advisory Commission for the Qualification of Disappeared Detainees, Executed Prisoners, and Victims of Political Imprisonment and Torture. She also established the Presidential Advisory Committee on Human Rights to find mechanisms to improve the identification of deceased victims of the dictatorship (Borzutzky, 2017: 189). However, one of Bachelet's first government's most significant contributions to human rights issues was its commitment to memorialization, in particular the inauguration of the Museum of Memory and Human Rights in February 2010. This museum has become an important symbol and resource for collective memory about the traumas of the past. The documentation and archives of the Pinochet-era repression—guarded by the Vicarage of Solidarity—have been designated as UNESCO Patrimony of Humanity.

Bachelet's first presidency also marked the beginning of an important political turning point. In her first year of office, massive student protests broke out in protest of the poor quality of public education. In the words of Sofía Donoso, "the hundreds of thousands of students that mobilised in 2006 articulated a heartfelt discontent with the segregating effects of the education system" (2013: 2). This marked the first protest movement of such a magnitude in many years. The movement was known as the March of the Penguins because of the black and white mandatory uniforms worn by secondary school student in Chile. These mass protests marked the beginning of the re-awakening of Chilean civil society and its social movements.

It was also the start of an increasingly urgent citizens' demand for reform of the political and economic systems that the political elite had so far failed to change. In the second year of President Sebastian Piñera's first term, student protests once again filled the streets of Chile's main cities for seven months. According to Alberto Mayol, the main cause of the university students' riots was uneasiness with the existing economic model (2012). The criticism made by college students was also a protest against the unequal distribution of wealth, social segregation, and inequality of opportunity in Chilean society.

In 20 years and 4 Concertación governments, the pending problems of the transition, such as the 1980 Constitution and the neoliberal economic system, under which pensions, healthcare, education, and water continue to be privatized, remained unaddressed, and still proved to be a source of great frustration and political disillusionment for many Chilean voters. The political challenges that marked Bachelet's first government, specifically the mass protests and corruption scandals, have become recurring difficulties that subsequent governments have continued to face. As there has been no symbolic rupture with the constitution and economic system imposed by the dictatorship, the links between the state and civil society have never been properly rebuilt on new foundations of trust (Delamaza, 2016: 116).

After its failure in the 2010 elections, the *Concertación* coalition reinvented itself as the *Nueva Mayoría*, and Michelle Bachelet easily won the presidential election in 2014. The Bachelet's administration sought to fulfil the promises made during the campaign, such as the discussion of a new Constitution, and the reform of labor and employment laws, but the renaming of the coalition did not solve the deeper issues that had been plaguing the *Concertación*. Namely, the loss of trust of the electorate in the country's political institutions. The growing trend of political disillusionment and anti-establishment sentiment from the electorate in Chile has revealed major failures on the part of the country's political elite.

Throughout its political transition, Chile was characterized by the continuity of its political-economic strategies of development, which improved the quality of life of the majority of the population. Chile has grown economically in the last 30 years and is an example for many countries in terms of institutional stability and democratization. For instance, Chile has signed 26 free-trade agreements with more than 60 countries from all continents and is the first Latin American country to have been invited to participate as a member of the OECD. At a glance, the numbers say that Chile's economic policies have been a success: GDP has grown at an average rate of 5.6 percent in the last 25 years (Friedman & Hofman, 2013), and the income per capita has quintupled, increasing from US$4700 in 1990 to US$25,000 in 2019. Poverty has decreased from 38.6 in 1990 to 7.8 percent in 2013 (Ministerio de Desarrollo Social, CASEN, 2013). According to the Human Development Index (HDI) of the United Nations, Chile should be considered the best case of all Latin American countries. However, with a Gini coefficient of 0.50 (OECD, 2014: 111), Chile is also a country with severe economic inequalities (Engel & Navia, 2006).

The *Concertación*, Piñera, and *Nueva Mayoría* governments focused on macroeconomic stability at the cost of income inequality (Solimano, 2012). As Edgardo Boeninger shows, between 1990 and 2006, "the country has permanently lived the tensions between continuity and change; between state, market and regulation; between national coherence and decentralization; between growth and equity" (2007: 250). While absolute poverty has indeed decreased in Chile, the gap between the richest and the poorest has remained incredibly wide. According to the

OECD, 77.5 percent of Chileans are poor or economically vulnerable (OECD, 2017). The private education, healthcare, and the pension systems mean that many people find themselves living precariously close to the edge of poverty: a loved one falling seriously ill can send a family deep into debt. In terms of education, anyone who can afford to pay for the tuition fees sends their children to private or semi-private school, because public schools fare poorly on post-secondary level entrance exams.

Pinochet's free market ideology continues to have a strong influence on economic decision-making at La Moneda. However, while Piñera's reelection in 2017 appeared to confirm the triumph of neoliberalism in Chile, the primacy of the neoliberal model and the persistence of economic inequality has been challenged yet again by the Chilean population. Building on the momentum of the 2006 and 2011 protests, social unrest broke out in 2019 at a level that had not been seen since the end of the dictatorship, calling attention to many of the unfinished elements of the transition. The severity of the response from the government, imposing a curfew and calling in the army to impose order, as well as the excessive violence used by the police forces against the protesters (OHCHR, 2019), illustrates that the institutional reforms required to ensure the respect of human rights and commitments to the non-repetition of state violence and human rights abuses were not fully completed.

Citizens' anger and dissatisfaction with the political-economic model inherited from the dictatorship, as well as their dwindling patience with the impunity of corporations, politicians and state institutions with regard to accusations of corruption and recent human rights abuses, should be analyzed carefully by Chilean society. The protests are a call to discuss the kind of country Chileans want to live in in the future; one where precarity is not part of everyday life, economic background does not dictate the quality of education or healthcare available, and older generations can retire with dignity, and not into poverty. The strong demand for a new constitution which reemerged in the 2019 protest movement, and was confirmed in the October 2020 referendum and the May 2021 elections for the Constitutional Convention, suggests that this new political pact, that is the result of a broad process of deliberation, could be the symbolic act that puts end to the transition. The 2020 pandemic increases the lack of certainty regarding the socio-political future of Chile, since the mismanagement of the emergency by the Piñera administration has mainly affected the most vulnerable sectors.

As the Chilean transition progresses, fears of a return to authoritarianism are vanishing, but many accounts with the past remain outstanding, particularly structural and institutional changes. The memory of human rights violations committed in the past is at a crossroads in Chile, as these tensions are playing out in the current climate of political unrest facing the country. Carlos Nino (1996) and Jon Elster (2004) argue that demands of transitional justice are higher when memories of atrocities are fresh. It is interesting to confront this argument with the Chilean case where the demands for justice seem to be stronger in the last years than they were in the 1990s. As Chile grapples with how best to settle the remaining legacies of its unresolved past, the elements of transitional justice that we will explore in the coming chapters can provide a framework for understanding the relationship of past injustices to the complicated problems of the present.

Bibliography

Agnic, O. (2006). *Pinochet S.A. La base de la fortuna*. RIL editores.

Agüero, I. (2008). *El Diario de Agustín*. Documentary, 80 m.

Ahumada, J. (1958). *En vez de la miseria*. Editorial del Pacífico.

Albertus, M., & Menaldo, V. (2018). *Authoritarianism and the Elite Origins of Democracy*. Cambridge University Press.

Amorós, M. (2019). *Pinochet. Biografía militar y política*. Ediciones B.

Angell, A. (1971, February). Chile: From Christian Democracy to Marxism? *Current History*: 84–89.

Angell, A. (2009). Chile desde 1958. In L. Bethel (Ed.), *Chile desde la Independencia* (pp. 167–255). Ediciones Universidad Católica Silva Henríquez.

Aranda, G. (2004). *Vicaría de la Solidaridad: Una experiencia sin fronteras*. Ediciones ChileAmérica – CESOC.

Atria, F., Larraín, G., Benavente, J. M., Couso, J., & Joignant, A. (2013). *El otro modelo: Del orden neoliberal al regimen de lo público*. Debate.

Becker, N. (2011). *Una mujer en Villa Grimaldi*. Pehuén.

Bellisario, A. (2006). The Chilean Agrarian Transformation: The Pre-Agrarian Reform Period (1955–1965). *Journal of Agrarian Change, 6*(2), 167–204.

Bellisario, A. (2007). The Chilean Agrarian Transformation: Agrarian Reform and Capitalist 'Partial' Counter-Agrarian Reform, 1964–1980. Part 1: Reformism, Socialism and Free-Market Neoliberalism. *Journal of Agrarian Change, 7*(1), 1–34.

Bengoa, J. (1988). *Historia Social de la Agricultura Chilena, Vol. I El Poder y la Subordinación*. Ediciones Sur.

Blanco, F. (2010). *Desmemoria y perversión: privatizar lo público, mediatizar lo íntimo, administrar lo privado.* Editorial Cuarto Propio.

Boeninger, E. (2007). *Políticas Públicas en Democracia. Institucionalidad y experiencia chilena, 1990–2006.* Uqbar editores.

Borzutzky, S. (2017). *Human Rights in Chile: The Unfinished Struggle for Truth and Justice.* Palgrave Macmillan.

Brunner, J. J. (1986). De la universidad vigilada a la universidad empresa. La educación superior en Chile. *Nueva Sociedad, 84,* 140–146.

Carlin, R. E. (2006). The Decline of Citizen Participation in Electoral Politics in Post-Authoritarian Chile. *Democratization, 13*(4), 632–651.

Casals, M. (2014). "Chile en la Encrucijada". Anticomunismo y propaganda en la campaña del terror de las elecciones presidenciales 1964. In T. Harmer & A. Riquelme (Eds.), *Chile y la guerra fría global* (pp. 89–111). RIL editores.

Casassus, J. (2013). *Camino en la oscuridad.* Debate.

Cassidy, S. (2002 [1977]). *Audacity to Believe.* Darton, Longman and Todd Ltd.

Collins, C. (2013). La política de la justicia: Chile más allá del caso Pinochet. In C. Collins, K. Hite, & A. Joignant (Eds.), *Las Políticas de la Memoria en Chile: Desde Pinochet a Bachelet* (pp. 85–115). Ediciones Universidad Diego Portales.

Collins, C. (2014). Los Derechos Humanos durante la Concertación. In K. Sehnbruch & P. M. Siavelis (Eds.), *El Balance: Política y Políticas de la Concertación 1990–2010* (pp. 143–166). Catalonia.

Collins, C., Hite, K., & Joignant, A. (2013). Introduction. In C. Collins, K. Hite, & A. Joignant (Eds.), *Las Políticas de la Memoria en Chile: Desde Pinochet a Bachelet* (pp. 25–54). Ediciones Universidad Diego Portales.

Comisión Nacional de Verdad y Reconciliación. (1991). *Informe Rettig.* Gobierno de Chile.

Contreras, D., & Ffrench-Davis, R. (2012). *Policy Regimes, Inequality, Poverty and Growth: The Chilean Experience, 1973–2010* (WIDER Working Paper No. 4), available at https://www.econstor.eu/dspace/bitstream/10419/81078/1/682723371.pdf

Contreras, G., & Navia, P. (2013). Diferencias generacionales en la participación electoral en Chile, 1988–2010. *Revista de Ciencia Política, 33*(2), 419–441.

Cortés Terzi, A. (2000). *El circuito extrainstitucional del poder.* Ediciones Chileamérica-CESOC.

Crispi, J. (1982). El agro chileno después de 1973: expansión capitalista y campesinización pauperizante. *Revista Mexicana de Sociología, 44*(2), 481–514.

de la Parra, M. A. (1997). *La mala memoria.* Planeta.

Delamaza, G. (2016). Sociedad Civil, Ciudadanía y Movimientos Sociales en el Chile de Hoy. In M. A. Garretón (Ed.), *La Gran Ruptura: Institucionalidad política y actores sociales en el Chile del siglo XXI* (pp. 109–131). LOM ediciones.

Donoso, S. (2013). Dynamics of Change in Chile: Explaining the Emergence of the *Pingüino* Movement. *Journal of Latin American Studies, 45*(1), 1–29.

Drake, P. W. (2004). Foreword. In P. Winn (Ed.), *Victims of the Chilean Miracle. Workers and Neoliberalism in the Pinochet Era, 1973–2002* (pp. ix–xiii). Duke University Press.
Echeverría, M. (2008). *Krassnoff.* Catalonia.
Elster, J. (2004). *Closing the Books: Transitional Justice in Historical Perspective.* Cambridge University Press (Spanish trans. Elster, J. (2006). *Rendición de cuentas: la justicia transicional en perspectiva histórica.* Katz).
Engel, E., & Navia, P. (2006). *Que gane "el más mejor": Mérito y competencia en el Chile de hoy.* Debate.
Escudero, M. (2018). Congreso Nacional: Organización y funciones. In C. Huneeus & O. Avendaño (Eds.), *El Sistema Político de Chile* (pp. 119–151). LOM Ediciones.
Fermandois, J. (2013). *La revolución inconclusa. La izquierda chilena y el gobierno de la Unidad Popular.* Centro de Estudios Públicos.
Foxley, A. (1982). Experimentos Neoliberales en América Latina. *Colección Estudios CIEPLAN*, 7.
Friedman, J., & Hofman, A. (2013). *Inequality and the Top of the Income Distribution in Chile 1990–2012: Questioning the Consensus*, available at https://doi.org/10.2139/ssrn.2242259
Fuentes, C. (2013). *El Fraude.* Hueders.
Gárate, M. (2013). *La Revolución Capitalista de Chile 1973–2003.* Ediciones Universidad Alberto Hurtado.
Garretón, M.A. (1989). La Posibilidad Democrática en Chile. *Cuadernos de Difusión*, FLACSO-Chile.
Gómez-Barris, M. (2009). *Where Memory Dwells: Culture and State Violence in Chile.* University of California Press.
Góngora, M. (1988). *Ensayo histórico sobre la noción de estado en Chile en los siglos XIX y XX.* Editorial Universitaria.
González, M. (2013). *La Conjura: Los mil y un días del golpe* (2nd ed.). Catalonia.
Grupo de Investigaciones Agrarias de la Academia de Humanismo Cristiano. (1979). Tenencia de la tierra en Chile. *Cuadernillo de Información Agraria*, 1.
Gustafson, K. (2007). *Hostile Intent: U.S. Covert Operations in Chile, 1964–1974.* Potomac Books Inc.
Harmer, T. (2013). *El gobierno de Allende y la Guerra Fría interamericana.* Ediciones Universidad Diego Portales.
Haslam, J. (2005). *The Nixon Administration and the Death of Allende's Chile.* Verso.
Hidalgo, P. (2011). *El Ciclo Político de la Concertación (1990–2010).* Uqbar editores.
Hite, K. (2000). *When the Romance Ended: Leaders of the Chilean Left, 1968–1998.* Columbia University Press.

Hojman, D. E. (1996). Poverty and Inequality in Chile: Are Democratic Politics and Neoliberal Economics Good for You? *Journal of Interamerican Studies and World Affairs, 38*(2/3), 73–96.

Huneeus, C. (2000). *El Régimen de Pinochet.* Editorial Sudamericana.

Huneeus, C. (2003). *Chile, Un País Dividido. La Actualidad del Pasado.* Catalonia.

Jadresic, E., & Zahler, R. (2000). *Chile's Rapid Growth in the 1990s-Good Policies, Good Luck, or Political Change?.* IMF Working Paper No. 00/153. Available at: https://www.imf.org/en/Publications/WP/Issues/2016/12/30/Chile-s-Rapid-Growth-in-the-1990-s-Good-Policies-Good-Luck-or-Political-Change-3789

Jocelyn-Holt, A. (1998). *El Chile Perplejo: Del avanzar sin transar al transar sin parar.* Planeta.

Joignant, A. (2002). La democracia de la indiferencia. Despolitización, desencanto y malestar en el gobierno de Eduardo Frei Ruiz-Tagle. In O. Muñoz & C. Stefoni (Eds.), *El Periodo del Presidente Frei Ruiz-Tagle* (pp. 83–106). FLACSO-Chile & Editorial Universitaria.

Kay, C. (2000). Latin America's Agrarian Transformation: Peasantization and Proletarianization. In D. Bryceson, C. Kay, & J. Mooij (Eds.), *Disappearing Peasantries? Rural Labour in Africa, Asia and Latin America* (pp. 123–138). Intermediate Technology Publications.

Kornbluh, P. (2003). *Los EEUU y el Derrocamiento de Allende. Una historia desclasificada.* Ediciones B.

Kornbluh, P. (2004). *Pinochet. Los archivos secretos.* Ed. Crítica.

Kunstmann, W., & Torres, V. (Eds.). (2008). *Cien Voces Rompen el Silencio: Testimonios de Ex-Presos Politicos de la Dictadura Militar en Chile 1973–1990.* Dirección de Bibliotecas, Archivos y Museos.

Lagos, R. (1961). *La concentración del poder económico.* Editorial del Pacífico.

Lagos, R. (2013). *Mi vida. De la infancia a la lucha contra la dictadura.* Debate.

Larrañaga, O., & Rodríguez, M. E. (2014). Desigualdad de Ingresos y Pobreza en Chile 1990 a 2013. *Documento de Trabajo*, UNDP – Chile, available at http://www.cl.undp.org/content/dam/chile/docs/pobreza/undp_cl_pobreza_cap_7_desiguypob.pdf

Lechner, N. (1998). Modernización y Democratización: Un dilema del desarrollo chileno. *Estudios Públicos, 70*, 231–242.

Lessa, F. (2019). Operation Condor on Trial: Justice for Transnational Human Rights Crimes in South America. *Journal of Latin American Studies, 51*(2), 409–439.

Lira, E., & Castillo, M. I. (1991). *Psicología de la amenaza política y del miedo.* Instituto Latinoamericano de Salud Mental y Derechos Humanos.

Lira, E., & Loveman, B. (2014). *Poder Judicial y Conflictos Políticos (Chile: 1925–1958).* Lom ediciones.

Lira, E., & Rojas, H. (Eds.). (2009). *Libertad Sindical y Derechos Humanos: Análisis de los Informes del Comité de Libertad Sindical de la OIT (1973–1990)*. Lom ediciones.

Loveman, B., & Lira, E. (2000). *Las ardientes cenizas del olvido: Vía chilena de Reconciliación Política 1932–1994*. Lom Ediciones.

Magasich, J. (2020a). *Historia de la Unidad Popular* (Tiempos de preparación: de los orígenes al 3 de septiembre de 1970) (Vol. 1). Lom ediciones.

Magasich, J. (2020b). *Historia de la Unidad Popular* (De la elección a la asunción: los álgidos 60 días del 4 de septiembre al 3 de noviembre de 1970) (Vol. 2). Lom ediciones.

Mayol, A. (2012). *El Derrumbe del Modelo. La crisis de la economía de mercado en el Chile contemporáneo*. Lom ediciones.

Montealegre, J. (2003). *Frazadas del Estadio Nacional*. Lom ediciones.

Moulian, T. (2002 [1997]). *Chile Actual: Anatomía de un Mito* (3rd ed.). Lom Ediciones.

Navia, P. (2004). Participación electoral en Chile, 1988–2001. *Revista de Ciencia Política, 24*(1), 81–103.

Nino, C. (1996). *Radical Evil on Trial*. Yale University Press.

Novoa, E. (1992). *Los Resquicios Legales*. Ediciones Bat.

O'Shaughnessy, H. (2000). *Pinochet: The Politics of Torture*. New York University Press.

Ochoa, G., & Maillard, C. (2011). *La Persistencia de la Memoria: Londres 38, un espacio de memorias en construcción*. Londres 38, espacio de memorias.

OECD. (2014). *Society at a Glance 2014: OECD Social Indicators*, available at https://doi.org/10.1787/soc_glance-2014-en

OECD. (2017). *How's Life? 2017: Measuring Well-Being*. OECD Publishing, available at https://doi.org.proxy.bib.uottawa.ca/10.1787/how_life-2017-en

Office of the High Commissioner of Human Rights, OHCHR. (2019). *Informe sobre la Misión a Chile, 30 de octubre – 22 de noviembre de 2019*, available at https://www.ohchr.org/Documents/Countries/CL/Report_Chile_2019_SP.pdf

Orellana, M. E. (2002). *Allende. Alma en Pena*. Editorial Cuatro Vientos.

Otano, R. (2006). *Nueva crónica de la transición* (2nd ed.). Lom ediciones.

Passmore, L. (2017). *The Wars Inside Chile's Barracks: Remembering Military Service Under Pinochet*. University of Wisconsin Press.

Peña, J. C. (2007). *Los Fusileros: Crónica secreta de una guerrilla en Chile*. Debate.

Pino-Ojeda, W. (2011). *Noche y niebla: neoliberalismo, memoria y trauma en el Chile postautoritario*. Editorial Cuarto Propio.

Policzer, P. (2009). *The Rise and Fall of Repression in Chile*. University of Notre Dame Press.

Presidential Advisory Commission for the Qualification of Disappeared Detainees, Political Executed, and Victims of Political Imprisonment and Torture. (2011). *Final Report*. Santiago (in Spanish).

Riquelme, A. (2014). La Guerra Fría en Chile: Los intricados nexos entre lo nacional y lo global. In T. Harmer & A. Riquelme (Eds.), *Chile y la guerra fría global* (pp. 11–43). RIL editores.
Rojas, F. (2001). La Detención del General Pinochet: Notas para su interpretación y evaluación del impacto en el sistema político chileno. In F. Rojas & C. Stefoni (Eds.), *El "caso Pinochet": Visiones hemisféricas de su detención en Londres* (pp. 21–39). FLACSO-Chile.
Ruiz-Tagle, J. (1973). Huelga en El Teniente: Un conflicto mal planteado. *Revista Mensaje, 219*, 216–218.
Salazar, M. (2011). *Las letras del horror: La DINA*. Lom ediciones.
Salazar, M. (2012). *Las letras del horror: La CNI*. Lom ediciones.
Sanabria, H. (2007). *The Anthropology of Latin America and the Caribbean*. Pearson Allyn and Bacon.
Sands, D. R. (1982). Chile Under Frei: The Alliance for Progress. *The Fletcher Forum*, 33–60.
Sanhueza, G. (1999). La Crisis Financiera de los Años 80 en Chile: Análisis de sus Soluciones y su Costo. *Economía Chilena, 2*(1), 43–68.
Schlotterbeck, M. (2018). *Beyond the Vanguard: Everyday Revolutionaries in Allende's Chile*. University of California Press.
Sepúlveda, A. (2020). *La Unidad Popular. Los mil días de Salvador Allende y la vía chilena al socialismo*. Sudamericana.
Silva, P. (1991). Technocrats and Politics in Chile – From the Chicago Boys to the CIEPLAN Monks. *Journal of Latin American Studies, 23*(2), 385–410.
Skoknic, F. (2013). El rol de Agustín Edwards antes y después del 11 de septiembre de 1973. *CIPER Chile*, available at http://ciperchile.cl/2013/09/10/el-rol-de-agustin-edwards-antes-y-despues-del-11-de-septiembre-de-1973/
Solimano, A. (2012). *Chile and the Neoliberal Trap the Post-Pinochet Era*. Cambridge University Press.
Sorensen, K. I. (2011). Chilean Print Media and Human Rights: Mainstream Silence Versus Satirical Subversion. *Peace and Change, 36*(3), 400–426.
Spooner, M. H. (2011). *The General's Slow Retreat: Chile After Pinochet*. University of California Press.
SQC. (2012). *Transición en la medida de lo posible: entrevista a Ricardo Lagos*, available at https://www.youtube.com/watch?v=9sME3GcTP94
Stern, S. (2009). *Recordando el Chile de Pinochet: en vísperas de Londres 1998*. Ediciones Universidad Diego Portales.
Stern, S., & Winn, P. (2014). El Tortuoso Camino Chileno a la Memorialización. In P. Winn, S. Stern, F. Lorenz, & A. Marchesi (Eds.), *No hay mañana sin ayer: Batallas por la memoria histórica en el Cono Sur* (pp. 205–326). Lom ediciones.
Tironi, E. (2013). *Sin Miedo, Sin Odio, Sin Violencia. Una Historia Personal del No*. Ariel.

Tricot, T. (2015). *Un Sociólogo en el Frente Patriótico Manuel Rodríguez. Testimonio de un Militante*. Ceibo Ediciones.
United States Senate Select Committee to Study Governmental Operations with Respect to Intelligence Activities Report. (1975). *Covert Action in Chile, 1963–1973 (Church Report)*, available at https://fas.org/irp/ops/policy/church-chile.htm
Valdés, H. (1996 [1974]). *Tejas Verdes. Diario de un Campo de Concentración en Chile*. Lom ediciones/Ediciones CESOC.
Valdés, J. G. (1995). *Pinochet's Economists. The Chicago School in Chile*. Cambridge University Press.
Westad, O. A. (2018). *La Guerra Fría: Una historia mundial*. Galaxia Gutenberg.
Wilde, A. (1999). Irruptions of Memory: Expressive Politics in Chile's Transition to Democracy. *Journal of Latin American Studies, 31*(2), 473–500.
Winn, P. (2013). *La revolución chilena*. Lom Ediciones.
Wright, T. C., & Oñate, R. (2007). Chilean Political Exile. *Latin American Perspectives*, 155, *34*(4), 31–47.

CHAPTER 3

Searching for the Truth

Answering the question "what happened?" is one of the biggest challenges societies must face after a period of conflict and violence. The question is broad: it encompasses both the demand for a clear description and explanation of the facts of the events, especially given the difficulty of accessing information during periods of conflict or state repression, but it also implicitly asks, why? Why did this conflict occur? Why were human rights violations committed? Why were certain people in particular targeted? Why was the conflict not stopped sooner? Attempting to answer these complex questions and clarify the truth of what occurred is at the core of transitional justice processes. Without confronting the past, it is difficult to restore democratic institutions and rebuild people's trust in those same institutions. While it is impossible to uncover and confirm the "full truth" and every detail about traumatic events such as human rights violations and armed conflict, collective efforts to reconstruct a narrative that is as close as possible to the truth can begin to repair the social fabric of post-conflict societies. This collective truth-seeking effort is important not only for victims and their families, who have a right to know the truth about what happened to them or their loved ones, but also for the wider society. The truth can contribute to reconciliation efforts on many levels; it helps achieve justice by combatting impunity, it helps in memorializing the horrors of the past, and it helps establish what sorts of reparations are

H. Rojas, M. Shaftoe, *Human Rights and Transitional Justice in Chile*, Memory Politics and Transitional Justice,
https://doi.org/10.1007/978-3-030-81182-2_3

necessary, all of which contribute to ensuring that the abuses suffered never occur again.

The right to the truth has become an important norm in international law. It was first established in Articles 32 and 33 of the Additional Protocol I to the Geneva Convention (1977), which established the general principle of "the right of families to know the fate of their loved ones" (International Committee of the Red Cross, 1977), but also emphasized the particular case of missing persons and established the obligation of the conflicting parties to search for those considered missing. The right to the truth and the ensuing obligation to investigate were further reinforced by international organizations such as the Inter-American Court of Human Rights. The concept was expanded to include not only victims and their families, but all of society, and the obligation to investigate and pursue the truth was explicitly defined as being a duty of the state (IACtHR, 2014). Various mechanisms exist to elucidate the truth, and they can be official methods driven by the state, or more informal truth-telling mechanisms. Combining a number of different techniques provides a more complete picture of the events that took place. Some of the mechanisms that are often used include truth commissions of various formats and attributes, criminal trials, investigative journalism, official reports, opening the archives of repressive organizations, academic research, victims' testimonies, perpetrators' confessions, and so on.

In this chapter, we will examine the main challenges and successes of the search for the truth in Chile. First, we will analyze the particularities of the Chilean case that made the search for the truth difficult. Next, we will assess the mechanisms that were used in the truth-seeking process. In particular, we will focus on the two main official truth commissions: the Report of the National Commission of Truth and Reconciliation and the Report of the National Commission on Political Imprisonment and Torture. Finally, we will analyze torture survivors' published testimonies, both as an example of civil society truth-telling and in order to assess Chile's search for the truth from a survivor's perspective.

3.1 Hidden Truth: Censorship

Disinformation, censorship, and control of the media were a key feature of the dictatorship from the moment the military junta took power (Sorensen, 2015: 17). While many people knew about the human rights abuses, state propaganda and censorship were very strong, and accurate information about what was going on was difficult to access. According to Bastías, "The military regime exercised tight control over the press in the years after the coup d'état...In addition to radio stations, the military junta closed down fifteen mass media, including newspapers, magazines, and press agencies" (2013: 150). A governmental department called the Division of Social Communication (DINACOS) worked to authorize and censor the content generated by all audiovisual and written mass media from 1973 until 1990. DINACOS also revised cultural works and oversaw the dictatorship's official communications. Freedom of expression was severely limited, and the only directly available information was that which the dictatorship had authorized.

The military junta used their control of the media to create an official narrative about the coup and to claim that the country was at war against communist subversives. In order to justify their repressive actions, they created a fake news campaign about an alleged communist plot *Plan Z*, which was a supposed initiative by left-wing extremists to overthrow the government and kill the elite in a violent socialist revolution (Stern & Winn, 2014: 263). But the military regime not only used their control of the media to manipulate the official narrative of events, they also used the media as a distractor. They would artificially generate media buzz about events like the 1986 passing of Halley's Comet or the supposed sightings of the Virgin Mary by a young man named Miguel Ángel Poblete, between 1983 and 1988, in order to move public focus away from other more serious events and issues. While several media organizations actively collaborated in the dictatorship's disinformation efforts, such as *El Mercurio*, *La Segunda*, and *Las Últimas Noticias*, many magazines and media organizations risked a lot by publishing and circulating unauthorized information underground.

Civil society resisted censorship by generating alternative media or coming up with creative ways to get around the censorship. For instance, in the Jesuit magazine *Revista Mensaje* some blacklisted intellectuals wrote under pseudonyms, using indirect language to explain what was happening. The magazine even revealed the signs of prior censorship to their readers by leaving in the darkened the sections that were not authorized to be published as evidence that it had been redacted. A number of magazines were founded during the dictatorship in order to resist the censorship efforts and circulate unauthorized information, such as *Revista APSI* in 1976, *Revista Análisis* in 1977, *Revista Cauce* in 1982, and *Fortín Mapocho* and *Revista Hoy* in 1984. The Vicariate of Solidarity, which was an important civil society religious organization involved in the defense of human rights throughout the course of the dictatorship, published the magazine *Solidaridad* from 1976 and distributed it in parishes. To get around the prohibition of films and music, pirated copies of censored or banned movies would often be circulated secretly. For instance, the 1982 movie "*Missing*," directed by Costa-Gavras based on the disappearance of American reporter Charles Horman, was banned until 2000, but thousands of illicit copies were still distributed widely on VHS tapes. Just before and after the 1988 plebiscite, several books investigating the human rights abuses under the Pinochet regime were published in installments in newspapers. Journalist Patricia Verdugo published the book *Los Zarpazos del Puma* (The Blows of the Puma) in 1989, which narrates the "Caravan of Death" massacre led by General Sergio Arellano Stark's entourage in 1973, and *La Historia Oculta del Régimen Militar* (The Hidden Story of the Military Regime), a work by journalists Ascanio Cavallo, Manuel Salazar, and Óscar Sepúlveda, appeared as press articles published in the newspaper *La Época* in 1988. These articles were later compiled in book format.

After 17 years of state censorship, Chilean society was deeply misinformed about the human rights abuses perpetrated by the military regime. The strong propaganda push about *Plan Z* and the regime's claim of being "at war" against left-wing subversives meant that many civilians, especially those who supported at least some aspects of Pinochet's government, truly believed that part of the repression that had taken place was necessary. Even those who followed alternative media and were able to access more information about the dictatorship's repressive activities had an incomplete picture of what had happened. The effects of years of state censorship persisted in the media long after the end of the dictatorship, particularly in the early years of the transition, due to the auto-censorship and unwritten norms that many who worked in the media continued to follow about what was acceptable or not to publish or air on TV (Sorensen, 2015: 48). In a continuation of the history of resistance to censorship under the dictatorship, many civil society actors stepped in during the transition to fill in the gaps of official truth-telling and combat the spread of indifference. However, in a context where the state apparatus spent years actively blocking access to the truth, there was an important obligation that the governments of the transition undertake state-led truth-seeking initiatives. In the complex political context of the pacted transition from the dictatorship, the official truth-telling process took many years.

Two main truth commissions of different scopes, created years apart, have investigated the abuses of the Pinochet regime.

3.2 What Is a TRC?

Truth and Reconciliation Commissions (TRCs) are important and widely used mechanism in societies that have suffered serious human rights violations or conflict. The most widely cited definition of a truth commission includes five main characteristics. First, it is focused on the past and not the present. Second, it investigates patterns of abuse and not specific events. Third, it engages directly with the affected population. Fourth, it is a temporary mechanism that concludes with an official report, and finally, it is authorized officially by the state (Hayner, 2011: 12). This definition is that of truth commission expert Priscilla Hayner, who has undertaken a comprehensive analysis of 40 truth commissions that have been created throughout the world.

According to Hayner, the most common objectives of TRCs are sanctioned fact-finding, hearing and responding to the needs of survivors, countering impunity, evaluating institutional responsibility, and promoting reconciliation. These goals are quite ambitious within the context of a post-conflict society (2011: 20). While they may not achieve all these goals within the short mandate of the investigation, truth commissions can establish a strong beginning for the protracted process of transitional justice and often continue to have an impact over time. For instance, commissions often compile evidence that could later be used in criminal trials and engage directly with the victims to fully understand their needs, thus helping the state determine the best course of action in terms of reparation measures.

There are four main elements that if considered could contribute to the success of a Truth Commission:

1. The participation and representation of victims and the general public is essential to the success of any TRC process (UN, 2010). Truth Commissions should implement public consultations and publicly discuss the powers and procedures of the commission prior to its creation, with special attention and priority given to victims, survivors, and their families. Special efforts should be made by commissioners to ensure the participation of men and women. Gender aspects must be visible in the composition and work of the

Commission. The wellbeing of the victims must be kept in mind throughout the process of the commission, for instance, by having qualified personnel to provide psychological assistance to victims and their family members. In addition, when the report is finished and conclusions are published, the report must be made public and diffused widely within the population. Broad public discussion about the results of the report can contribute to reconciliation efforts and gives civil society stakeholders an opportunity to bring forward suggestions about the next steps to be taken.

2. The manner by which the commission handles the participation of perpetrators is another key element to consider. Perpetrators are essential to uncovering the truth of what took place as they are often involved in hiding the evidence of crimes and seek to avoid being held accountable. As such, the commission must consider what incentives will be offered to the perpetrators to declare and break the pacts of silence and whether amnesties or pardons will be offered. Perpetrators are also important because while Truth Commissions do not have the power to condemn anyone criminally, they do often serve to combat impunity. As such, perpetrators are sometimes named in TRC reports. If the names of the perpetrators will appear in the report, it must be ensured that they had the possibility to testify before the commission and give their version of the facts.
3. The authority of the commission is another element that must be decided when establishing a truth commission. The TRC, as well as its powers and the types of crimes it will investigate (favouring the most serious), should be established by law. It is important to clarify that the commission report does not establish *res judicata*. In other words, it cannot establish criminal guilt or innocence, and does not replace the criminal process, where evidentiary standards are higher. Truth commissions must be independent, impartial, and objective to the greatest degree possible (UN, 2010). Commissioners must be immovable in office in order to ensure they cannot be replaced by state officials if they do not like the findings of the investigation, and the state must establish protection measures for commissioners, officials, declarants, and witnesses.
4. The extent of state support for the commission is another important aspect to consider. The state must grant financial and technological resources to the commission so that it can carry out its activities. If necessary, the state should also provide support from the police

force, for instance, to access sites where crimes were committed. Finally, all documentation generated during the commission's work must be preserved, ideally by the state, as it is part of a society's collective memory and can be helpful in further transitional justice processes. It should be established who can access the information and under what conditions, as well as what will be the professional use of the information. With this in mind, the state should also consider means to mitigate the conflicts that may arise between the freedom of information and privacy rights.

These are some of the key elements to take into consideration when tailoring a truth commission to suit the specific circumstances of the society in transition.

3.3 The Rettig Commission

Almost immediately after coming into power, President Aylwin created the National Commission on Truth and Reconciliation by Supreme Decree No. 355. Under pressure from human rights organizations and seeking to fulfill the promises of both his political campaign and that of the *No* campaign in 1988, Aylwin chose to create a truth commission as a first step to address the dictatorship's abuses and strengthen democratic institutions, without endangering the fragile newfound democracy. The short text of just nine articles established the limits and objectives of the commission and named the eight commissioners, who were political moderates hailing from parties on both sides of the political spectrum. Raúl Rettig of the Radical Party was named president, and Jorge Correa of the Christian Democratic Party was named secretary. The remaining commissioners were Jaime Castillo Velasco (Christian Democratic Party), Mónica Jiménez (Christian Democratic Party), José Zalaquett (Party for Democracy), José Luis Cea (center-right), Ricardo Martín (right-wing), Laura Novoa (right-wing), and Gonzalo Vial (right-wing).

The final report came to be known as the Rettig Report, named after its president. It had a staff of 60 people and a maximum of 9 months to complete its task. The focus of the commission was narrowed to investigating the most serious human rights violations: disappeared detainees, forced executions, and victims of violence/torture resulting in death. Its objectives were fourfold:

1. To establish as complete a picture of the past human rights violations as possible, as well as the antecedents and circumstances of these violations.
2. To gather evidence that may make it possible to identify the victims by name and determine the fate or whereabouts of said victims.
3. To recommend such measures of reparation and reinstatement as it sees fit.
4. To recommend the legal and administrative measures which should be adopted in order to prevent or deter the perpetration of new, serious human rights violations.

The Rettig Report investigated a relatively small number of cases as it focused on only the most serious human rights violations. This meant that the cases of tens of thousands of torture survivors were excluded from the investigation. Several reasons explain this limitation of the commission's investigation and mandate. It was done partially because of the fear as to how the military would respond (Borzutzky 2017: 69) but also for more practical reasons: firstly, it was thought that an investigation of all human rights violations would take far too long (pragmatism) and, secondly, that the State would have to finance too many reparations (austerity).

Some of the main technical limitations of the Rettig Report were that it could not compel anyone to testify before it, nor did it did not impose any measures that would encourage perpetrators' confessions. This is in contrast to other truth-seeking processes which put a stronger emphasis on perpetrator engagement. For instance, the South African TRC had the power to grant individual amnesties to perpetrators of politically motivated crimes if they fully confessed to their actions and required perpetrators of human rights violations to attend public hearings as a condition for amnesty (Hayner, 2011). In addition, the Rettig Report was not permitted to name the perpetrators, which other TRCs such as that in El Salvador had done, as a means to provide some measure of accountability in the face of the likelihood that the justice system would prove to be incapable of doing so (Collins et al., 2016: 181). Another relevant limitation of the Rettig Commission was that the hearings were not public, an aspect which, in commissions such as the Peruvian TRC, had a very significant impact in allowing those who were from less affected regions or who were less aware of the conflict to learn about the extent of the violence (Hayner, 2011: 36).

Furthermore, to appease the opposition, the commission's founding decree reiterated explicitly that truth commission does not replace the judiciary, where the evidentiary standards are higher: "In accordance with a solid and well-established principle in the area of human rights, it was determined that in no case was the Commission either to take on legal functions proper to the courts or to interfere in cases already pending. In order to make the matter even more explicit, the Commission was expressly prohibited from making pronouncements on whether and to what extent particular persons might be responsible for the events it investigated" (TRC Report, Vol I, part 1: 14). In spite of these limitations, the commission undertook a diligent and expansive investigation, based on the archives of the *Vicaría de la Solidaridad*, an entity of the Archbishopric of Santiago created by Cardinal Silva Henríquez with the support of the Pope, as well as numerous testimonies from the relatives of the victims, and information provided by international organizations.

President Aylwin presented the Truth and Reconciliation Report to the nation in a public address on March 4, 1991. The final report provided a summary of the context of the dictatorship and the main trends of violence, presented the numbers and details of the several thousand cases of executions and disappearances, provided recommendations, and then provided a short explanation of each of the victims' cases. On behalf of the state, Aylwin officially acknowledged responsibility and apologized to the victims and their families for the suffering they experienced and called on the armed forces and other state institutions named in the report to do the same (Spooner, 2011: 80). The information gathered by the Commission (subsequently supplemented by the National Corporation for Reparation and Reconciliation between 1992 and 1997) recorded 2014 people executed and 1183 detainees disappeared, with a total of 3197 victims. The report found that 95% of the abuses that had been evaluated were committed by state agents, while 4% of the cases were committed by the armed left.

One particularly important and controversial conclusion of the Rettig Report was that there had been no war in Chile in 1973 and, therefore, that the "state of war" had in fact been used to limit citizens' rights and justify the violence of state forces. To declare that there had been no internal war was a powerful conclusion, particularly as it came from a group of well-respected, moderate commissioners at both ends of the political spectrum. In a deeply divided society, only one year after the end of Pinochet's rule, the Rettig Report officially disproved and rejected the narrative that had been pervasive throughout the military regime to justify the violence and repression citizens suffered at the hands of the state. Aylwin's apology and the results of the report legitimized the alternative discourses and histories that had been suppressed during the dictatorship. The Commission also proposed several important recommendations for legal and institutional reforms and victims' reparations, such as a monthly pension for the victim's relatives, as well as symbolic measures to redeem the dignity and good name of the victims, and so on (TRC Report, 1991: 836). These will be further explored in Chap. 4 (*see* Reparations Law No. 19,123).

The Rettig Report was released in a political climate where Pinochet continued to be a powerful and disruptive presence and where the army maintained significant independence from government. The most negative reaction to the Rettig Report came from the armed forces (Loveman & Lira, 2000: 520–523). In particular, "the reactions of the army and the navy were […] very strong and the most critical of the report. The army severely contested the truthfulness, as well as the impartiality of the report" (Ferrara, 2015: 50). The military went as far in their denial as to argue that they had saved the Homeland, maintaining that any violence had been justified. Another important institution which had been criticized in the report was the Supreme Court: the Rettig Report accused the judiciary of being too cautious and failing to fulfill its duty to protect citizens from excessive use of power throughout the course of the dictatorship. Like the armed forces, the Supreme Court refused to acknowledge nearly all of the criticisms and declared the report to be too passionate, reckless, political, and biased.

Despite these institutional rejections of its results, the report was well received by the public. It likely would have had a more significant impact on Chilean society had it not been overshadowed by the assassination of Jaime Guzmán, a right-wing senator, by left-wing extremist group FPMR hardly a month after its release. The ensuing media outcry led to a lack of public discussion and engagement with the Rettig Report, and its strong declaration that there had been no internal war was diluted by counter-terrorism discourse, a lack of circulation of the results, and outright denial by the right-wing and the armed forces. Consequently, mere weeks after the release of the report of the Truth and Reconciliation Commission, public discussion around the issue of human rights violations was frozen (Ferrara, 2017).

Political parties on both sides of the spectrum showed a desire to frame the Rettig Report as the definitive answer to the issue of human rights and declare the problem dealt with and the transition over (Ruderer, 2010).

What could have been an important moment of national reckoning and discussion about how best to continue addressing the country's complex history and difficult political present instead resulted in a veil of silence falling over any discussion of human rights abuses. This silence lasted for nearly seven years. After the report, human rights cases were filed in courts and were considered a matter of victims and perpetrators and not a problem of Chilean society as a whole. Between 1991 and 2004, the right-wing and the armed forces referred to human rights violations as "isolated excesses" committed by state agents. There were only a few sporadic episodes where the dictatorship's violent past came back into the spotlight, such as the 1995 conviction of former General Manuel Contreras and former Brigadier Pedro Espinoza for the homicide of Orlando Letelier in Washington, D.C., a case that was only able to move forward because it had been expressly excluded from the Amnesty Law due to pressure from the US administration.

In 1997, Tomás Moulian was one of the first to lift the veil of silence regarding human rights by publishing "Current Chile, Anatomy of a Myth" (*Chile Actual, Anatomía de un Mito*), a harsh criticism of the first years of the transition. His book is a clear example of civilian truth-telling in the face of inaction from the state. He unflinchingly delivered a worrying diagnosis of Chile's process of democratic transition and its failure to address the abuses of the past. To those who considered the Rettig Commission the "final answer" to Chile's human rights problem, Moulian pointed out its "two large gaps: its investigations do not lead to judicial proceedings and do not include those affected by prolonged torture and abusive imprisonment" (1991: 70). He vocally condemned the political elite for attempting to bury memory of the past, denouncing the authorities for promoting a "compulsion to oblivion" and for "invoking 'reasons of State' to achieve forgetfulness and demobilization of society." He exposed the pervasive culture of impunity, declaring that "the supposed political-economic miracle of Chile is nothing more than a plastic surgery. Pinochet is still the *factotum* that makes decisions in the shadows" (1997: 39). Moulian described Chilean democracy as an iron cage in which the transitional governments were trapped, unable or unwilling to do the work necessary to hold the armed forces and other sectors of society accountable.

Moulian had both the lucidity and the audacity to share a social diagnosis that nobody wanted to make at the time: "When the Commission released its report [the Rettig Report] President Aylwin apologized, with tears in his eyes, on behalf of the State. A great symbolic act through which the nation assumed its responsibility, but also a spectacular act of evasion" (1997: 70). In other words, by trying to walk the fine line of protecting their newfound democracy and confronting the past, the transitional governments abandoned their responsibility to take on the challenge of building a process of reconciliation grounded in justice and instead opted for the easy path of forgetting. Moulian's book was an immediate hit and spent an entire year in the top 10 best selling books' list of the newspaper *El Mercurio*. The success of Moulian's sociological essay shows that although the problems of the past were removed from the public agenda, they never disappeared from the social agenda. Years later, and mainly because of this book, Moulian received the National Prize in Social Sciences and Humanities.

Nonetheless, it is fair to say that the Rettig Report was an essential first step in the long process of transitional justice that has taken place over the last three decades and has had quite a significant long-term impact on Chilean society (Ferrara, 2015). The commission has helped advancements in the realms of justice and reparations, as background information it compiled served as evidence in the trials for human rights violations, and its recommendations formed the basis of Chilean reparations policy. The Rettig Report has been incorporated into multiple memorializing initiatives, such as the Museum of Memory and Human Rights, as well as guarantees of non-repetition policies. It has also been the base platform from which it was later possible to advance in the struggles for the truth in the Corporation for Reparation and Reconciliation, the Roundtable Dialogue, and the Political Imprisonment and Torture Commission.

3.4 The Mesa de Diálogo

A year after the publication of *Chile Actual, Anatomía de un Mito*, Pinochet's arrest in London brought these problems back to the surface and kick-started a new wave of public discussion around human rights issues in Chile. There was a push for new truth-seeking initiatives, to which the government responded with Frei administration's *Mesa de Diálogo* (Roundtable Dialogue) in August 1999. This initiative sought to decisively establish what had happened to the bodies of the disappeared and make progress toward the recognition of individual and institutional responsibilities (Lira, 2005: 157). This was the first time the armed forces recognized any responsibility in the killings. On January 5, 2001, the armed forces reported that 180 bodies were thrown into rivers or the ocean (Ferrara, 2017: 225). While it succeeded in bringing together opposing parties in discussion, it was discovered that the information provided by the armed forces was inaccurate and fragmented (Lazzara, 2006: 21). Overall, the results of the Roundtable Dialogue were disappointing for many human rights activists and organizations.

Yet, after more than ten years of transition in which the armed forces had adopted obstructive positions, one of the main contributions of the agreement of the Dialogue Table was the express recognition of the armed forces in the commission of arrests, homicides, and later cover-up of those crimes (Lira, 2005: 163). The renewed public push for truth brought the gaps in the Rettig Report back to the surface, particularly the lack of discussion surrounding the issue of torture. As a result, many survivors began to speak out publicly about their experiences, and in 2003, President Ricardo Lagos announced a broad new human rights policy "*No hay mañana sin ayer*" (There is no tomorrow without yesterday), which included the proposal of creating a second truth commission to investigate torture and political imprisonment.

3.5 The Valech Commission

Crimes of torture were silenced during the first years of the transition. Torture, unless it resulted in death, was omitted from the Rettig Commission, and when discussions of human rights abruptly ended in 1991, torture became a taboo topic in Chilean society. Many torture victims faced social stigma and felt a sense of isolation because of what they had suffered. They could not speak about their traumatic experiences and many faced employment discrimination as well as suspicion from co-workers and acquaintances (Rojas, 2012: 381). The complete lack of recognition of the horrors they suffered at the hands of the state meant that in some cases survivors were not able to have their names cleared of the criminal associations of the political imprisonment they had suffered during the dictatorship. This lack of acknowledgment of the crimes committed against them reinforced a deep sense of injustice in survivors and their families.

Paradoxically, while torture was becoming a taboo topic in Chile, the prohibition of torture was becoming an increasingly recognized norm in international law: the UN Convention against Torture and Other Cruel, Inhuman or Degrading Treatment or Punishment was drafted in 1984 and came into force in June 1987 (Chile ratified that same year), and the Inter-American Convention to Prevent and Punish Torture was adopted in 1985. These international treaties included important state obligations to investigate any claims of torture, as well as victims' right to compensation. This international norm against torture would become an important tool for local activists advocating for justice for survivors of torture and a source of pressure for governments later on in the transition.

The silence regarding crimes of torture began to change after Pinochet's arrest in London (Passmore, 2017: 8). Chilean torture survivors organized themselves to send background information to Spanish Judge Baltasar Garzón, who had issued the arrest warrant and extradition request to have the former Chilean dictator judged for crimes against humanity in Spain. These testimonies were used to help the prosecutors argue against Pinochet's state immunity as a diplomat and former head of state, as it was argued that international crimes such as torture are not the function of a head of state, and as such, a former head of state who has committed these crimes should not be granted immunity (Evans, 2006: 289). Torture victims' testimonies played a decisive role in this landmark case in international law, and the Pinochet case was the beginning of a recognition in Chile of the crimes that torture victims had suffered.

Around this time, more torture victims began to speak out publicly about their experiences as well. An important figure in breaking the silence was Felipe Agüero, Professor of Political Science at the University of Miami at the time. Agüero wrote a letter to the Director of the Institute of Political Science at the Catholic University of Chile, explaining the difficulty of attending conferences on international relations and civic-military relations, when he would constantly come face to face with Emilio Meneses, a professor at the Institute, who had participated in the acts of torture he had suffered at the National Stadium after September 11, 1973. The letter was made public, and Dr. Meneses sued Dr. Agüero for infamy and slander. In the ensuing legal battle, Professor Agüero was able to prove that he was a victim of torture, and the courts rejected the lawsuit against him, which prompted an administrative investigation of Professor Meneses at the Catholic University and ultimately resulted in his resignation. This case caught the attention of acclaimed journalist Patricia Verdugo, winner of the 1997 National Prize for Journalism, who was inspired to write the bestselling book *De la tortura no se habla*, (2004), (We don't talk about torture) in which various torture survivors including Agüero participated. Verdugo's investigation is another excellent example of how civil society stepped in to tell the truth when the state would not. The arrest of Pinochet in London thus sparked a series of events on the ground in Chile which brought the issue of torture and political imprisonment back into the spotlight and put it onto the public agenda.

In August 2003, in commemoration of the upcoming 30th anniversary of the coup, President Ricardo Lagos gave the speech "There is no tomorrow without yesterday," in which he presented a human rights policy that had an enormous resonance in Chile. This human rights policy was the result of long-term advocacy by groups of former political prisoners and Chilean human rights groups alike, who argued that addressing the issue of torture was a moral obligation of the state, as well as an obligation under the international treaties Chile had signed (Lira & Loveman, 2013: 116). One of the measures proposed as part of this initiative was to create another truth commission to investigate crimes of torture that had been neglected for so many years. The Commission on Political Imprisonment and Torture was created on November 11, 2003, through Supreme Decree No. 1040. It became known as the Valech Commission, as it was chaired by Monsignor Sergio Valech, who had been the chair of the human rights defending organization Vicariate of Solidarity. Other commissioners were Miguel Luis Amunátegui, Luciano Fouillioux, José Antonio Gómez, Elizabeth Lira, Lucas Sierra, and Álvaro Varela. María Luisa Sepúlveda was the Executive Vice President of the Commission. The Valech Commission had a timeline of 1 year to complete its investigation—but was reopened again in February 2010 for another 18 months—and had the following objectives: (1) to determine who suffered political imprisonment and torture for political reasons, committed by state agents or others; (2) to propose the conditions, characteristics, and forms of reparations.

The task of the Commission was challenging, as they were investigating crimes that had taken place 30 years prior. Besides the declaration of the victim, the Commission asked or searched for information and documents to support their claim. The Commission defined torture to be any act that caused severe pain or suffering to a person, whether physical or mental, for the purpose of obtaining information, a confession, punishing him/her for committing an act or coercing him/her or others, diminishing his/her physical or mental capacity, or for reasons based on any type of discrimination, committed by a state agent or another person (Valech Report, 2005: 24). The Valech Commission based its methodology on the Rettig Commission. Just like its predecessor, it did not publish the names of the perpetrators, nor did it include public hearings. It was relatively easy for the commissioners to reach a conclusion about the cases of political imprisonment, as there was usually documentary evidence, but cases of torture were more difficult to prove. While they could not prove that torture was suffered by every single victim who testified, the consistency between victims' testimonies allowed the Commission to come to the conclusion that the practice was widespread (Ferrara, 2015: 174).

The final report was released in November 2004 and summarized its results in one particularly important new conclusion: that political violence and torture had been an institutional and systemic policy of the dictatorship. This was a significant statement, as it brought an end to the discourse that the human rights abuses had been "isolated excesses." The Commission received a total of 36,035 testimonies and recognized 27,255 victims and found that more than 94% of those who testified had experienced torture. The Commission identified 1132 political prisons and torture centers with 15 victims or more and outlined the 3 main objectives of the regime's policy of using torture: to generate fear within the population, to suppress the opposition (the left), and to obtain information. The most widely used methods of torture were described in detail.[1]

The majority of victims (44%) were between 21 and 30 years old, with another 25% between 31 and 40 years old. However, there were 1244 victims who had been minors at the time of their political imprisonment or torture. More than half of the victims were working class, while 15% were professionals and technicians, and 15% were students, and most victims either had no direct political affiliation (31%) or were associated with the Socialist Party (22%). The Commission also revealed the gendered nature of torture, unveiling horrifying practices of sexual violence used against women. The victims who testified in the Commission had been 87.5% men and 12.5% women: 3399 women testified as having experienced some form of sexual violence, 316 of whom were raped; 13 women became pregnant because of violations by state agents during detention, and 229 women who were pregnant lost their babies because of torture. The details and the sadism of state agents shocked Chilean society, as the extent and widespread use of torture were far greater than anyone had thought (Sierra, 2005; Oteíza 2009).

[1] For example, the grill, Pau de arara, the phone, the submarine (wet or dry), rape, and sexual abuse (e.g., German shepherd "Volodia," owned by policewoman Ingrid Olderock, was trained to rape at Venda Sexy torture center in Santiago).

In comparison to the Rettig Commission, the Valech Commission was far more explicit in its condemnation of state institutions. While the Rettig Commission declared there had been no war, thus condemning state violence as being unjustified, the Valech Commission declared that violence and repression had been systemic policies of the government and its institutions such as the police, the secret police, and the armed forces, aided by complicit institutions such as the media and the courts. This took the condemnation a step further, stating that not only had violence been unjustified, but it had been purposeful and planned. In some ways the Valech Commission was able to be more explicit in its conclusions due to the different political climate in which it was created, one where Pinochet's influence had significantly decreased. The changes in the political climate were also evident in the very different institutional responses to the Commission. Unlike the Rettig Commission, all the branches of the armed forces and the police accepted responsibility and accepted the report as being a truthful account of events to varying extents. Political parties of the right also declared their support of the Commission and its report. The institution most unwilling to accept the criticisms of the report was the Supreme Court, and even then, they still accepted more responsibility in comparison to their response to the Rettig Report (Ferrara, 2015: 181). The Valech Commission also proposed several reparation measures in order to recognize the role of the state in what had happened to the victims. The main measures proposed were monthly pensions, health benefits, housing benefits, and educational benefits. Memorials were also a symbolic form of reparation proposed by the report.

While it was an improvement in further unveiling the truth of what took place during the dictatorship, and it received a much greater number of testimonies in comparison to the Rettig Commission, the Valech Commission was criticized for two main limitations: it excluded a number of victims, and it imposed a 50-year confidential status on victims' testimonies. First, many victims were excluded for not having enough evidence, particularly if their torture took place outside of a torture center as in that case there were no supporting documents or other victims who could corroborate their presence (Borzutzky, 2017: 150). The short timeline to process the large number of testimonies ended up creating a significant demand for the Commission to extend its mandate.

The Valech Commission also included a significant exclusion of Mapuche testimonies. The Mapuche people experienced significant repression and violence during the Pinochet dictatorship. Decree Law

2568 enacted in 1979 under the Pinochet dictatorship abolished collective land rights and led to an erasure of indigenous rights (Aylwin, 2000: 277–300). These policies were a continuation of long-term processes of ethnic assimilation and displacement from the land (Gomez-Barris, 2015). Mapuche land was given to timber and forestry corporations, and the loss of land impoverished Mapuche communities and disrupted their social fabric (Goicovic Donoso, 2015). The exclusion of the Mapuche from the Valech Commission occurred in the larger context of a lack of consideration for the violence against Mapuche and a lack of methodologies suitable to their inclusion within past truth and reconciliation initiatives (Jara et al., 2018). However, in the specific case of the Valech Commission, over 5000 testimonies from Mapuche victims and survivors were excluded. Mapuche representatives wanted to provide a collective account of the events their communities had experienced, which was more in line with their cultural practices and experiences, but the Commission only accepted individual testimony (Borzutzky, 2017: 151). Jara et al. argue that by failing to consider the cultural specificities of the Mapuche people in official truth commissions, the Chilean state lost an opportunity to establish spaces of dialogue with them and advocate for a broader conception of justice and human rights (2018).

Second, after the publication of the Valech Report, Law No. 19,992 was passed. Article 15 of this law established that the testimonies of the torture victims who had spoken in the Valech Commission would be given a 50-year confidential status. This constituted a big step backward from the Rettig Commission, which had handed over its testimonies to the courts where they had played an important role in the judicial process and were used as evidence in several trials. This 50-year secret status not only reduced the impact of the Commission with regard to helping victims bring perpetrators to justice in the courts (Ferrara, 2015: 176) but also drew anger and frustration from many victims who had testified in order to make Chilean society aware of what had happened to them. In response to this law, many victims have mobilized, and groups such as *Desclasificación Popular* and the Londres 38 memorial site are currently campaigning to demand the 50-year secret clause be withdrawn. Many survivors have issued court challenges, worked to have their own testimony declassified, or directly published their testimonies in books or online archives for public access. However, the documents collected by the Commissions in the process of their work continue to be classified. In September 2021 this discussion was again brought to the table, although this time at the Constituent Assembly (*Convención Constitucional*).

After the Valech Report was published in 2004, many survivors came forward saying they had not testified and still hoped to. The mandate of the Commission was extended, until May 2005, recognizing another 1204 victims (Valech II Report, 2005). In February 2010, due to continued pressure and demand, President Michelle Bachelet issued Supreme Decree No. 43 and created the Presidential Advisory Commission for the Qualification of Disappeared Detainees, Executed Prisoners, and Victims of Political Imprisonment and Torture, known as Valech III. Until August 2011, the Commission heard 31,831 new testimonies and recognized 9795 new victims (Valech III, 2011). This report was delivered to President Piñera and promoted online by the INDH. The Valech II and III Commission followed the same process and methodology as Valech I. The main difference being that the testimonies gathered after Valech I were not made secret by law. In total, through the Valech Commission, its extension, and the Presidential Advisory Commission, the state of Chile has officially recognized 40,018 victims of political imprisonment or torture.

3.6 Torture Victims' Testimonies

The Valech Commission, and its extensions, played an important role in bringing the experiences of victims of torture to the light. However, because it took 30 years for the Commission to be created, and because the testimonies of victims in the Commission were made secret for another 50 years, many victims took it upon themselves to come forward and publish their experiences in their own words. Within this context of taboo and silence, more than 500 testimonial documents of survivors were published in Chile. An especially significant book of testimonies is *Cien Voces Rompen el Silencio* (One Hundred Voices Break the Silence), edited by Wally Kuntsman and Victoria Torres in 2008. This book collected the testimonies of one hundred survivors. Many of those who chose to participate in the book had been outspoken about their experience and involved in torture survivors' groups who had undertaken initiatives such as sending testimonies to Judge Baltasar Garzón during Pinochet's detention in London and the recovery of former torture center, the National Stadium, as a site of memory and historical monument.

The testimonies were written between 2002 and 2007 by 61 men and 39 women, and only 700 copies of the book were published. Reading and analyzing the testimonies of survivors such as the ones in Kunstman and

Torres' book is an important way to better understand why survivors have come forward and how they have been affected by the horrific and systemic violence they experienced. Understanding the victims' perspective can also help in analyzing the successes and failures of state-led truth-seeking initiatives and how to continue working to heal these deep societal wounds. There are several elements that emerge in most victims' testimonies: their motivation for writing the testimony, the conditions and their experiences during the detention, their lives after liberation, and their evaluation of their lives and recent Chilean history (Rojas, 2012).

The most common motivations survivors cited for writing their testimonies were to leave a historical record and publicize the horrific events they endured so that they would never happen again. Many survivors stated that they felt an obligation to tell their story as they felt that the majority of Chileans were ignorant of this significant and tragic part of their national history and as such did not understand the importance of reparations. In the same vein, some also hoped their testimonies would help the state assess and improve reparation policies. Others cited a desire to honor victims who did not survive the torture, as well as a desire to hold perpetrators accountable for their actions (Peris Blanes, 2005). The motivation of survivors for writing a testimony can help us understand what they would like to see from society, within the pursuit of truth and a collective national narrative. The fact that so many cited leaving a historical record or informing Chileans of the truth as their motivation for writing a testimony indicates that social recognition of their experiences is very important to survivors (Rojas, 2012).

Survivors also delved into the painful details of their experiences, giving an account of the unlimited and inhuman cruelty of state agents. Apart from the physical and emotional torment inflicted upon them, many survivors also recounted how terrible it was to hear the screams of other detainees or to have to witness a loved one be tortured. In particular, the testimonies of women who were sexually abused were horrifying. It is worth mentioning that some survivors mentioned in their stories gestures of generosity and solidarity of other prisoners. The details of what happened to survivors of torture are important because it is impossible to fully understand the horrors that they went through, but the closest one can get to understanding is by reading or hearing their version of events from their own perspective (Rojas, 2012). These testimonies therefore have significant historical value in ensuring that Chilean society never forgets what took place.

Many survivors also expressed in their testimonies how incredibly difficult their life was after liberation (Rojas Baeza, 2004: 165). They were victims of social discrimination and employment discrimination, often facing social stigma in the workplace or being let go from their job. Many survivors felt isolated not only because of the traumatizing experiences they suffered but also because others avoided them or regarded them with great suspicion as if they were dangerous criminals. Most victims had high expectations of the transition and Chile's newly recovered democracy, but were deeply disappointed and frustrated by how quickly human rights issues fell off the public agenda and the government's priority list, so much so that the crimes committed against them were ignored or considered taboo. This part of survivors' testimonies indicates how deeply their experience of torture has affected their lives, not only during their detention but afterward as well. Survivors' testimonies make it clear that their experiences of isolation and discrimination did not end with their release from torture and detention centers. In fact, the lack of government action and social recognition of their struggles prolonged and deepened the trauma and the hurt they felt: they were submitted to cruel and degrading treatment at the hands of the state, and yet this assault on their dignity was neither acknowledged nor apologized for. Instead, they were treated like social pariahs (Rojas, 2012).

Finally, victims reflected upon their lives as well as how the state and society have addressed the experiences they have felt. For most of them, the old wounds of the past remain open. The long years of inaction of government and indifference of Chileans hurt them. Survivors feel that they have received insufficient compensation and that they are neither understood nor respected by the majority of the population. There is an overwhelming sense that while Chileans believe they know the stories of the dictatorship, they have no real understanding of the experiences of victims. They have never read a testimony, and the reality of what occurred in torture centers is widely unknown. The physical, psychological, and emotional damage that experiences of torture have left on people's lives is irreversible, and for this reason the state and society have a responsibility to support them through their healing process. The conclusion of most survivors' testimonies is that, while they experienced a living nightmare which has left an indelible mark on their lives, they survived it, and continue to survive it, with strength and resilience. By not acknowledging their stories and perspective, their dignity and strength as survivors of state terrorism are not being sufficiently recognized by Chilean society as a whole (Rojas, 2012).

3.7 Conclusion

The search for the truth in Chile has been a long and complicated process. Despite the limits imposed by the fragile state of democracy in the first years of the political transition, the Rettig Commission established by President Aylwin had an important impact in revealing the truth about the repression and violence under the Pinochet regime, specifically political executions and disappearances. In particular, the conclusion of the Rettig Report that there had been no internal war was very significant as it officially established that the suspension of citizens' rights and the use of state violence against them had been unjustified. The search for the truth after the release of the Rettig Report was interrupted for many years, which was particularly difficult for survivors of torture and state violence, many of whom spent 30 years campaigning for the process of truth-seeking to continue and for their experiences and trauma to be recognized by the state. The efforts of the Mesa de Diálogo in 1999, though inconclusive, did lay the groundwork for some institutional recognition of responsibility by the armed forces.

Valech Commission released its report in 2004, completing in many ways the results of the Rettig Report 13 years earlier. The conclusion of the Valech Report indicated that torture had been a widespread and systemic policy of the dictatorship and strongly condemned all state institutions that had been involved in torture or complicit in allowing it to occur. Together, these two reports form the main body of official "truth-telling" about the human rights abuses of the dictatorship in Chile. However, civil society initiatives such as journalistic investigations, books, and academic investigations like those of Tomás Moulian and Patricia Verdugo undertook important work to fill the gaps in official truth-telling during the 30 years between the two commissions and also with regard to the 50-year confidential status imposed by the state on the testimonies of torture victims to the Valech Commission. While these various mechanisms and initiatives greatly contributed to the search for the truth in Chile, it is not yet fully complete. For example, the location of many of the disappeared has yet to be established.

Years of campaigning by survivors of torture finally succeeded in expanding the official search for truth in 2003. Testimonies of these survivors reveal that their experience of exclusion from truth and reconciliation efforts was deeply painful and it compounded their situation of social isolation and stigmatization. Many survivors have a deep desire for a social recognition of the profound physical, psychological, and emotional damage their experiences of torture have inflicted on their lives. Uncovering the truth about the extent of human rights violations under the dictatorship was a positive step toward recognition and acknowledgment of survivors' stories. Yet, many feel it is not enough if not accompanied by other efforts to help them in their recovery. Reparations are one of the ways that a state can both symbolically and materially seek to repair the harm caused by human rights violations. The wounds inflicted on victims of state terror are irreversible, and the state and society have a responsibility to support them as they seek to heal from these traumatic experiences.

Bibliography

Aylwin, J. (2000). Los conflictos en el territorio Mapuche: Antecedentes y perspectivas. *Perspectivas, 3*(2), 277–300.

Bastías, M. (2013). *Sociedad civil en dictadura: relaciones transnacionales, organizaciones y socialización política en Chile.* Ediciones Universidad Alberto Hurtado.

Borzutzky, S. (2017). *Human Rights in Chile: The Unfinished Struggle for Truth and Justice.* Palgrave Macmillan.

Collins, C., Garcia-Godos, J., & Skaar, E. (Eds.). (2016). *Transitional Justice in Latin America: The Uneven Road from Impunity Towards Accountability.* Routledge.

Comisión Nacional de Verdad y Reconciliación. (1991). *Informe Rettig.* Gobierno de Chile.

Comisión Nacional sobre Prisión Política y Tortura. (2005). *Informe de la Comisión Nacional sobre Prisión Política y Tortura*, available at https://bibliotecadigital.indh.cl/handle/123456789/455

Evans, R. (2006). Pinochet in London: Pinochet in Chile: International and Domestic Politics in Human Rights Policy. *Human Rights Quarterly, 28*(1), 207–244.

Ferrara, A. (2015). *Assessing the Long-term Impact of Truth Commissions: The Chilean Truth and Reconciliation Commission in Historical Perspective.* Routledge.

Ferrara, A. (2017). El Largo Camino a la Verdad en Chile. Una Perspectiva Histórica. In R. Jimeno (Ed.), *Justicia Transicional: Historia y Actualidad* (pp. 213–239). Thomson Reuters Aranzadi.

Goicovic Donoso, I. (2015). Campos conceptuales, perspectivas de análisis y ciclos históricos en el estudio del movimiento Mapuche. In J. Pinto (Ed.), *Conflictos étnicos, sociales y económicos: Araucanía 1900–2014* (pp. 19–44). Pehuén.

Gómez-Barris, M. (2015). Mapuche Mnemonics: Beyond Modernity's Violence. *Memory Studies, 8*(1), 75–85.

Hayner, P. (2011). *Unspeakable Truths: Transitional Justice and the Challenge of Truth Commissions* (2nd ed.). Routledge.

Inter-American Commission on Human Rights (IACHR). (2014). *The Right to the Truth in the Americas*, available at https://www.oas.org/en/iachr/reports/pdfs/Right-to-Truth-en.pdf

International Committee of the Red Cross (ICRC). (1977), *Protocol Additional to the Geneva Conventions of 12 August 1949, and relating to the Protection of Victims of International Armed Conflicts (Protocol I)*, 8 June 1977, 1125 UNTS 3, available at https://www.refworld.org/docid/3ae6b36b4.html

Jara, D., Badilla, M., Figueiredo, A., Cornejo, M., & Riveros, V. (2018). Tracing Mapuche Exclusion from Post-Dictatorial Truth Commissions in Chile: Official and Grassroots Initiatives. *International Journal of Transitional Justice, 12*(3), 479–498.

Lazzara, M. J. (2006). *Chile in Transition. The Poetics and Politics of Memory.* University of Press of Florida.

Lira, E. (2005). Mesa de Diálogo de Derechos Humanos. In E. Lira & G. Morales (Eds.), *Derechos humanos y reparación: una discusión pendiente* (pp. 152–164). Lom ediciones.

Lira, E., & Loveman, B. (2013). Torture as Public Policy. In C. Collins, K. Hite, & A. Joignant (Eds.), *The Politics of Memory in Chile from Pinochet to Bachelet* (pp. 91–132). First Forum Press.

Loveman, B., & Lira, E. (2000). *Las ardientes cenizas del olvido: Vía chilena de Reconciliación Política 1932–1994.* Lom Ediciones.

Oteíza, T. (2009). De "la conspiración de silencio" al reconocimiento de voces alternativas. Las violaciones a los derechos humanos en Chile según el Informe Valech (2003). *Revista Latinoamericana de Estudios del Discurso, 9*(1), 87–111.

Passmore, L. (2017). *The Wars Inside Chile's Barracks: Remembering Military Service Under Pinochet.* University of Wisconsin Press.

Peris Blanes, J. (2005). *La imposible voz: Memoria y representación de los campos de concentración en Chile: la posición del testigo.* Cuarto Propio.

Presidential Advisory Commission for the Qualification of Disappeared Detainees, Political Executed, and Victims of Political Imprisonment and Torture. (2011). *Final Report.* Santiago (in Spanish).

Rojas Baeza, P. (2004). Romper el silencio. In P. Verdugo (Ed.), *De la tortura no se habla: Agüero versus Meneses* (pp. 161–180). Catalonia.

Rojas, H. (2012). Torture in Chile (1973–1990): Analysis of One Hundred Survivors' Testimonies. *California Western International Law Journal, 42*, 353–392.

Ruderer, S. (2010). La política del pasado en Chile 1990–2006: ¿Un modelo chileno? *Revista Universum, 25*(2), 161–177.

Sierra, L. (2005). Reabrir y Cicatrizar: Notas sobre el *Informe Valech* y sus Reacciones. *Anuario de Derechos Humanos* (pp. 157–166). Universidad de Chile.
Sorensen, K. I. (2015). *Los Medios, La Memoria y los Derechos Humanos en Chile*. RIL Editores.
Spooner, M. H. (2011). *The General's Slow Retreat: Chile After Pinochet*. University of California Press.
Stern, S., & Winn, P. (2014). El Tortuoso Camino Chileno a la Memorialización. In P. Winn, S. Stern, F. Lorenz, & A. Marchesi (Eds.), *No hay mañana sin ayer: Batallas por la memoria histórica en el Cono Sur* (pp. 205–326). Lom ediciones.
United Nations. (2010). *Guidance Note of the Secretary General: United Nations Approach to Transitional Justice*, available at https://www.un.org/ruleoflaw/files/TJ_Guidance_Note_March_2010FINAL.pdf

CHAPTER 4

Reparations for the Victims

The dictatorship devastated many people's lives. Families were forced to flee the country and leave everything they knew behind; workers were unfairly dismissed from their job because of their political affiliation; political activists were imprisoned, tortured, and killed; and many people lost loved ones to violence and repression. Victims of these human rights violations experienced serious physical injuries and psychological trauma and in many cases suffered social and economic consequences stemming from these same horrible events (Rojas, 2012). In many cases, these are tragedies and losses that can never be undone: loved ones cannot be brought back and traumatic experiences cannot be erased. In order to rebuild the relationship between the state and victims of repression and restore trust in government, the state must make efforts to recognize the profound impacts these human rights violations will have on victims for the rest of their lives. The search for the truth is often the first step in this process, but beyond establishing the true events in the context of human rights abuses, the state also has a responsibility to *repair* the wrongs done to those who have suffered most, and to support them in their healing. Mending the relationship between the state and victims is an essential part of broader efforts of social reconciliation.

Reparations programs are one of the means states can use to officially recognize the abuses that have taken place and seek to compensate victims. Reparations can take both material and symbolic form and work best

H. Rojas, M. Shaftoe, *Human Rights and Transitional Justice in Chile*, Memory Politics and Transitional Justice,
https://doi.org/10.1007/978-3-030-81182-2_4

when the two types are combined. Symbolic reparations, such as memorials or official apologies, work to repair the moral wrong done to victims by officially acknowledging and taking responsibility for human rights abuses, while material reparations aim to provide economic compensation for the damage caused. Pablo de Greiff notes that for many victims, material reparations programs are often "the most tangible manifestation of the efforts of the state to remedy the harms they have suffered" (2006: 1), as economic compensation tends to have a direct and immediate impact on their lives. In this chapter we will focus on the material reparations policies implemented in Chile, and we will explore symbolic reparations in depth in the following chapter (Memorialising and Commemorating).

It is important to ensure that reparations policies are implemented alongside other elements of transitional justice such as truth, memory, justice, and guarantees of non-repetition, as there is a danger that material reparations appear empty if they are not accompanied by the pursuit of truth, justice, and other transitional justice initiatives. For instance, conflicts can emerge when victims perceive economic compensation from the state as a means for authorities to evade accountability by buying their silence or bribing them not to pursue justice through the courts (Lira, 2006: 10).

The concept of a victim's right to reparations has been consolidated through international treaties such as the UN Convention against Torture, and the rulings of international tribunals such as the Inter-American Court of Human Rights. It has become an important legal principle which establishes that reparations for victims should be "proportional to the gravity of the violations and the harm suffered" (UN, 2005). The right to reparations is thus often interpreted to mean that the state should seek to return the victims' lives to how they were before the violation occurred. However, the concept is expanding and evolving rapidly in many ways, and broader understandings of reparations now seek to recognize the preexisting inequalities which often result in the most marginalized and vulnerable populations being most affected by conflicts and human rights violations.

In this context, authors such as Rodrigo Yepes (2009) and Lauren Balasco (2017) argue that reparations should not seek to return victims to their previous lives, but to improve them, by designing reparations programs which seek to compensate for the harm done to victims by addressing structural inequalities and injustices that continue to cause suffering. Another important expansion of the concept of reparations is the idea of collective reparations, which has been established through key rulings in the Inter-American Court of Human Rights such as the 2004 ruling in the *Case of Plan de Sánchez Massacre v. Guatemala*, where compensation is made collectively to a whole community. This is an important development especially for indigenous communities, where collective reparations are often considered a more culturally appropriate means of compensation.

Due to the diverse nature of the harms suffered by victims, reparations programs and initiatives can take a wide variety of different shapes and forms. Pablo de Greiff (2006) suggests that there are seven main elements which can be used to analyze and evaluate the reach and success of reparations programs. The first three elements help assess who is able to access the program, and how well it covers all the different types of victims: the **scope** of a program refers to how many beneficiaries there are, **completeness** addresses how accurately it covers the whole range of those affected, and **comprehensiveness** indicates which types of crimes a reparations program ultimately seeks to address. These elements can help assess whether reparations programs address the wide range of harms caused to various groups of victims, as well as who is being included and excluded.

The last four elements focus on how well the benefits address the harms caused. The **complexity** of a program denotes the different ways in which the reparations seek to repair the harm done, in other words, the combination of distinct types of benefits it provides. The fifth element, **integrity or coherence**, is the relationship between the various types of benefits provided by a reparations program, and how well they complement each other. This element can also be used to assess how the reparations program fits within and relates to the broader context of other transitional justice elements and policies. Sixth, **munificence** indicates the magnitude of the benefits, or their monetary value. The final element **finality** refers to how and whether receiving benefits limits other avenues of civil redress or not (2006: 5–12). These seven elements of reparations are useful tools for assessing how effectively reparations programs achieve their purpose of compensating for the harms done and supporting the whole spectrum of victims in their recovery.

Reparations policy in Chile has gone hand in hand with the search for the truth, as reparations initiatives for the relatives of the executed and disappeared, as well as survivors of torture and political imprisonment have been largely based on the recommendations of the official truth commissions. Most of the initiatives in the Chilean reparations system were initially designed and implemented by the first democratic government, which sought to create a comprehensive reparations framework to compensate the wide range of different victims. Subsequent criticisms of the reparations framework were then left unaddressed for several years, as political leaders on both sides of the political spectrum sought to declare the issue of human rights dealt with. Renewed momentum for human rights policy after Pinochet's detention in London in 1998 resulted in an improvement and reevaluation of Chile's reparations systems at the time, and new programs were created to fill gaps in the initial reparations landscape, particularly the exclusion of torture victims.

In this chapter, we will review the extensive reparations policies implemented in Chile over the years, and then we will seek to evaluate the Chilean reparations framework using Pablo de Greiff's seven elements of reparations, outlined above.

4.1 Laying the Foundations of a Comprehensive Reparations Framework

During the dictatorship, the vast majority of the victims of state repression had nowhere to turn for help but to a handful of human rights organizations, such as the *Vicaría de Solidaridad*, the Social Aid Foundation of Christian Churches (FASIC), the Committee for the Defense of People's Rights (CODEPU), and the Chilean Human Rights Commission. In many ways, the actions of these groups in providing economic, social, medical, psychological, and legal support foreshadowed much of the work which the state would later take on through reparations programs (Lira, 2006: 24). When the dictatorship ended in 1990, President Aylwin declared a major focus of his administration would be taking responsibility for the damages done by the state to its citizens, by providing moral and material reparations to the victims of state repression. The first reparations programs of the Chilean government thus emerged from the recommendations published in the Rettig Report (1991), which outlined the findings of the Truth and Reconciliation Commission created to investigate the crimes committed under the dictatorship. The report proposed establishing various symbolic reparations measures to recognize the dignity of the victims and allow their relatives a means of honoring them, as well as providing economic compensation for the damage caused to these families. Two main reparations initiatives were based on the recommendations of the commission's report; Law No. 19,123 established the *Program of*

Reparations for the Relatives of the Executed and Disappeared and created the National Corporation for Reparations and Reconciliation, while the *Program of Reparations and Comprehensive Healthcare for Victims* (PRAIS) was created under the Ministry of Health and aimed to provide health assistance to victims of all different types of human rights abuses.

As part of their efforts to address and repair the wrongs of the past, the Aylwin administration also undertook reparations initiatives for victims of other types of human rights abuses. Programs were established for those forced into exile, through the *National Office of Returns*, for those who were politically dismissed from their jobs, through the *Program for the Recognition of Political Exoneration*, and the *Peasant Reparations Program* for peasants expelled from their lands or excluded from land reform. These reparations programs took various forms, such as monthly pensions, social services, as well as educational and health benefits for the designated groups of victims. The state paid out 52 billion pesos in reparations pension payments between 1992 and 2001, as well as an additional 7 billion pesos to educational institutions, including universities, for the studies of the victims' children until they reached the age of 35 (INP, 2021). While this spending was significant and appreciated, some significant gaps and omissions remained. The most glaring issue was the lack of government recognition or support for torture victims and political prisoners, who were excluded not only from material reparations such as monthly pensions programs, but also from symbolic reparations measures such as the Truth and Reconciliation Commission.

A sense of insufficiency permeated the perception many victims held of the reparations efforts. While beneficiaries were grateful for the benefits and pensions they received, there was an overwhelming sense that these efforts were empty if not accompanied by a more serious search for truth and justice. Allowing perpetrators to go free was therefore another major factors which caused victims to feel the government's efforts were not sufficient. Yet despite these significant pending issues, at the beginning of Frei's mandate various political actors wanted to close the issue of human rights. Legislative initiatives were even presented that sought to enact an Expiry or Endpoint Law for victims to come forward with claims and for benefits to be distributed. Proponents of this legislation argued that it was not good for society to remain stuck in the past, that the page had to be turned, and that the moral debt owed by the state had already been assumed by all sectors.

These attempts to legislate an endpoint for reparations programs collapsed after Pinochet's arrest in London in 1998, which infused new momentum into discussions of human rights policies in Chile, culminating shortly after the election in 2000 of Socialist President Ricardo Lagos, with the announcement of a broad new human rights proposal in 2003, entitled *No Hay Mañana sin Ayer* (There is no tomorrow without yesterday). This proposal was the direct result of many years' worth of advocacy from human rights organizations and the work of human rights experts, and it sought to improve upon earlier public reparations policy and rectify the exclusion of torture survivors and political prisoners. A new truth commission was created that would finally investigate cases of torture and political imprisonment during the dictatorship (Valech Commission), and the *Program of Reparations for Victims of Political Imprisonment and Torture* was subsequently established. The new measures and improvements in reparations policy were becoming increasingly technical, and as such social welfare experts and economists were involved in debates on reparations. Among the measures announced were an increase in reparations pension amounts by 50 percent, increasing the payments received by unmarried partners of victims to be equal to that of husbands and wives, the establishment of a one-off payment of 10 million pesos for children who had not previously received benefits, the granting of grace pensions through the President's Scholarship Fund, the improvement of educational benefits, and improvements to healthcare programming through PRAIS.

The Chilean reparations landscape thus includes a wide variety of different types of reparations policies and programs, most notably pensions, educational benefits, and health services, and has sought to provide support and recognition to victims of all kinds of human rights abuses including execution, forced disappearance, exile, political dismissal, the expulsion of peasants from their land, and finally political imprisonment and torture.

Program of Reparations for the Relatives of the Executed and Disappeared

The report of the Truth and Reconciliation Commission included a reparations proposal, which proposed recommendations for symbolic reparations initiatives, suggestions as to how to handle legal and administrative issues affecting victims, and a series of social welfare initiatives such as pensions, healthcare assistance, education benefits, and housing (TRC

Report, Vol II, part 3: 823–836). Law No. 19,123, passed in early 1992, was the main bill seeking to implement the reparations recommendations of the Rettig Report. It initially faced some pushback from families of the victims related to declaring the presumed death of victims and the single pension, which didn't take into account the number of members of families affected. Aylwin's government worked with the Group of Families of Disappeared Detainees (AFDD) to incorporate their proposals into the reparations bill (Lira, 2006: 4).

The law established a reparations system of monthly pensions for relatives of the executed and disappeared amounting to $ 226,667 Chilean pesos (US$ 537), which would be split between the different beneficiaries. It also included educational benefits for the children of victims as well as healthcare benefits. The initial number of beneficiaries of the program was 5794 people. Law No. 19,123 also created the National Corporation for Reparations and Reconciliation as the governing body which would oversee and promote the reparations programs and would function until 1996. The Corporation determined who qualified to receive the monthly pensions and benefits, as well as undertaking other important reparations efforts such as investigating the whereabouts of the disappeared, human rights outreach, and education, among others.

The reparations program was well received overall but excluded certain groups of potential beneficiaries, for instance, unmarried partners of victims and children out of wedlock had difficulty accessing monthly pensions (Lira, 2006: 10). Families of victims also criticized the lack of coherence of reparations initiatives with pending truth and justice issues. Notably, certain key promises made under the umbrella of reparations, such as the investigation into the whereabouts of missing detainees, also continued to be woefully unmet. The Frei government created the Human Rights Programme in the Ministry of Interior, which sought to follow up on the pending objectives of the Corporation for Reparation and Reconciliation after it was dissolved in 1997, in particular continuing to investigate unsolved cases of forced disappearances. This program still exists to this day in the Under Secretariat for Human Rights; however, more recent measures have failed to create much significant advancement: as of September 2019, of the 1210 people recognized as disappeared during the dictatorship, the remains of only 235 had been identified (Rojas & Suárez, 2019).

Program of Reparation and Comprehensive Health Care for Victims

Arguably the most significant Chilean reparations initiative is the Program of Reparation and Comprehensive Health Care for Victims (PRAIS), as it provided reparations to all kinds of victims of human rights abuses, and accounted for intergenerational trauma by including up to the third-generation relatives of victims. This program built on the work of the network of professionals in human rights organization such as the Vicaría de Solidaridad and FASIC, who had offered mental health support to victims during the dictatorship (Lira, 2016: 203–206). Some of these mental health professionals worked with the Rettig Commission and collaborated in creating the recommendations related to physical and psychological healthcare for victims.

The PRAIS program was thus created in 1991 as a program of the ministry of health, seeking to address the significant, lasting mental and physical health problems experienced by victims of human rights violations. The loss of a loved one in horrifying circumstances, the trauma caused due to torture, and the difficult experience of being forced into exile all leave significant marks on people's bodies and minds. PRAIS was not limited only to the victims identified in the Rettig Report and instead works in conjunction with other programs; a victim's qualification for any established reparations programs was enough to allow them to qualify as a beneficiary and access physical and mental health benefits. PRAIS is the Chilean reparations program with the broadest reach in terms of which victims can qualify (Lira, 2006: 56). It is accessible to the families of executed and disappeared detainees, those who were fired for political reasons, those who were exiled, former political prisoners, torture victims, and any other person who had been recognized by the state as having suffered a human rights violation under the dictatorship. The program was officially institutionalized in 2004, as part of President Ricardo Lagos' project to update earlier public reparations policies.

The PRAIS program is therefore an impressive example of reparations as a form of rehabilitation (Lira, 2016), which provides free lifetime physical and psychological healthcare through the public health system to help victims of human rights abuses heal from experiences of trauma. To this day, PRAIS provides free healthcare to victims and their families, and as of 2015, it has 784,300 beneficiaries. In terms of providing psychosocial care as an integrated aspect of the national reparations framework, this program goes beyond what was adopted in most other reparations systems in Latin America, where rehabilitation was provided to victims mainly through the work of NGOs, such as Anti-Drug Foundation of El Salvador (FUNDASALVA). Recently, in 2011, mental health and rehabilitation initiatives for victims of state repression and armed conflict have been established in Argentina and Colombia as well (Lira, 2016: 202). There have recently been some important critiques, however, as to how well PRAIS actually benefits the victims who are accessing it, particularly as there have been no official government evaluations of the program since 1994 (Yaikin, 2016).

National Office of Returns

Along with health benefits and monthly pensions for victims' families, President Aylwin also prioritized the return of exiles within his reparations framework. Thousands of Chileans fled the country or were expelled during the course of the dictatorship, forced to leave their entire life behind and start anew. Many had to leave friends and loved ones behind, and spent their years in exile waiting to be able to return. In some cases, they didn't even fully unpack their suitcases. In August of 1990, Law No. 18,994 was adopted to establish the National Office for Returns. This agency provided support to all those who had been expelled or had fled the country, as well as their children born in exile, in their efforts to return to Chile. It assisted in the return of 52,557 Chileans from 70 different countries, where they had been exiled or sought asylum. However, many in exile chose not to return, as the emotional strain of uprooting themselves again would have been too difficult. The Office operated until 1994, and over four years, the program received funds totaling US$ 20.8 million, US$ 19 million of which came from international cooperation. Several other laws were passed to complement the efforts to reintegrate exiles, for instance, to recognize academic degrees completed by Chileans while in exile abroad and allow them to work in Chile with their foreign qualifications. Services were also provided to assist newly returned Chileans with incorporating themselves back into the workforce, as well as referring them to social services (Wright & Oñate, 2007: 46).

Program for the Recognition of Political Exoneration

Through the Program for the Recognition of Political Exoneration, the government also sought to compensate those who had lost their jobs for political reasons. After the military coup, there had been a major purge of anyone in government agencies, the public service, or universities, who was known to be politically affiliated with the Allende government or spoke out against the military regime. This had major economic consequences on peoples' lives as well as exposing them to social stigma and isolation. After the return to democracy, as much as possible, the government sought to rehire and reinstate those who had been fired for political reasons to their original positions. Through Law No. 19,234, it was established that those who had been politically dismissed from their jobs would be granted pension benefits. The program benefited 14,508 people and involved an expenditure of 20 billion pesos.

Due to pressure and lobbying from groups representing the politically dismissed, it was later complemented by Law No. 19,583, which expanded the program's reach to include members of certain public service sectors who had been excluded from the previous iteration of the program, and extended the time period for applicants requesting benefits (Lira, 2006: 28). The second iteration of the program benefited 59,444 people, with a total expenditure of 90 billion pesos. By 2003, the state had recognized the wrongful political dismissal of 86,208 people and 305 billion pesos had been paid out.

Despite the broad reach to beneficiaries, there have been concerns that the reparative aspect of this particular program was diluted, due to a technicality which allowed some members and collaborators of the military regime to apply for and be granted pensions (CGR, 2013; Case 1254-2011).

Reparations for Rural Communities

Another complicated case in the context of Chilean reparations efforts is repression in rural communities during the dictatorship. The experience of abuse of peasants and agrarian reform activists under the dictatorship was a particularly complicated and violent one. Agrarian reform was an exceedingly polarizing and controversial issue in the years leading up to the military coup. As such, the persecution of leaders of organizations such as land cooperatives and unions was immediate, widespread, and brutal as soon as the military junta took power. When the military regime changed the regulations for assigning land, many activist leaders and organizers were excluded from land reform initiatives, expelled from their lands and forcibly disappeared. Many rural Chileans experienced serious economic hardship due to the loss of their lands and their livelihoods, as well as persecution (Hite, 2013: 95), and due to this, some were forced to leave their home villages and communities to seek better opportunities elsewhere in the country.

During the transition to democracy, the government entered into discussions with peasant organizations to develop an effective reparations program. Many ideas were proposed by the organizations, such as the allocation of productive plots of land to those who had lost them, as well as educational and housing benefits, but these were not ultimately included (Lira, 2006: 37). The program was not established until 1996, under President Frei. Pensions were granted through the Peasant Reparation Program to compensate for the harms caused to many who had lost their land, and with it their homes and livelihoods. In cases of extreme need, the Presidency of the Republic could also grant grace pensions. Law No. 19,568 was passed in 1998 to further the efforts to restore property and compensate the injured parties.

While beneficiaries have expressed gratitude for the pensions, many also felt the reparations were grossly insufficient (Lira, 2006: 37). In this particular case where victims were already economically disadvantaged, a greater participation and inclusion of the proposals of victims, as well as a more innovative approach to reparations would have been appropriate, to seek to not only compensate for the losses of victims but improve their current situation in the way they most deemed necessary, for instance, through educational assistance and housing benefits.

Alongside peasant activists, Mapuche communities suffered from the impacts of the reversal of agrarian reform during the dictatorship. For example, according to Richards, "at the end of the counter-reform, Mapuche families kept only 16 percent of the land they had recovered between 1962 and 1973" (2016: 87). Yet the significant abuses and collective experience of violence experienced by the Mapuche under the military regime was situated within a long and violent history of dispossession from their lands (Bengoa, 2004: 419–433). The dictatorship exacerbated structural and historical injustices by abolishing the right to collective land ownership. In addition to this, they suffered from political persecution, executions, and disappearances, which were again worsened by a history of racial discrimination. For instance, land occupations and defense of traditional territories by the Mapuche were branded as "terrorism" during the dictatorship (Borzutzky, 2017: 151). Unfortunately, this terminology has persisted in some sectors, who to this day consider the leaders of the

Mapuche communities who are fighting for the recovery of their lands as terrorists. This accumulation of historical injustices has led to a recognition that Chile has a historical debt toward the Mapuche (Di Giminiani, 2018).

Despite the specific nature of the abuse and violence experienced by the Mapuche, no separate culturally appropriate reparations model was developed or considered to seek to redress the harms done to Indigenous communities. As a result, material reparations programs caused further harm by disrupting Mapuche community networks, causing feelings of guilt and "a state of imbalance within the delicate web of intra-family relationships at the heart of these communities" (Durán et al., 2000). Key historical demands of the Mapuche include the return to their ancestral lands, the right to jurisdictional autonomy, and the recognition of cultural identity (Jara et al., 2018). An approach such as collective and community-based reparations measures devised in collaboration with Mapuche leaders and communities, and rooted in addressing structural and historical injustices which originated long before the Pinochet dictatorship, would likely have had a much more positive impact in repairing the harm done in this particular, hard hit, community (Durán et al., 2000). Given the ongoing nature of state repression in these communities, and the continued use of Pinochet-era anti-terrorism laws to repress the Mapuche community (Ancalao Gavilán, 2018; UN, 2017), such an approach may still be worth considering.

Program of Reparations for Political Imprisonment and Torture

The journey to recognition and reparations for victims of political imprisonment and torture has been a long one. Aylwin's government partially tried to address the situation of political prisoners as part of their reparations efforts. During the years of the dictatorship, the military justice system was used to circumvent just trials in civilian courts in order to convict many political activists and adversaries of the regime. Without due process, people were convicted in military courts right after the coup. Others were detained and imprisoned in detention centers and denied their right to a free trial. Torture and degrading treatment of prisoners was commonplace. Many prisoners and detainees were released over the course of the dictatorship, but in 1989, there were still 397 identified political prisoners in jails across Chile. In the 1990 presidential campaign, the *Concertación* coalition explicitly stated its intention to free these political prisoners.

However, due to legal complications related to military law, only 45 of the 397 identified political prisoners could be freed immediately when the democratic transition took place.

To address the situation of political prisoners, the Aylwin administration passed the Cumplido Laws, named after the main author of the regulations, Minister of Justice Francisco Cumplido. These laws authorized the president to issue pardons for political prisoners, amended the Code of Military Justice, the Criminal Code, the State Security Act, the Arms Control Act, and the Terrorist Conduct Act, among other measures. These reforms had a significant impact in helping secure the release of political prisoners who had committed non-serious crimes, and clearing their names through the issuing of presidential pardons. Once the Cumplido Laws were passed, procedures were expedited to free and pardon the remaining political prisoners. However, once they had been pardoned and freed, there was very little state support for them in comparison to other victims of the dictatorship. The crimes of torture and political imprisonment were not recognized by the government in any official capacity. There was no acknowledgment of the suffering any former detainees had experienced or any significant effort to compensate them for it.

The only reparations program to which survivors of political imprisonment and torture had access was PRAIS, and that was only if they had proof of their detention. Former political prisoners were not eligible for monthly pensions unless they were specially granted grace pensions by the president. Given the widespread nature of torture and political imprisonment during the dictatorship, this exclusion of thousands of victims was a major oversight in the Aylwin administration's reparations framework and contributed to further stigmatizing the experiences of torture victims (Rojas, 2012).

This major limitation in Chilean reparations policy was addressed in 2003, when President Lagos presented a new and wide-ranging human rights proposal to the country, entitled *No Hay Mañana sin Ayer* (There is no tomorrow without yesterday). Reparations for victims of political imprisonment and torture were significantly improved through the creation of the Valech Commission, which provided symbolic reparations by finally officially acknowledging these crimes, and also provided recommendations for material reparations. On December 24, 2004, Law No. 19,992 was published (which has since been amended by Law No. 20,405). It establishes reparation pensions for the victims mentioned in the Valech Report and their spouses, as well as a bonus for persons who were born while their parents were in prison. Educational benefits were granted, including the payment of tuition and annual fees at institutions of higher education. This benefit is also extended to the descendants of victims of torture and political imprisonment.

The new reparations measures and improvements created through the *No Hay Mañana sin Ayer* human rights initiative measures have rectified some of the glaring omissions and problems of the earlier reparations' framework. They have sought to finally recognize the dignity of survivors of torture and political imprisonment, as well as include sectors of victims who were excluded from earlier versions of reparations programs, such as unwed partners of the people who had been disappeared and executed, and children out of wedlock. However, the Valech commission and reparations initiative was criticized on several counts: the 50-year confidentiality clause on testimonies led some potential beneficiaries to boycott the commission as they felt their silence was being bought, the closing of the victim and survivors lists prevented new cases or new information to be considered, and the material reparations were criticized as insufficient as they were significantly lower in value than Rettig reparations (approximately US$ 217 for individuals names by the Valech commission, and approximately US$ 666 for families named by the Rettig commission) (Collins et al., 2016).

4.2 Evaluation of Chilean Reparations Policy

Much money and time has been spent since 1990 on devising and distributing reparations programs in Chile, but how effective have these programs been? In this section, we will use the seven elements of reparations suggested by Pablo de Greiff (2006)—scope, comprehensiveness, completeness, complexity, integrity, munificence, and finality—as a framework to evaluate the successes and limitations of the wider landscape of the main six material reparations initiatives included in Chilean reparations policy.

Scope Throughout the transition, hundreds of thousands of victims have accessed some form of reparations through the Program of Reparations for the Relatives of the Executed and Disappeared, the Program of Comprehensive Healthcare for Victims, the National Office of Returns, the Program for the Recognition of Political Exoneration, the Peasant Reparations Program, and the Program of reparations for Political

Imprisonment and Torture. As such, Chile's system of reparations has been large in scope, or the number of beneficiaries. Completeness and Comprehensiveness Completeness refers to whether reparations succeed in covering the whole wide range of potential beneficiaries. Among Chilean reparations policies, the Rettig reparations' initial exclusion of unmarried partners and children out of wedlock caused it to be incomplete for several years. Valech reparations also struggled with completeness, as the 50-year confidentiality clause dissuaded some potential beneficiaries from participation and attempts to close the victim and survivors lists to new cases and new information restricted the program's ability to be fully complete. In terms of comprehensiveness, or the recognition of all the victims of different types of violations, the Chilean reparations landscape has become more comprehensive since the inclusion of political prisoners and torture survivors. The lack of recognition of some of the most serious and widespread human rights violations for nearly ten years was a major deficit in Chilean reparations policy for a long time. In addition, the lack of recognition of the Mapuche as a distinct group of victims resulted in a culturally inappropriate approach to reparations which ultimately caused these communities harm.

Complexity Chilean reparations policy is fairly advanced when it comes to complexity, because it makes use of a variety of different types of programs and forms of compensation. As a whole, the broad use of benefits programs, educational credits, and monthly pensions, as well as symbolic measures such as the truth commissions and official state apology, make the Chilean reparations system quite complex. In comparison, Argentinian reparations initiatives favored more heavily a quite large one-time payment, in the form of government bonds, and provided far fewer benefits-style programs (Guembe, 2006). When one takes a closer look, however, some of the individual programs lack complexity. The reparations program for peasants, for instance, provided a simplistic response to a very complex experience of lasting economic, social, physical, and psychological harm caused by repression and loss of land. The payment of monthly pensions in this particular case seems far from proportional to the harm caused.

Integrity (Internal and External Coherence) The integrity of a reparations program has two aspects to it: its internal and external coherence.

The Chilean reparations system is quite internally coherent. The various reparations measures complement each other as a general rule, for instance, by allowing beneficiaries to access PRAIS healthcare benefits if they have already qualified for any of the other reparations' programs. However, the external coherence of different reparations programs with other transitional justice elements has been very mixed, and a key distinction must be made in terms of the external coherence of Rettig and Valech reparations. Rettig reparations have been fairly externally coherent in the sense as they went hand in hand with truth-seeking initiatives; their policies and programs stemmed from the recommendations of the TRC. They were also accompanied by symbolic reparations and memorializing initiatives such as the official state apology and the Memorial for the Detained and Disappeared in the General Cemetery. However, victims criticized the lack of attention and effort made by the state to bring perpetrators to justice, as well as the failure to locate and identify the remains of the disappeared, as major problems of coherence with the elements of truth and justice. These limitations made other reparations efforts appear empty. Cath Collins notes, however, that the door was left open to the pursuit of justice by forwarding background information to the courts on cases submitted to the Rettig commission (Collins et al., 2016: 64).

Valech reparations faced more issues of external coherence, as the links between truth, justice, and reparations were less clear than their Rettig predecessors. The commission sought to link reparations explicitly to truth while severing them from connections to justice. 50-year confidentiality clause imposed a limit on the dissemination of the truth, while simultaneously inhibiting justice by removing the possibility of forwarding information to the courts (Collins et al., 2016: 72). This experience in Chile, of reverting toward less external coherence in the Valech reparations process, contrasts with that of Brazil where reparations have been the main driver of transitional justice. The two Brazilian reparations commissions have fed demands for truth, justice, and memory and were instrumental in leading to the full-fledged Truth Commission (Abrão & Torelly, 2011: 481–485).

Furthermore, locating the whereabouts of the disappeared is an issue of enormous importance to families in order to have closure and be able to properly mourn their lost loved one. The lack of progress made on this front over the past 30 years is highly frustrating for families. This pending issue of disappearances is a significant problem of coherence between the elements of reparations and truth, as it is difficult for the state to effectively compensate a moral wrong which it has not even fully clarified yet.

Munificence In terms of the sixth element, munificence, a modest to medium sum of money was awarded to beneficiaries through most of Chile's reparations programs. The fact that reparations were awarded through monthly pensions and went hand in hand with social benefits meant it would be a consistent source of economic support throughout the course of victims' lives. However, there have been some criticisms of Valech reparations sums for being insufficient in terms of compensation.

Finality The lack of finality is significant in the Chilean case, as there have been many limitations to the pursuit of justice and accountability, particularly in the early years of the transition. As such, allowing victims the possibility to continue to pursue civil redress through other means even after having accepted benefits may have reduced the likelihood of beneficiaries feeling like their silence was being bought. It is certainly not perfect, but all things considered, the Chilean system of reparations has worked to provide compensation to a great number of victims for a wide variety of different types of human rights abuses. The many initiatives undertaken during the early years of the transition worked to reverse some of the damage of the dictatorship, for instance, by facilitating the return of exiles, and established an important basis of reparations policy with programs such as PRAIS. Over the years, Chilean reparations efforts have closed some of the important gaps and exclusions that initially emerged in their reparations policies, through the reforms and new initiatives introduced in 2003 by President Lagos to support and acknowledge victims of torture and political imprisonment.

However, the efficiency and success of the Chilean reparations system as a whole has not been recently evaluated, and as such many of the programs that are still ongoing have not updated in many years. The lack of follow-up on locating the bodies of the disappeared has been a major pending issue ever since the very first reparations policies were created. Some remaining gaps, such as meaningful reparations for the Mapuche and rural communities who experienced counter land reform have yet to be addressed. As Loveman and Lira point out, "Many of the peasants expelled from the land of the agrarian reform (1964–1973), excluded from the benefits of Law No. 19,234, aged in poverty and misery, without any reparation before their death" (2021: 21).

These limitations undermine the coherence of the reparations system as a whole and create a sense of insufficiency among victims and beneficiaries about the extent to which their dignity is being recognized. Recognition is at the core of reparations efforts, as symbolic reparations, such as memorials or official apologies, work to repair the moral wrong done to victims by officially acknowledging and taking responsibility for human rights abuses. Chapter 5 will explore more deeply the concept of memory, and how human rights violations are memorialized and commemorated in Chile in a national context where multiple and conflicting memories exist.

Bibliography

Abrão, P., & Torelly, M. (2011). The Reparations Program as the Lynchpin of Transitional Justice in Brazil. In F. Réategui (Ed.), *Transitional Justice Handbook for Latin America* (pp. 443–485). Brazilian Amnesty Commission, Ministry of Justice/International Center for Transitional Justice.

Ancalao Gavilán, D. (2018). *Violación a los derechos humanos de la nación Mapuche en Chile*. Fundación Instituto de Desarrollo y Liderazgo Indígena, available at https://media.elmostrador.cl/2018/05/392175.pdf

Balasco, L. M. (2017). Reparative Development: Re-Conceptualising Reparations in Transitional Justice Processes. *Conflict, Security & Development, 17*(1), 1–20.

Bengoa, J. (2004). *La Memoria Olvidada. Historia de los Pueblos Indígenas de Chile*. Publicaciones del Bicentenario.

Borzutzky, S. (2017). *Human Rights in Chile: The Unfinished Struggle for Truth and Justice*. Palgrave Macmillan.

Case 1254-2011. 34th Criminal Court of Santiago, Judge Mireya López Miranda (*Ministra en Visita de la Corte de Apelaciones de Santiago*).

Collins, C., Garcia-Godos, J., & Skaar, E. (Eds.). (2016). *Transitional Justice in Latin America: The Uneven Road from Impunity Towards Accountability*. Routledge.

Comisión Nacional de Verdad y Reconciliación. (1991). *Informe Rettig*. Gobierno de Chile.

Contraloría General de la República (CGR). (2013). Informe final sobre examen de cuentas relativo a los pagos de pensiones no contributivas a Exonerados Políticos del sector civil efectuados a través del Instituto de Previsión Social, IPS (Informe No. 81-2012).

De Greiff, P. (Ed.). (2006). *The Handbook of Reparations*. Oxford University Press.

Di Giminiani, P. (2018). *Sentient Lands: Indigeneity, Property, and Political Imagination in Neoliberal Chile*. University of Arizona Press.

Durán, T. et al. (2000). *Muerte y Desaparición Forzada en La Araucanía: Una Aproximación Étnica*, available at http://www.derechos.org/koaga/x/mapuches/

Guembe, J. (2006). Economic Reparations for Grave Human Rights Violations. In P. De Greiff (Ed.), *The Handbook of Reparations* (pp. 22–51). Oxford University Press.

Hite, K. (2013). *Política y arte de la conmemoración. Memoriales en América Latina y España*. Mandrágora Ediciones.

Instituto de Previsión Social (INP). (2021). *Leyes de reparación*, available at https://nuevo.ips.gob.cl/servlet/internet/inicio/beneficios-y-pensiones/leyes-de-reparacion

Jara, D., Badilla, M., Figueiredo, A., Cornejo, M., & Riveros, V. (2018). Tracing Mapuche Exclusion from Post-Dictatorial Truth Commissions in Chile: Official and Grassroots Initiatives. *International Journal of Transitional Justice, 12*(3), 479–498.

Lira, E. (2006). The Reparations Policy for Human Rights Violations in Chile. In P. de Greiff (Ed.), *The Handbook of Reparations* (pp. 55–99). Oxford University Press.

Lira, E. (2016). Reflections on Rehabilitation as a Form of Reparation in Chile after Pinochet's Dictatorship. *International Human Rights Law Review, 5*(2), 194–216.

Loveman, B., & Lira, E. (2021). *Los campesinos "exonerados de la tierra". Leyes y políticas de reparación y clientelismo político en Chile*. Der Ediciones.

Richards, P. (2016). *Racismo: el modelo chileno y el multiculturalismo neoliberal bajo la Concertación, 1990–2010*. Pehuén.

Rojas, H. (2012). Torture in Chile (1973–1990): Analysis of One Hundred Survivors' Testimonies. *California Western International Law Journal, 42*, 353–392.

Rojas, H., & Suárez, R. (2019, September 12). *Registros de detenidas/os desaparecidas/os y su incorporación en expedientes judiciales sobre violaciones a los derechos humanos en Chile*. Presentation at "Encuentro Internacional sobre Procesos de Documentación de Desaparición y Desaparición Forzada de Personas. Perspectivas Comparadas: México, Chile y Colombia". Universidad Iberoamericana de México.

United Nations. (2005). *Basic Principles and Guidelines on the Right to a Remedy and Reparation for Victims of Gross Violations of International Human Rights Law and Serious Violations of International Humanitarian Law*, available at https://www.ohchr.org/en/professionalinterest/pages/remedyandreparation.aspx

United Nations. (2017). *UN Experts Urge Chile Not to Use Anti-Terrorism Law Against Mapuche Indigenous Peoples*, available at https://www.ohchr.org/en/NewsEvents/Pages/DisplayNews.aspx?NewsID=22209&LangID=E

Wright, T. C., & Oñate, R. (2007). Chilean Political Exile. *Latin American Perspectives*, 155, *34*(4), 31–47.

Yaikin, B. (2016). Las cifras ocultas del PRAIS: El programa de salud para víctimas de la dictadura con fecha de vencimiento. *El Desconcierto*, available at https://www.eldesconcierto.cl/2016/08/22/las-cifras-ocultas-del-prais-el-programa-de-salud-para-victimas-de-la-dictadura-con-fecha-de-vencimiento/

Yepes, R. U. (2009). Transformative Reparations of Massive Gross Human Rights Violations: Between Corrective and Distributive Justice. *Netherlands Quarterly of Human Rights, 27*(4), 625–647.

CHAPTER 5

Memorializing and Commemorating

The social divisions caused by periods of protracted conflict and repression run deep. When the past is one of conflict and polarization, different sectors of society remember it in different ways, and conflicting memories of the past emerge. In these circumstances, the question of how to remember the conflicted past becomes quite contentious. Controversies about memorialization and commemoration often re-emerge with just as much force, if not more, many years down the line. Whereas history tells us what happened in the past, memory deals with how we understand the past in the present: what we remember, and what we forget. Collective memory is the significance a society, or a group of people within a society, attributes to the past. This significance creates a narrative of the past that is deeply tied to identity and thus inevitably political. Memory is particularly important in the aftermath of conflict and human rights violations, mainly due to the gravity of these events and the lasting impact they have on society and on individuals.

Victims and future generations, as well as society as a whole, not only have a right to know what happened, but also a right to remember. The importance of memorializing and commemorating, and with them the right to memory, is increasingly being recognized in international norms of transitional justice. For example, the UN Guiding Principles and Framework for the Processes and Mechanisms of Transitional Justice suggests that museums, memorials and days of commemoration can be an

H. Rojas, M. Shaftoe, *Human Rights and Transitional Justice in Chile*, Memory Politics and Transitional Justice,
https://doi.org/10.1007/978-3-030-81182-2_5

important element of reparations, reconciliation and the preservation of historical memory (2010: 8). Memorialization has been a recurring theme in many rulings in the Inter-American Court of Human Rights, rulings which have established various memorialization and commemoration initiatives as part of a state's international responsibility to provide reparations for victims (Castro Valdebenito, 2019: 22). The state plays an important role in establishing an official account of the past, which can contribute to creating greater social acceptance, understanding, and recognition of this shared history. Official acts of memorialization and commemoration can have a symbolic reparative role. This is particularly important for victims, as the way others value and recognize their experiences can contribute to either restoring or undermining their dignity. For instance, many victims fight to protect and restore sites of human rights abuses, in order for the population at large to better understand what happened to them. Memorializing initiatives can also have an educational role in transmitting the past and establishing the narrative which future generations will use to learn about and build their understanding of a country's historical traumas. Memory is always selective however, and in choosing to commemorate certain things, others are forgotten. Memory is constantly evolving as time goes by and political contexts change, and it is for this reason that sites of memory are an important means of ensuring certain historical events do not slowly fall into oblivion.

The foundations of the concept of the right to memory can be found in a long history of studying memory within the social sciences. Among the abundant literature on this subject, the works of several authors are particularly significant to understanding this concept, and the role it plays in transitional justice processes. Maurice Halbwachs argues in his two salient works, *The Social Frameworks of Memory* (1925) and *The Collective Memory* (1950), that memory is socially constructed, delimited, and interpreted. Memory is the result of social interaction, thus making collective memory something that is acquired and situated within a social group, reinforced through social rites and commemorations. Halbwachs also argues that there can be multiple collective memories within one society, as different social groups are socialized in different ways, inevitably constructing different interpretations of the past.

Elizabeth Jelin takes advantage of these earlier European reflections on collective memory to explore the role of memory within the Latin American social project of *Nunca Más* ("Never Again"), which is the continent's response to its experience of political violence and repression. In

Los Trabajos de la Memoria (2002), she seeks to create a theoretical framework for memory within the Latin American context. According to Jelin, collective memory is a space in dispute and in permanent construction. Battles over historical memory occur, and "memory entrepreneurs" use the controversial nature of memory for political gain. Society's interpretation of collective memory is constantly being challenged and updated. Steven Stern further explores the controversial nature of memory in his trilogy about collective memory in Chile. His works demonstrate that there are dominant collective memories and dissident ones, which compete for social acceptance. Stern demonstrates that multiple, conflicting collective memories exist in Chile. He argues that silence and oblivion are also types of collective memory, as the exclusion of certain memories indicates a social significance in as much as they are frameworks of interpretation promoted by social groups that do not wish to remember.

In this chapter, we analyze the multiple, conflicting collective memories in Chile, and how they have affected official memorialization efforts such as sites of memory, and memory in pedagogy and curriculum. Given the strong culture of forgetfulness and oblivion that existed in the early years of the transition, civil society took on a number of major roles to combat the attitude of indifference that had permeated much of Chilean society. Members of the public, in particular survivors and their families, have carried out strong advocacy work in order to demand the opening of and construction of memorial sites. Furthermore, memorialization in the form of media and popular culture has played a significant role in efforts, only partially successful, to construct an official collective memory regarding human rights abuses during the military dictatorship.

5.1 Collective Memory in Chile: Multiple Conflicting Narratives

In characterizing the memory of Chilean society in the last 50 years, the first thing that should be established is that multiple collective memories coexist, some of which are intransigent. There are clear differences in interpretation between those who still applaud the Pinochet dictatorship, those who oppose and criticize it, and the full range of views in between, including those who are indifferent to the past and its importance (Piper, 2005; Bucciferro, 2012; Peñaloza, 2015: 17–35; Rojas, 2017). These memories are in constant confrontation, both in the public and the private sphere. Collective memories in Chile are dynamic and evolving, and between different generations there are different interpretations of the past (Arnoso et al., 2012; Jara, 2013). From an early age, Chileans are exposed to these conflicting interpretations of the dictatorship, and processes of socialization in family, at school and in social and professional life, have an important effect on the way each Chilean remembers or understands the past. The multiple different memories that currently exist in Chile began to develop during the dictatorship, and the relative dominance of different narratives has changed over time.

During the 17 years of the dictatorship, there were two opposing poles of memory: the dominant collective memory, created and spread by the military junta, and the dissident one, articulated in private and spread through clandestine media. The official memory propagated by the dictatorship through propaganda and censorship painted the military junta as saviors of the nation. This narrative was one that emphasized the chaos of the *Unidad Popular* government and claimed that the coup had prevented the outbreak of a civil war and the installation of a Marxist dictatorship. The memory of "salvation" had broad popular support at the time, it survived as the official narrative of the military regime and its supporters until 1990, and even persists in certain sectors of society today. Until 1990, any alternative point of view was suppressed: memories about the shared sense of hope and change that many felt under the UP government, the global significance of the first democratically elected Marxist government, and the active efforts to destabilize the UP, funded by the CIA and implemented by the army and the center-right, were excluded and contradicted by the official narrative.

In response to this suppression, a clandestine counter-memory began to develop during the dictatorship. Through unauthorized media and alternative popular culture, knowledge and memory of state terrorism was transmitted. The culture of resistance gradually generated an alternative collective memory associated with human rights violations, while maintaining a positive memory of Allende and the *Unidad Popular*. This memory was shared through underground media, such as the programs *Escucha Chile* (Listen Chile) and *Radio Magallanes* transmitted by Radio Moscú (Radio Moscow), or through uncensored, clandestinely circulated magazines and publications (Sorensen, 2015). Memory forms identity, and many politically engaged citizens based their identity during the dictatorship in resistance. This dissident memory was also articulated in exile. The music of Víctor Jara, Inti Illimani, Quilapayún, and Illapu, among other artists who denounced the dictatorship or were associated with the UP, was listened to. These musicians and their music were popular symbols of resistance to the dictatorship.

These two opposing interpretations of the past finally confronted one another on the country's television screens during the run-up to the 1988 plebiscite election. The television campaigns of both Pinochet's supporters and his opponents presented two opposing interpretations of the past, which portrayed the military alternatively as "saviors of the nation" or as violators of human rights. In a way, society's understanding of the past was to determine its future. The *Yes* campaign reignited their messages from the past, pushing the dominant memory of the chaos of the Allende government that they had pushed for years to keep Pinochet in power. The *No* campaign, on the other hand, focused on the future, on what society would be like without the repression of the dictatorship. They evoked the dissident memory of struggle and pain that many experienced under Pinochet's rule. The *Concertación* coalition's marketing experts successfully put forward a new idea during the televised *No* campaign: "without hate, without violence, without fear, vote No." Relying on hope, and the desire for a more democratic and peaceful society to win the election, Pinochet's opponents did eventually bring the dictatorship to an end. The 1988 referendum shows how collective memory is always selective; memory can be edited and influenced by the messaging of those promoting a particular interpretation. Above all, the referendum is an excellent example of how memory is shared, as it has anchored a certain interpretation of the events leading to the end of the dictatorship in the collective consciousness of the nation.

Yet, the end of the dictatorship did not bring an end to the battle for memory in Chile. Since the return to democracy, memorializing initiatives have been a source of tension and conflict. Under the early governments post-dictatorship, those of Presidents Aylwin and Frei Ruiz-Tagle, few memorializing initiatives were carried out. The most significant initiatives in this period were Salvador Allende's state funeral, the Memorial for the Detained and Disappeared in the General Cemetery, and the restoration of former torture center, Villa Grimaldi. After the Rettig report was released in 1991, collective memory of oblivion dominated, and the main narrative was to leave the past behind as it risked re-igniting tensions and endangering democracy. Civil society activists thus took the work of collective memory into their own hands, fighting to establish sites of memory and creating films and books that addressed Chile's violent past. The later governments of Presidents Ricardo Lagos and Michelle Bachelet invested more state resources into the already established sites of memory, and created many new ones during their respective mandates. Navigating the tensions between the multiple collective memories that exist within different social sectors meant managing the conflicts between the government and civil society's often differing views on how best to remember the past (Pino-Ojeda, 2011: 150–4).

It is interesting and important to note that even so many years after the end of the dictatorship, memory remains divided and divisive in Chile. Steve Stern analyzes this reality of multiple collective memories in post-dictatorship Chile and identifies four main "emblematic memories" (2006). The first is memory as salvation, the official memory promoted during the dictatorship. While it is significantly less common nowadays, this interpretation of the past continues to justify the human rights violations of the military junta and the Pinochet dictatorship to varying extents. The second is memory as an open wound, what had been the dissident memory during the dictatorship: the painful experiences of death, torture, loss, and heartbreak suffered by the victims of state repression. This memory is far more widely accepted than it was at the time, although many victims still feel that their experiences of persecution are not well understood.

Third is the idea of memory as a democratic and ethical challenge, which puts to the test the ethics of those confronted with the reality of widespread violations of human rights. This memory is widespread among young people, and it suggests that there is a responsibility within a democratic society to commemorate serious human rights violations, inform future generations, and confront this difficult past, regardless of political affiliation. The fourth and final emblematic memory is that of the closed box, or memory as oblivion. This is the memory of those who believe the past to be too difficult or dangerous to confront as it would risk re-opening old wounds and was the dominant memory for the early years of the transition. These four "emblematic" memories show how there is no collective narrative about the past that is widely accepted in Chile. Instead, there are many clashing memories of the past, which continue to compete for social acceptance.

The existence of different viewpoints about the past is in many ways unavoidable, particularly in a democracy where free speech and freedom of the press are protected. Leigh Payne argues that a "contentious coexistence," where the conflicting understandings of the past are debated and broad sectors of society engage in dialogue around these issues, is healthy for society and for democracy (2008: 21). These kinds of debates can allow people of all walks of life to come to their own conclusions about what took place and why it is important to remember. However, in Chile, there is still a reluctance to engage in these kinds of broad, open public discussion related to the past (Rojas, 2017; López, 2018), in the media and in other public spheres (Sorensen, 2015: 23). This reticence means that even while there are conflicting narratives about the past, they rarely confront each other in public.

This has caused, and continues to cause, political and social conflict, creating difficulties in efforts to build a healthier and more open democratic debate about the past and its legacy. This has prevented the development of a more cohesive political reality, and legislation relating to memorializing the past continues to be polarizing and paralyzing. The challenges caused by this conflicting collective memory and lack of discussion can be clearly understood through an analysis of sites of memory and the difficulties of memorialization in Chile.

5.2 Sites of Memory

A site of memory is a place where memory is put into action and takes material form. According to Pierre Nora (1996), sites of memory have a material, functional, and symbolic meaning. The material experience of a site, its functional purpose in transmitting memory, and its symbolic importance within the context of a greater narrative of memory are interconnected elements, which together give the site its meaning. When it comes to memorializing human rights violations, the Fundamental Principles for Public Policy on Sites of Memory of the Mercosur Institute of Public Policy on Human Rights states that "sites of memory are considered to be all those places where serious human rights violations were committed, or where these violations were resisted or confronted, or which for some reason are associated by the victims, their families or communities with these events, and which are used to recover, rethink and transmit traumatic processes and/or to pay homage and reparation to the victims" (IPPDH, 2012: 21). Sites of memory are a means to evoke the memory of serious human rights violations that occurred in the past and to convey it to the generations that did not experience these events (ib.: 16). Sites of memory therefore seek to transform the traces of the past by placing them within the framework of a broader narrative, making them intelligible and evoking memories directly and purposefully.

Steve Stern and Peter Winn suggest that sites of memory have two main roles: a symbolic role in terms of reparations and recognition of victims, along with a pedagogical role in terms of transmitting public history (2014: 322). On the one hand, these sites are significant for local communities and those most affected. They can act as a space of reflection for victims and their families, and recognize and restore the dignity of victims, as well as explicitly or implicitly acknowledge the responsibility of perpetrators. On the other hand, sites of memory can promote the communication and construction of collective memory and simultaneously provide a space for the educational aspect of memory work. While these two roles of sites of memory often reinforce each other, they can sometimes collide as well: tensions can emerge between preserving the site exactly as it was, creating contemporary memorializing elements, and adding structural elements that can contribute to the educational function of the site. Memorials often appeal most to those intimately connected with them, but there are also memorials that appeal to the entire population. The location of the site and its symbolic significance can broaden its impact. For example, the Constitutional Court of South Africa is located next to a prison compound where Mahatma Gandhi, Nelson Mandela, Winnie Mandela, Fatima Meer, among others, were imprisoned, which has the symbolic effect of tying together current efforts to seek justice with those in the past (Madikida et al., 2008).

Public policies regulating sites of memory can function as tools for protecting and promoting principles of human rights. By helping to protect, support, and regulate memorializing initiatives, sites of memory can be established in an official capacity and with the resources needed to operate. In 2014, Argentina passed the Law No. 26,691 on the Preservation, Signage and Dissemination of Sites of Memory of State Terrorism. In 2018, Uruguay passed the Law No. 19,641 on Sites of Historical Memory of the Recent Past. These laws define what is considered a site of memory, explicitly recognize human rights violations as the product of state terrorism, and outline the periods in which recognition is due (Escáriz Oñate, 2020: 26–27). Having a specialized legal framework has created a clear process in Argentina and Uruguay for the establishment, protection, and management of sites of memory through a human rights lens.

In contrast, Chile does not have specialized legislation on sites of memory. At present, Law No. 17,288 (1970) on National Monuments and Supreme Decree No. 259 (1980) on the Protection of Municipal Cultural and Natural Heritage are in force. The Technical Secretariat of the National

Monuments Council has an area specialized in historical heritage, which prepares technical reports that allow the Council to grant the status of national monument to 41 sites of memory or historical heritage, including constructions, archives, memorials, or monuments. Article 9 of Law No. 17,288 establishes the definition of historical monuments as "places, ruins, constructions and objects of fiscal, municipal or private property that, because of their quality and historical or artistic interest or because of their antiquity, are declared such by supreme decree, issued at the request and prior agreement of the Council."

Given the lack of specialized legislation, sites of memory in Chile are very diverse. Some sites are well institutionalized, while others are precarious and humble. In the worst cases, the dictatorship tried to erase the sites that accused it of committing crimes. Whether a site is able to achieve official designation as a site of memory depends largely on the advocacy of survivors and families of the victims, and access to funding in order to maintain the site once it is established can also present an important challenge. The creation of a specialized legal framework to regulate sites of memory in Chile would considerably improve the recognition and protection of sites of memory and provide greater support to human rights organizations in terms of financing and management of sites (Escáriz Oñate, 2020: 29–30). In this section, we will look at three important sites of memory in Chile as examples to illustrate the difficulties of memorializing in the transitional justice process: Villa Grimaldi Park for Peace, the Museum of Memory and Human Rights, and Venda Sexy.

Villa Grimaldi Park for Peace

Villa Grimaldi is an excellent example of the tensions of the early transition with regard to memorialization. The Villa was a torture center used by the secret police DINA from 1973 to 1978 (Toledo et al., 2009: 122). Approximately 4500 prisoners passed through this detention center (Spooner, 2011: 147), and at least 234 people are known to have been executed or disappeared there (López & Hevia, 2016: 107). After the dissolution of the notorious secret police agency the DINA, and its replacement by the CNI, the site was closed off, and certain buildings were demolished to hide evidence of its use as a torture center. At the end of the dictatorship, the Villa Grimaldi was fraudulently "sold" to the relatives of a top official of the CNI, General Hugo Salas Wenzel, who had plans to knock down what remained and develop the site (Lazzara, 2006:

132). News of the construction plans prompted survivors and neighborhood activists to mobilize in order to block construction (Rojas, 2015: 263). With the help of the local mayor, they were able to get the attention of the Human Rights Commission of the Chamber of Deputies, which enabled them to accuse the new "owners" of the site of fraud and halt construction.

Civil society activists and local government officials worked to convince the Minister of Housing to buy the site in order to convert it into a "park for peace" and memorial site, and it was nationalized in 1994. The restoration and transformation of the site lasted 2 years, and the Villa Grimaldi Park for Peace was inaugurated in 1997 (Spooner, 2011: 147), becoming the first former detention site in South America to be restored as a site of memory (Collins & Hite, 2009: 385). The recuperation and creation of this site of memory was led almost entirely by civil society activists, with strategic help from municipal and low-level government authorities. President Aylwin and many members of his government feared that openly supporting such a controversial project would endanger the fragile state of early democracy. The political climate of fear and excessive caution continued into the subsequent administration as well, evidenced by the fact that not a single senior government official of President Frei Ruiz-Tagle's government attended the inauguration ceremony (Stern & Winn, 2014: 328).

The site was not allocated significant government funding, which made it difficult to maintain. Villa Grimaldi thus had a relatively low profile during the first eight years of its existence. Government politics shifted in favor of memorialization and commemoration in the intermediate years of the transition under Presidents Lagos and Bachelet. The site was declared a national monument in 2005, and Villa Grimaldi began to receive more abundant and permanent government funding. This allowed the site to be better maintained, as well as to expand its reach to undertake various educational and restoration projects, which have converted it into an important cultural and education center. It is now one of Chile's best-known sites of memory about the human rights violations under the dictatorship.

This case illustrates the difficulties of memorializing initiatives in the transition (Gómez-Barris, 2010). The conflict between the different collective memories—those of human rights violations and those that favored forgetting—is evident in the development of Villa Grimaldi. The existence of this site of memory is owed to a small group of dedicated activists whose experiences in this torture center caused them to feel strongly about its importance and preserving the memory of those who suffered and were killed there. The salvaging and transformation of Villa Grimaldi received little aid from the government, due to fears within the *Concertación* of the reigniting of tensions. However, later government support allowed the site to amplify its reach and impact in terms of public education and communication of the history and significance of this particular space within the broader context of the Pinochet dictatorship. The slow shift from a dominant memory of oblivion toward one in favor of remembering human rights was therefore crucial in allowing the site to grow in influence and impact, as it brought funding and support.

Villa Grimaldi Park for Peace. (© Fernando Rojas Corral, with permission)

Museum of Memory and Human Rights

The difficulties of the transitional justice process in Chile are evident in the creation of the Museum of Memory and Human Rights (MMHR), even 20 years after the end of the dictatorship, when the threat of a return to authoritarianism was non-existent. During the government of President Lagos, human rights organizations proposed the creation of a House of Memory. As some organizations saw their sources of funding gradually diminishing, they were concerned about the preservation of their archives. When Michelle Bachelet was elected President in 2006, she took on the project of creating a Museum of Memory and Human Rights. This initiative was the result of pressure from a small group of human rights experts and activists, as well as the crowning initiative within her broad policy of supporting memorializing efforts. In order to ensure the Museum would be able to have a lasting impact, the Bachelet government opted to establish a foundation that receives public funds to ensure a source of permanent funding for the museum. The Bachelet administration intended to inaugurate the museum before the end of the President's mandate. As such, the decision-making process around many elements of the museum was rushed as a result of the short timeline of only four years.

A good example of this rushed decision-making process is the decision as to where the Museum was ultimately located. The idea of building the museum in the center of the city or in a location of symbolic importance such as a detention center like Villa Grimaldi or the National Stadium was ruled out. It was decided that a deteriorated public property located next to Quinta Normal Park would be recovered as the site for the museum. The benefit of the site was its easy access via the metro, despite being at some distance from downtown Santiago. An international competition was called to design the museum, and the Brazilian architectural firm "Estudio America" quickly won: its model was that of a giant glass and crystal container, superimposed as if it were a bridge with its bases surrounded by water. The main building seems to be an ark where the memories of the horrors lived are deposited, whose doors lead to a public square that invites commemorative events.

The interior of the museum includes an auditorium, as well as rooms for activities with students. The Museum's permanent exhibition invites visitors to follow two main routes: the military dictatorship and the human rights defense movement in Chile. A common criticism leveled by the right wing was that nothing was said about what was happening in Chile before 1973, nor was there sufficient detail given about the context surrounding the coup. From the left- wing, it faced some criticism for basing its exhibitions heavily on what had been established in the Rettig and Valech reports, and therefore only including the official, state narrative. In 2013, when the meaning of the exhibition's content was publicly discussed, the justification for the timeline was that the museum did not want to allow any space for arguments justifying the human rights abuses or the coup. In response to the criticism that the content was relied too much on the Rettig and Valech reports, it was argued that this allowed the museum to be seen as objectively presenting the official facts of what took place (Stern & Winn, 2014: 348–349).

While Villa Grimaldi was established mainly through the efforts of civil society activism and later benefited from government support, the Museum of Memory was established through institutional means, propelled by the Bachelet government. Due to the political considerations and the short timeline that the Bachelet administration had to work with, the museum has been criticized for lacking in symbolism. Human rights activists did not initially play an important role in deciding the format, design, or content of the museum. However, despite the rush in its creation, and the criticisms from both the left and the right regarding its content, the museum has had a tremendous social impact. It hosts over 100,000 visitors—both Chileans and foreigners—every year (Museo de la Memoria y Derechos Humanos, 2014), as well as organizing numerous educational and cultural events.

Museum of Memory and Human Rights. (© Hugo Rojas Corral, 2020)

Venda Sexy

Venda Sexy is an example of a site that is still in dispute, and which demonstrates the challenges and limits of current legislation related to sites of memory in Chile. This site was a center of detention, torture, and forced disappearance in the early years of the dictatorship, used by the DINA secret police in Santiago (Echeverría, 2008: 92). It was a house located in a middle-class residential neighborhood, which received its name due to the sexual torture techniques that were used on the detainees (Guzmán, 2014: Ch. 3). Loud music was played to muffle the sounds of prisoners' screams. Women prisoners in particular were submitted to especially horrifying types of sexual abuse, including electric shocks and sexual assault. Due to the shockingly sadistic torture techniques and the gendered nature of the abuses, this site has been a flashpoint of activism of female survivors. After the closing of the site as a torture center, it was sold to private owners who rented it out to students and to families and at one point, even used it to open a nursery and day care for children. However, once the history of the site was known, renters abandoned it, and parents sought other day care facilities. After years of fighting by women's survivor groups for the recuperation of this house as a "site of active memory for women survivors" (Mujeres Sobrevivientes y Siempre Resistentes Collective, 2016), in 2016 the site was declared a national monument.

The Bachelet government sought to purchase the house in 2016, but the owner asked for more than the government had offered, in spite of the fact that the offer was already much higher than the market valuation of the house. Curiously, the site was subsequently sold to a real estate company for less than its market price. Even though it was declared a national monument, which supposedly protects the site from being modified, a swimming pool has since been installed on the grounds, and there is no official signage indicating the relevance of the site. There are fears among survivor groups that the site could face demolition, erasing the story of female resistance to the dictatorship and along with it the suffering and subsequent strength that women survivors have demonstrated in enduring and overcoming the horrors of Venda Sexy. The challenges faced by survivors in seeking to have this site protected emphasize the need for specialized legislation creating a clear process for the establishment, protection, and management of sites of memory related to human rights violations and state terrorism.

5.3 Counter-Memory

The complex landscape of collective memory in Chile also includes pro-regime sites of memory, for example, the Jaime Guzmán Memorial in Santiago, the Augusto Pinochet Foundation, the Augusto Pinochet Square in Linares, and the José Toribio Merino Hall in the Naval Museum in Valparaíso. However, the low-profile nature of many of these sites suggests that they are directed toward previous subscribers to this particular collective memory rather than being broadly influential. The Jaime Guzman memorial is a good example of how this memory has lost ground and public appeal and is now far from being the dominant narrative in Chile. The Jaime Guzmán memorial came about as part of a negotiation between the *Concertación* coalition and the right, when the *Concertación* sought to erect a memorial to Salvador Allende in Plaza de la Constitución, across from La Moneda Presidential Palace. The right eventually agreed in exchange for a monument to Senator Jaime Guzmán, an important figure on the right. Known as one of the most high-profile civilian Pinochet supporters, Guzmán was killed by left-wing extremist group FPMR.

The proposed location for this monument was *Plaza Italia*, the most popular square in Santiago, and home to frequent political mobilizations and protests, recently nicknamed *Plaza de la Dignidad* (Dignity Square). Inaugurated in 2008, the Guzmán monument was ultimately installed in the financial district in front of the US Embassy, as there were protests and complaints against the original location suggested by the right wing (Hite & Collins, 2009: 395). The monument itself is not particularly conspicuous and does not detail much about Guzmán apart from stating he was killed by terrorists. According to Steve Stern and Peter Winn, "if this is the main memorial of the right-wing counter-memory, it is one that hides its identity, obscures its objectives, and masks its significance" (2014: 287). The forced relocation of the monument indicates how much this particular memory has lost the battle for public space and support. However, the fact that it exists in and of itself is testament to the multiple and conflicting memories that continue to endure in Chile.

The stark differences between the stories of these different memorials illustrate just how necessary it is for the Chilean government to implement legislation specifically regulating sites of memory: Villa Grimaldi, a site established by civil society activism and then bolstered by government support; the Museum of Memory and Human Rights, inspired by civil society activism but implemented and led by the Bachelet government; Venda Sexy, given state protection through the declaration of the status of national monument but which remains vulnerable to demolition; and the Jaime Guzmán memorial, a counter-memorial site whose intent and message are ambiguous to the average onlooker.

These sites reveal the complexity of memorialization in Chile, the persistence of multiple conflicting collective memories, and their evolution in dominance and acceptance over the years. Greater state engagement in this area is needed, as legislation regulating the preservation, recovery, ownership, access, financing, and management of the site is necessary if Chilean society is to continue creating and improving sites of human rights memory. In addition, stronger laws would also help regulate the use and political exploitation of sites of memory. The fact that victims and families so often fight to preserve the sites where they and their loved ones suffered serves as an indicator of the importance of sites of memory to the symbolic reparations for victims, and therefore the important responsibility of the state in terms of the reparative function of memorialization.

5.4 Media, Culture, and Memory

Despite the intense state censorship during the dictatorship, dissident, alternative memories were spread through media and popular culture. Programs like *Escucha Chile* on Radio Moscow, and magazines like *Revista Solidaridad*, published by the Vicariate of Solidarity, as well as *Cauce* and *Análisis*, addressed the repression and shared information and news about the human rights abuses taking place. Near the end of the dictatorship, several long form journalistic investigations about state violence and repression were published. These include Patricia Verdugo's *Los Zarpazos del Puma* ("The claws of the Puma") and *La historia oculta del régimen militar* ("The hidden history of the military regime") by Ascanio Cavallo et al., which exposed the repression and violence of the dictatorship. After the return of democracy, one might have expected the opening of a space in the media to address the human rights violations that occurred. However, the remains of state censorship and the climate of fear about a return to authoritarianism continued to have an important impact on the media. Many media organizations continue to self-censor, and according to Kristin Sorensen, there are unwritten norms in Chile about what is acceptable for public discussion. To disrespect these norms means to risk one's job as well as being put on the blacklist (Sorensen, 2015: 34). Mainstream media therefore did not address human rights abuses often, especially crimes of torture, even after the return to democracy.

With the arrest of Pinochet in London in 1998, there was a proliferation of human rights-related coverage in the media. New alternative publications emerged, such as the satirical magazine *The Clinic*, which on top of political cartoons and satire included a regular section covering the detained and disappeared, along with other human rights abuses (Sorensen, 2015: 150). Given its popularity and the fact that it was directed at a younger audience, this magazine brought the issue of human rights into the spotlight for a generation that had not been exposed to much public discussion of this topic before. Between its jokes and satire, *The Clinic* continues to publish serious political criticisms in articles and opinion columns.

Music was also an important way of keeping dissident memories alive during the dictatorship. Musicians like Víctor Jara, who was killed by the military regime for his political activism, and the group Inti Illimani, whose song "Venceremos" (We shall overcome) had been the anthem of the *Unidad Popular*, were listened to clandestinely. Songs by popular artists from other countries, such as "Santiago de Chile" by Cuban singer Silvio

Rodríguez, "Yo pisaré las calles nuevamente" (I will walk the streets again) by Pablo Milanés, and "They Dance Alone (Cueca Solo)" by Sting, denounced the repression of the dictatorship and expressed solidarity and support for the people of Chile in their resistance against state violence. In the later years of the dictatorship, when censorship was not quite as strong and the repression was less intense than it had been in the 1970s, "El baile de los que sobran" (The dance of those left over) by Los Prisioneros rock band became an iconic song of protest and dissidence for younger generations. In the late 1980s and early 1990s, many exiled musicians began to return to Chile: Illapu's "Vuelvo para Vivir" (I return to live) became an anthem for those who had lived in exile, or who had been separated from their families. As such, music was an important means of keeping alternative and dissident memories alive, with the clandestine circulation of banned albums and songs being a key part of the resistance. Certain bands and songs have thus become an important element of Chile's collective memory of its violent past.

Cinema and television also played an important role in developing Chile's collective memory of the dictatorship years. According to Marc Ferro, there are three dimensions through which cinema and memory are linked: cinema can be an auxiliary source of history, an agent of history, and a didactic resource for teaching history (1988). Banned films such as *Missing*, about an American journalist murdered by the military regime, were circulated clandestinely during the dictatorship. Yet it wasn't until the 2000s that films became especially influential in terms of memory in Chile. Both documentary and fiction films addressing the recent past have been screened in Chilean cinemas to large audiences, as well as being played on TV channels. One of the most influential is Andrés Wood's *Machuca*, a 2004 film about two young boys from different economic backgrounds living through the social tension in the lead up to the military coup. Other notable works include Patricio Guzmán's documentary trilogy *La Batalla de Chile* (The Battle for Chile), and *Memoria Obstinada*, among others. These films were widely viewed and have brought the issues of the dictatorship into the public eye (Barraza, 2018). It was only in September 2021 that a television channel dared to broadcast for the first time *La Batalla de Chile*, losing an important sponsor.

More recently, popular TV series like *Los Archivos del Cardenal* (The Cardinal's Files) based on the human rights defense of the Vicariate of Solidarity; *Ecos del Desierto* (Echoes of the Desert) about human rights lawyer Carmen Hertz; and *Los 80*, a show about a middle-class family and their experience of the historical events of the 1980s, such as the repression and the plebiscite, have brought stories of the dictatorship to various audiences (Acuña, 2018: 13). Moreover, they have been an influential force in transmitting collective memory to younger generations, by sharing stories based on the true historical events (Mateos-Pérez & Ochoa, 2018: 292). Popular culture in Chile, from journalism and media to music, cinema, and television, have therefore played an important role in the creation of collective memory in Chile. By broadly diffusing fictional and real stories about Chilean history to a wide-ranging audience, directors and screenwriters alike have made these stories accessible and attractive to a vast number of Chileans, who might not otherwise have been exposed to these stories, or been curious enough to investigate their past.

5.5 Pedagogy of Memory

The polarization over the recent past in Chile has influenced what is taught in schools, and how (Magendzo & Toledo, 2009). Teachers fear the reactions they will receive when teaching about the dictatorship: they are afraid of how families will react, how school leadership will react, and in public schools, about how the municipal government will react. In particular, there is fear of eventual parent complaints (Cardoch, 2014). The 2013 Pontifical Catholic University of Chile Bicentennial Survey clearly illustrates the divisions within Chilean society. Two thirds of those surveyed agreed or strongly agreed with the following statement: "It is important that what happened in Chile between 1973 and 1990 be taught in schools." However, it is worrying that 15.7 percent say they do not agree or disagree; while 16.1 percent say they disagree or strongly disagree (2.1 percent of respondents did not answer this question). This suggests that a third of Chilean adults do not attach importance to the teaching of Chile's recent past in schools. In this polarized and indifferent context, how do we motivate teachers, and how do we avoid neglect by teachers who do not want to teach these topics? How do we overcome the politics of forgetting in schools and involve the past in the formulation of future expectations? How do we assign meaning to the past? The pedagogy of memory seeks to respond to these questions, suggesting that we must study our recent history in order to promote a shared, nuanced memory, "built from the understanding of what we have been as a society and what we aspire to be; compassionate, and capable of integrating feeling and reflection as the basis of a citizenship that promotes being attentive to the other" (Rubio, 2013: 446).

Renato Gazmuri (2013) has investigated the ideological struggles in the construction of the curriculum in history and social sciences in Chile. According to Gazmuri, "the first school texts addressing the 1973 coup d'état were published in 2000"; before this, history textbooks stopped in 1973. The textbooks published in 2000 referred to the period 1970–1990 in a concise and careful way. Teachers taught with caution, worried about causing controversy. The debate over how to teach about the recent past returned in 2007 when history curriculum adjustments were discussed. The new curriculum was debated at the Higher Education Council. Disagreements existed regarding how to refer to certain facts of the past. For example, some people still protest or complain when books refer to the "coup d'état," or "dictatorship" (preferring "military pronouncement" or "military regime"), declaring them to be prejudicial or inaccurate terms. Therefore, some textbooks use the expression dictatorship, while others use the term military government. The new curriculum proposed in 2007 required that the following elements be covered: the political and economic crisis of 1970 to 1973, the military coup/intervention, human rights violations that occurred under Pinochet, and the neoliberal reforms to the economic model. Any publisher could publish a textbook to be used in schools, as long as it was approved by the Ministry of Education and included the above elements. The changes had only a small impact however, as the textbooks addressed the issue briefly and cautiously (Stern & Winn, 2013: 369).

The new curriculum was implemented, amid criticism from conservative sectors. Expressed in opinion columns published in the conservative newspapers *El Mercurio* and *La Segunda*, they argued that by including the dictatorship in the history curriculum, national reconciliation was being undermined, which in turn fostered hatred and sowed divisions. They also contended that there was historical proximity: that the events were too recent to be truly considered historical (Gazmuri, 2013: 46–47). For the traditional conservative sectors, history and social science subjects should be used to transmit the country's traditions and generate loyalty to the nation. These groups are fully aware that the definition of the history curriculum is something eminently political in Chile. According to this sector, through the teaching of history, national identity can be strengthened. As such, the historical narrative they favor is one that emphasizes nation building and patriotism. For the neoliberal center-right, history has no meaning. It is a distraction, because we need citizen-consumers, and productive citizens as opposed to engaged citizens. Neoliberalism is interested in the depoliticized present, and in that context, memory is an obstacle to reconciliation and to the tasks of economic development and modernization. It is against these forces that any changes to the history curriculum must contend.

With a neoliberal view of history in mind, in 2010 under the Piñera administration, the Minister of Education, Joaquín Lavín, announced that the number of hours of history and social sciences taught per week would be reduced from four to three in order to increase mathematics and language. The National Council of Education approved the measure, but the controversy escalated to the point that the government had no choice but to rescind it. Despite avoiding the decrease in hours, the teaching of recent history (post-1970) continues to lack depth, and many teachers continue to feel unprepared: not only unsure about what to teach about the dictatorship, but also how to teach it. The recent history of Chile is briefly taught in year 6 and then with a little more context and insight in secondary school, in year 10. Regrettably, the National Council of Education approved new changes to the curriculum in 2019 for the last two years of schooling. While their attempt to reduce history course hours in 2010 was defeated, this time they succeeded: History of Chile is no longer among the six compulsory subjects of the final two years of secondary school.

One reason for the difficulties in approving and making changes to the history curriculum is that the National Council of Education is comprised of part-time councilors. This affects the quality of decision-making as it limits discussion time and councilors cannot devote themselves fully to this duty. In addition, the council is deeply divided; there are councilors from all backgrounds, including Pinochet supporters. What is taught is therefore the result of a consensus among different sectors, and because there is very little consensus, very little is taught. The "consensus" only covers the most basic facts. Battles over the pedagogy of memory persist, to the detriment of generations of students who have grown up post-dictatorship and often have a limited understanding of what took place. The pedagogical discourses of memory have been affected by the ups and downs of memory battles between different social narratives (S. Infante, 2015: 79). Progress has not been made in the classroom but in public spaces: memorials, museums, cinema, and television.

5.6 Conclusion

Collective memory in Chile is deeply divided. Multiple conflicting interpretations of the past exist, and because these different narratives rarely confront each other in public debates and discussions, there is a lack of open democratic debate and memorializing continues to be a polarizing topic. While there has been a proliferation of memorials in the last years, Chile still lacks legislation to regulate more carefully the process of creating and managing sites of memory. Consequently, there is a great diversity in the condition of the many sites of memory and national monuments that exist to commemorate victims of human rights violations. Through their broad appeal, accessibility, educational programming, and cultural events, the Museum of Memory and Human Rights and Villa Grimaldi (former torture center) have played an important role in promoting and transmitting memory of human rights abuses and contributing to a more widespread acceptance of this memory. However, while the former dominant memory of Pinochet and the military junta as saviors of the nation has become much less popular, public monuments like the Jaime Guzmán memorial indicate that it still lives on.

Media and popular culture have also contributed in important ways to collective memory in Chile, as screenings of films and documentaries about the dictatorship, such as *Machuca* and *The Battle for Chile*, have drawn important audiences, as have TV series such as *Los 80* and *Los Archivos del Cardenal*. These films and TV shows have contributed to reflections about the recent past, reinforcing collective memory about the human rights abuses, repression, and social conflict caused by the dictatorship. While advances have been made in many regards, there is still much room for progress, particularly with regard to pedagogy of memory, and teaching Chile's recent history in schools. The deep divisions that remain in Chilean society are evident in the challenges of approving a curriculum that discusses the recent past, and the political difficulties that emerge whenever change is proposed.

It is interesting to note that while collective memory in Chile is clearly still disputed, the social unrest and mass protests that broke out in October 2019 have employed symbols and cultural elements that draw direct parallels between the Pinochet dictatorship and President Piñera's government. Iconic songs such as Víctor Jara's *El derecho de vivir en paz* (The right to live in peace), Los Prisioneros' *El baile de los que sobran*, and the anthem of the UP, *Venceremos*, were played and sung during the recent protests. Protesters have made signs and graffiti using the symbolism, slogan, and logos of the 1988 *No* campaign, such as ironic takes on the slogan *La alegría ya viene* ("Happiness is coming") which highlight the promises that were not kept in the return to democracy. The presence of these elements, which draw a direct line from the policies of the dictatorship to the problems of inequality and social injustice that protesters are currently facing, adds weight to the question as to why none of the governments since the return to democracy have fundamentally challenged the existing neoliberal economic system.

In addition, the military curfew declared on October 19, 2019, caused many Chileans to relive difficult memories of repression, and the ensuing police violence caused many protesters to draw links between the violence and human rights violations of the past and those of the present. The symbols and slogans of the activism of human rights activists during the dictatorship, especially the families of the disappeared and their demand *¿Dónde Están?* (Where are they?), have also been imitated during the 2019 protests. This has highlighted the ways in which the past is repeating itself, as many searched for family members detained or injured during the unrest.

The imagery of the 2019 protest movement is steeped in the past. The unresolved elements of the transition have not gone unnoticed by the Chilean people, and collective narratives of memory are playing an important role in bringing people together and shaping the demonstrations. Perhaps the protest movement of 2019 will be the catalyst for a broader debate and discussion about the events of the past and their importance. While there may not be a socially shared narrative about the dictatorship, the dominance of memories that either deny or seek to forget recent human rights abuses has significantly diminished. As the generations who experienced the dictatorship, and particularly those who survived state violence get older, it is increasingly important that memory of the past be transmitted to younger generations. The recent human rights abuses show just how easy it is to repeat the horrors of the past.

Bibliography

Acuña, N. (2018). Prólogo: Por el camino de las series. In J. Mateos-Pérez & G. Ochoa (Eds.), *Chile en las series de televisión: Los 80, Los archivos del Cardenal y El reemplazante* (pp. 9–14). RIL editores.

Arnoso, M., Cárdenas, M., & Páez, D. (2012). Diferencias intergeneracionales en la mirada hacia el pasado represivo chileno. *Psicología Política, 45*, 7–26.

Barraza, V. (2018). *El Cine en Chile (2005–2015): Políticas y poéticas del nuevo siglo*. Editorial Cuarto Propio.

Bucciferro, C. (2012). *For-Get: Identity, Media, and Democracy in Chile*. University Press of America.

Cardoch, N. (2014, September 11). *Entrevista a Ricardo Brodsky: La importancia de la memoria histórica en educación en Chile*. Facultad de Filosofía y Humanidades de la Universidad de Chile, available at http://www.filosofia.uchile.cl/noticias/105211/la-importancia-de-la-memoria-historica-en-educacion-en-chile

Castro Valdebenito, H. (2019). *Memoria, Patrimonio y Ciudadanías*. Editorial América en Movimiento.

Colectivo Mujeres Sobrevivientes Siempre Resistentes. (2016). *Comunicado Colectivo Mujeres Sobrevivientes Siempre Resistentes*, available at http://www.laizquierdadiario.cl/Comunicado-Colectivo-de-Mujeres-Sobrevivientes-Siempre-Resistentes-a-la-Opinion-Publica-Nacional-e

Collins, C., & Hite, K. (2009). Memorial Fragments, Monumental Silences and Reawakenings in 21st-Century Chile. *Millennium, 38*(2), 379–400.

Echeverría, M. (2008). *Krassnoff*. Catalonia.

Escáriz Oñate, M. (2020). *Regulación de los Sitios de Memoria en el Cono Sur: Análisis Crítico y Propuestas para Chile*. Law thesis, Alberto Hurtado University.

Ferro, M. (1988). *Cinema and History*. Wayne State University Press.

Gazmuri, R. (2013). *La construcción ideológica del curriculum chileno en historia y ciencias sociales*. Doctoral thesis, Universidad Autónoma de Barcelona.

Gómez-Barris, M. (2010). Witness Citizenship: The Place of Villa Grimaldi in Chilean Memory. *Sociological Forum, 25*(1), 27–46.

Guzmán, N. (2014). *Ingrid Olderock, La mujer de los perros*. Ceibo Ediciones.

Hite, K., & Collins, C. (2009). Memorial Fragments, Monumental Silences and Reawakenings in 21st-Century Chile. *Millennium: Journal of International Studies, 38*(2), 379–400.

Infante, S. (2015). *Del discurso al aula: recontextualización de textos escolares en materia de Dictadura militar y derechos humanos para sexto año básico en Chile*. Museo de la Memoria y los Derechos Humanos.

Instituto de Políticas Públicas en Derechos Humanos del Mercosur (IPPDH). (2012). *Principios fundamentales para las políticas públicas en materia de sitios de memoria*, available at https://www.ippdh.mercosur.int/principios-fundamentales-para-las-politicas-publicas-en-materia-de-sitios-de-memoria

Jara, D. (2013). *The Aftermath of Political Violence: The Opposition's Second Generation in the Post-Coup Chile and Its Familial Memory*. Ph.D. thesis in Sociology, University of London – Goldsmiths.

Lazzara, M. J. (2006). *Chile in Transition. The Poetics and Politics of Memory*. University of Press of Florida.

López, L. (2018). *"A mí no me pasó". Memorias del miedo en personas que no fueron víctimas de violaciones a los derechos humanos en la dictadura cívico-militar chilena (1973–1990)*. Ph.D. thesis in Social Sciences, University of Chile.

López, L., & Hevia, E. (2016). Archivo oral de Villa Grimaldi: experiencia y reflexiones. In M. G. Acuña et al. (Eds.), *Archivos y memoria de la represión en América Latina (1973–1990)* (pp. 107–129). Lom Ediciones.

Madikida, C., Segal, L., & van den Berg, C. (2008). The Reconstruction of Memory at Constitution Hill. *The Public Historian, 30*(1), 17–25.

Magendzo, A., & Toledo, M. I. (2009). Educación en Derechos Humanos: Curriculum Historia y Ciencias Sociales del 2° Año de Enseñanza Media. Subunidad "Régimen Militar y Transición a la Democracia". *Estudios Pedagógicos, 35*(1), 139–154.

Mateos-Pérez, J., & Ochoa, G. (2018). *Chile en las series de televisión. Los 80, Los Archivos del Cardenal y El Reemplazante*. RIL Editores.

Museo de la Memoria y los Derechos Humanos. (2014). *Memoria Anual del Museo de la Memoria y los Derechos Humanos*, available at https://ww3.museodelamemoria.cl/wp-content/files_mf/1460129457MEMORIA2014.pdf

Nora, P. (Ed.). (1996). *Realms of Memory. The Construction of the French Past* (Conflicts and Divisions) (Vol. I). Columbia University Press.

Payne, L. (2008). *Unsettling Accounts: Neither Truth nor Reconciliation in Confessions of State Violence*. Duke University Press.

Peñaloza, C. (2015). *El Camino de la Memoria. De la Represión a la Justicia en Chile, 1973–2013*. Editorial Cuarto Propio.

Pino-Ojeda, W. (2011). *Noche y niebla: neoliberalismo, memoria y trauma en el Chile postautoritario*. Editorial Cuarto Propio.

Piper, I. (2005). *Obstinaciones de la Memoria: La dictadura militar chilena en las tramas del recuerdo*. Ph.D. thesis, Universitat Autònoma de Barcelona.

Rojas, H. (2015). Biopolitics and Homo Sacer in a Torture Center in Chile. *Revista Direito GV São Paulo, 11*(1), 257–276.

Rojas, H. (2017). *Indifference to Past Human Rights Violations: The Impact of Transitional Justice Success*. Doctoral thesis, University of Oxford.

Rubio, G. (2013). *Memoria, Política y Pedagogía: Los caminos hacia la enseñanza del pasado reciente en Chile*. Lom ediciones.

Sorensen, K. I. (2015). *Los Medios, La Memoria y los Derechos Humanos en Chile*. RIL Editores.

Spooner, M. H. (2011). *The General's Slow Retreat: Chile After Pinochet*. University of California Press.

Stern, S. (2006). *Battling for Hearts and Minds: Memory Struggles in Pinochet's Chile, 1973–1988*. Duke University Press.

Stern, S., & Winn, P. (2014). El Tortuoso Camino Chileno a la Memorialización. In P. Winn, S. Stern, F. Lorenz, & A. Marchesi (Eds.), *No hay mañana sin ayer: Batallas por la memoria histórica en el Cono Sur* (pp. 205–326). Lom ediciones.

Toledo, M. I., Veneros, D., & Magendzo, A. (2009). *Visita a un lugar de memoria: Guía para el trabajo en derechos humanos*. Lom ediciones.
United Nations. (2010). *Guidance Note of the Secretary General: United Nations Approach to Transitional Justice*, available at https://www.un.org/ruleoflaw/files/TJ_Guidance_Note_March_2010FINAL.pdf

CHAPTER 6

Investigating and Condemning the Perpetrators

Justice presents a particular challenge in many political transitions. It is important that transitional governments hold perpetrators accountable in order to combat impunity and build people's trust in state institutions. This is no easy task, as perpetrators often actively seek to avoid punishment, using tactics such as self-amnesties in order to evade justice. In addition, state institutions are often eroded throughout long periods of conflict and violence, and in a volatile political climate where perpetrators still hold significant influence, it can be difficult to hold criminal trials. Transitional governments must often be creative in their initial approach to accountability, striking a balance between retributive and restorative justice approaches.

While retributive justice involves punishing perpetrators through judicial and legal measures such as criminal prosecutions, restorative justice is not focused on punishment, but rather on rectifying the harm caused by the crime. Restorative justice seeks to create accountability through a range of mechanisms which generally involve the participation of both victims and perpetrators and ultimately seek to further social reconciliation (Johnstone, 2013). In the difficult and unstable context of the transition, many governments initially opt to use alternative and restorative justice approaches, or a combination of retributive and restorative approaches. However, it is important to ensure that the most serious crimes do not go unpunished. Problems

H. Rojas, M. Shaftoe, *Human Rights and Transitional Justice in Chile*, Memory Politics and Transitional Justice,
https://doi.org/10.1007/978-3-030-81182-2_6

arise when governments mistake restorative justice to be synonymous with passivity or inaction. Choosing not to hold perpetrators accountable not only allows for impunity, but also ignores the fact that many victims strongly desire traditional justice processes (Laplante, 2009).

The state has an international responsibility to satisfy the victims' right to justice, and an important aspect of this right is the punishment of those responsible proportional to the gravity of the crime they committed. When it comes to human rights abuses, amnesty and prescription cannot be invoked. A number of different processes are involved in the formal mechanisms of investigating and condemning perpetrators, including the necessary institutional reforms which will allow the state to ensure impartial judicial investigations and the prosecution of those responsible. While in theory, justice should be sought immediately with the view of prosecuting as many perpetrators as possible and as soon as possible, the reality of post-conflict transitions is complex, and the process is often prolonged for an indefinite period of time. In Chile, roadblocks such as the Amnesty Law of 1978, a pro-Pinochet Supreme Court, and Pinochet's still strong influence, with the former dictator even going so far as declaring he would end the rule of law if any of his men were tried in court, have made the fight for justice a long, arduous, and ongoing process.

Upon becoming president, Aylwin was faced with a tense transitional atmosphere. Given this context, he favored a nontraditional approach to justice. This did not mean, however, dropping the pursuit of justice and accountability for perpetrators. His non-judicial first step toward justice was the Truth and Reconciliation Commission. Although it was not allowed to make pronouncements judging whether anyone was guilty or not, the TRC later helped in human rights cases by allowing the evidence collected during the investigation to be forwarded to the courts (Ferrara, 2015). In addition, lawyers and human rights organizations such as *Vicaría de la Solidaridad* had registered and processed complaints against the dictatorship throughout the 17 years of repression. These archives have proved to be invaluable throughout the pursuit of justice in Chile, providing evidence and register of the crimes committed, especially because one of the main difficulties in cases of human rights violations is the lack of evidence (Hau et al., 2019). Repressive agencies do not usually leave traces of the abuses committed, preferring to destroy anything incriminating.

Despite the many challenges, the governments of the transition sought to reform the judicial system in order to pave the way for an environment more favorable of accountability, particularly of those highest in the chain of command. With this national context in mind, the surprising arrest of Pinochet in London in 1998 acted as a catalyst for a stronger, more effective pursuit of justice in Chile: the prospective extradition of Pinochet resulted in the emergence of a strong argument that the dictator should be held accountable in Chile and allowed for several important reforms and changes which made the criminal investigation of Pinochet in Chile possible. The detention of the former dictator also instigated what Kathryn Sikkink (2011) calls a "cascade of justice," opening the door to more trials and convictions of those responsible for human rights violations.

6.1 Justice Under the Dictatorship

In the first 48 hours after the September 11 coup, 5373 people were arrested. Faced with the evidence of political persecution and brutal repression, the reaction was immediate: as early as September 14, 1973, lawyer and Christian Democratic Party deputy Bernardo Leighton presented the first habeas corpus (*recurso de amparo*) by a telephone call to the Court of Appeals of Santiago, for the arrest of seven leaders of the Socialist Party. Habeas corpus is used to secure the legal protection of a person known to be detained, by requiring they be brought before a judge and released unless lawful grounds for their detainment can be proven. Leighton's petition was denied because all civil and political rights had been suspended; Chile was allegedly under attack by an internal enemy. The first four months of the dictatorship were incredibly violent, and more than half of the disappearances and killings recognized in the Rettig report occurred during this period (Truth and Reconciliation Commission, 1991). In this repressive context, on October 4, 1973, a group of churches and religious communities mobilized to create the Committee of Cooperation for Peace in Chile, known as the Pro Paz Committee. This committee sought to provide medical, social, and legal aid to citizens in need, and through it many lawyers sought to mobilize to support detainees and their families (Bernasconi et al., 2019).

The main source of information for lawyers working in the Pro Paz Committee was the statements of the relatives of the detainees. Social workers listened to these statements, recorded the key details, and passed along the relevant information to the lawyers and their assistants. During the two years that it operated, the Pro Paz Committee provided legal aid to tens of thousands of Chileans, and presented 2342 habeas corpus, but a mere three cases were accepted by the Court of Appeals. This illustrates just how complicit the courts were in allowing state terrorism and violence to continue unchecked. In 1975, the DINA secret police intensified their efforts to eliminate left-wing extremist groups such as the MIR (*Movimiento de Izquierda Revolucionaria*). Around this time, Pinochet accused the Pro Paz Committee of being linked to left-wing extremist groups, pressuring Cardinal Raúl Silva Henríquez to shut down the committee by targeting and detaining professionals who worked there. Due to the increased danger faced by those involved in its activities, on December 31, 1975, the Pro Paz Committee was dissolved. This did not dissuade the Cardinal, however, and the very next day, January 1, 1976, he founded the *Vicaría de la Solidaridad* (Vicariate of Solidarity) to continue the work that the Pro Paz Committee had begun. The vicariate was founded by archiepiscopal decree and, as such, with the force of the Catholic Church behind it, was able to provide protection and aid to victims of the dictatorship until 1992.

The Vicariate of Solidarity became the most important human rights defense organization during the dictatorship years and a symbol of resistance to the Pinochet regime. The two main focuses of its work were legal action and outreach and human rights education (Del Villar et al., 2019). Lawyers and social workers of the vicariate continued file habeas corpus petitions and take legal action on behalf of victims and survivors throughout the entire course of the dictatorship. In addition to its legal branch, the vicariate organized educational workshops and meal programs for children in underprivileged neighborhoods. Its magazine *Solidaridad* spread information about human rights abuses, including information sheets about missing persons. The dedication of its staff as well as international support allowed the organization to sustain its important work for the duration of the Pinochet regime. When the legal action the vicariate undertook so rarely led to direct results such as the release of prisoners, why did they continue persistently for 17 years? According to Cath Collins, there are five main reasons. Firstly, the habeas corpus petitions did sometimes, although rarely, improve the conditions of prisoners who were being detained. Secondly, in order to bring a case to the regional courts, such as the Inter-American Court of Human Rights, domestic action had to be undertaken first. Thirdly, it allowed for a degree of domestic denunciation and awareness raising, as journalists were able to report about deaths and disappearances indirectly by reporting about the court proceedings or rejections of habeas corpus petitions. Fourthly, lawyers sought to shame judges into action by not allowing them to forget about the human rights violations. Finally, the legal process of filing habeas corpus petitions created significant evidence which many hoped would prove useful for future accountability processes (Collins, 2010a: 3–5; 2010b: 64–68). The archives of the vicariate have been an invaluable asset in both the truth and reconciliation commissions and in the justice process, by providing evidence for cases. However, the attitude of the vast majority of criminal judges was to apply the 1978 amnesty law decree or to declare that they had no jurisdiction and send the case files to the military justice system, where the denial of justice prevailed.

While the courts were complicit in the dictatorship, and by consistently rejecting habeas corpus petitions were "largely responsible for aggravating systematic human rights abuses" (Truth and Reconciliation Commision, 1991, vol. 1: 86), lawyers, social workers, doctors, religious leaders, survivors, and victims did not give up on fighting the injustices of the military regime. The archives that resulted from their dedication and hard work have proven exceedingly valuable not only as evidence for current justice processes, but also in the two truth and reconciliation commissions and in safeguarding collective memory of the abuses. The complicity of the courts in the repression of the dictatorship creates a significant responsibility for the state to engage meaningfully in the pursuit of justice.

6.2 Early Transition

When the dictatorship ended in 1990, many believed swift action would be taken to ensure that perpetrators would finally be held accountable; however, the reality proved to be far more complicated. The application of the Amnesty Act was the general rule during the dictatorship. This decree law, passed in 1978, made it impossible to take state agents to court for human rights crimes that took place between 1973 and 1978. Due to the Amnesty Act, and the fact that the courts had continuously upheld the interests of the dictatorship, most of the legal action on behalf of victims during the dictatorship was centered on emergency measures seeking to protect detainees rather than seeking to hold perpetrators accountable.

Many lawyers working with the Vicariate of Solidarity and other human rights groups believed that, once the dictatorship was over, they would be able to move forward with the thousands of cases of detained and disappeared and hold perpetrators accountable, as had occurred in Argentina with the fairly swift prosecution of members of the military junta in the Junta Trials only a few years into the transition (Collins et al., 2016: 60–61). This was certainly the belief of many politicians as well. In both the *No* campaign and the 1989 presidential election, seeking justice featured as a key element of the *Concertación* platform. In fact Aylwin's presidential campaign included the promise he would repeal the Amnesty law (Collins, 2010a: 6–9). The political climate in the early 1990s, however, proved far more volatile than many had expected. Pinochet's inflammatory statements suggesting that he would end the rule of law if they "touched any of his men" worried the newly elected government, and Aylwin was forced to make pragmatic decisions about what aspects of human rights action to prioritize. Ultimately, given the threats from the military, he chose to create a truth commission and implement reparations policies rather than focusing on the pursuit of justice.

The first stage of the transition was thus marked by a continued application of the 1978 Amnesty Act. Most of the time judges immediately closed judicial investigations if the crime had taken place during the period covered by the amnesty law, and the Supreme Court often sanctioned judges who took alternate stances on human rights or had looser interpretations of the Amnesty Act (Evans, 2006: 221). Between 1990 and 1998, only 12 convictions were handed down in Chile. The two highest profile trials were the *Orlando Letelier Case*, which led to the conviction of the former head of the DINA Manuel Contreras, and the so-called *Caso Degollados* (Slaughtered case), which led to the resignation of the Director of the Police, General Rodolfo Stange. These cases were widely followed by the media and the public, but it is important to note that both cases were only able to proceed as they both fell outside the 1978 amnesty law.

The Letelier case had been expressly excluded due to pressure from the United States, and the Degollados case occurred in 1985, after the period covered by the amnesty law. Contreras, while he was convicted, was not handed over to authorities by the armed forces for five months following his conviction, and carried out the beginning of his sentence in a military facility, guarded by his friends. The Degollados case did convict several police officers; however, General Rodolfo Stange, who the courts found had plotted to hide evidence, ignored the government's request for his resignation and returned to his post when it was ruled his actions had not been criminal (Evans, 2006: 227). In a sense both cases yielded significant results; they held important authorities to account, and Contreras was the first former head of a secret police force in South America to be convicted (Stern & Winn, 2014: 285), yet their limitations illustrate just how tense the atmosphere of the early transition was, in terms of civilian-military relations.

The main issue during the years of the early transition though was that convictions were few and far between. The continued application of the Amnesty law was an important roadblock to justice, as was the permanence of many pro-Pinochet Supreme Court justices. The government of Frei Ruiz-Tagle made several important reforms to the justice system, which would later have an important impact in terms of creating an environment more favorable to accountability, for instance, increasing the number of judges in the Supreme Court, offering retirement plans for the judges appointed by Pinochet to leave the courts, and establishing a retirement age of 75 for judges (Hilbink, 2014: Ch. 5). A constitutional reform was also approved so the Senate would participate in the process of appointing the judges of the Supreme Court. This had a very important effect on human rights cases, opening the Supreme Court to take a more liberal stance, ruling for example, that obligations under international humanitarian law negated the amnesty law, as well as invoking the "permanent crime" doctrine, which argued that if the remains of a disappeared person had not been found the crime was still ongoing. This allowed judges to sidestep the amnesty law and pursue investigations in cases of disappearances.

One of the most significant results of this opening of the judicial system was the acceptance of the first criminal complaint against Pinochet in January 1998, for crimes of genocide, kidnapping, illicit association, and illegal inhumation. The mere acceptance of this case by the courts shows just how much the environment for the pursuit of justice had changed by the late 1990s. The criminal complaint was filed by Gladys Marín, then general secretary of the Communist Party of Chile, who was personally motivated by the disappearance of her husband during the early years of the dictatorship. Another part of the impetus of the launching of this case was Pinochet's imminent changing of positions within government: in March he would be stepping down as commander in chief of the army and into a new role as senator-for-life. This was met with anger by many Chileans, who were becoming frustrated with the impunity enjoyed by the former dictator. In addition to Gladys Marín's judicial proceedings, others also sought to prevent Pinochet from entering into his new role as senator: a group of deputies from the *Concertación* coalition brought forward an ultimately unsuccessful petition to impeach him. Overall, these actions show that in the late 1990s, attitudes toward justice and impunity in Chile were beginning to open to the idea of greater accountability. The strict application of the amnesty law was being eroded, and legal and constitutional reforms created an environment much more favorable to holding perpetrators responsible.

6.3 Pinochet in London

The judicial scene in Chile changed drastically due to an unforeseen event on October 16, 1998: the arrest of Pinochet in London. The former dictator, now senator-for-life, Augusto Pinochet, traveled to London on September 22, 1998. It was his fourth trip to England during the transition. He was there for a hernia operation at the London Clinic and had also been invited to visit the country by a Syrian businessman dedicated to arms production and trade. In order to avoid inconveniences during his stay in Europe, he entered the country with a diplomatic passport that identified him as Antonio Ugarte, which declared that he was traveling as a representative of Chile on an official mission. He planned to leave the UK on October 17.

However, when staff of Amnesty International's London headquarters discovered that Pinochet was in London, they issued a statement reminding European governments of their obligation to detain Pinochet under international humanitarian law, in particular, the Convention Against Torture (Amnesty International, 2013). It so happened that since 1996, the 5th and 6th chambers of the *Audiencia Nacional* (National Court) of Spain had been investigating human rights violations committed by the Chilean and Argentinian dictatorships against Spanish citizens. Spanish lawyer and former political advisor of President Salvador Allende, Joan Garcés, had filed the original 1996 complaint against Pinochet (Dorfman, 2003: 31–32), and Judge Baltasar Garzón had been investigating crimes against Spanish citizens in Argentina, but extended his investigations to events in Chile because of the infamous Operation Condor, in which South American dictatorships cooperated in persecuting their political enemies across borders. Joan Garcés found out Pinochet was at the London Clinic and would be in England until October 17 and communicated the information immediately to Judge Baltasar Garzón, who issued the arrest warrant for the crimes of terrorism, genocide, and torture, and requested the extradition of Pinochet from the English government. Scotland Yard received the order and the London Metropolitan Police arrested Pinochet in the hospital (Spooner, 2011: 160).

The ensuing course of events caused a major commotion in international affairs and lasted for over a year. Pinochet's lawyers immediately submitted an appeal to the UK High Court of Justice, arguing for the former dictator's release on the grounds that he had diplomatic immunity as a former head of state. The High Court ruled in his favor; however, the prosecution appealed, and it was decided the case would be taken to the House of Lords. This case provoked major legal discussions (Byers, 2000; Woodhouse, 2003). The territoriality (*locus delicti*) and extraterritoriality principles were debated by criminal law experts; the territoriality principle holds that a sovereign state has exclusive authority to prosecute crimes which occur within its borders, while the extraterritoriality principle, also known as diplomatic immunity, holds that official representatives of foreign states are immune to the jurisdiction of other countries which they visit. Thus, the core of the debate was whether Pinochet enjoyed diplomatic immunity as a *former* head of state, and whether the principle of territoriality applied in the case of massive human rights violations and crimes against humanity. If the events occurred in Chile, then Chilean criminal law should be applied. On the other hand, it was argued that no justice had been served in the vast majority of human rights cases in Chile. In particular, the deaths of priest Joan Alsina and diplomat Carmelo Soria, both Spanish citizens, had been closed because they came under the Amnesty Act (Pigrau Solé, 2000: 663).

Meanwhile, Pinochet's detention caused an uproar in Chile, triggering intense legal and political debates. His supporters argued that the detention was an attack on national sovereignty and the principle of territoriality, while his opponents supported the extradition, arguing that the dictator had to be held accountable for his crimes under international human rights law, and pointing out that the Chilean judicial system had been thus far unwilling or unable to try him in Chile. Faced with these two extremes, the Chilean government adopted a third stance; they argued that Pinochet should be returned to Chile, but on the condition that he would be tried in his home country (Evans, 2006: 231). The government then used the extradition as an opportunity to take various steps that would ensure that a fair trial of Pinochet would in fact be possible in Chile. For instance, they worked hard over the course of his detention in London to repeal his parliamentary immunity (*fuero parlamentario*). The fact that Juan Guzmán, judge of the Court of Appeals of Santiago, was already investigating the criminal responsibility of Pinochet, in the context Gladys

Marín's complaint against the dictator, played in favor of the Chilean government, as it was an indication that steps were indeed already being taken to combat impunity.

In the meantime, the extradition situation escalated. Criminal proceedings were announced in eight different countries and France, Switzerland, and Belgium also requested Pinochet's extradition. Intense legal debates began on international law, European law, Spanish law, British law, and Chilean law. In November, the House of Lords reversed the High Court judgment and ruled that Pinochet was not immune from prosecution as a former head of state. However, one of the English judges, Lord Hoffman, had links with Amnesty International, an organization that participated in the accusation against Pinochet. Pinochet's lawyers in London used his connection to Amnesty International to argue that Lord Hoffman had not been impartial. Because of this, the decision was set to be reviewed in January 1999 (Amnesty International, 2008).

Various legal principles were used in the arguments for and against extradition. Criminal prescription was invoked, which is the idea that criminal complaints must be filed within a reasonable period of time after a crime is committed, that is, there is a time limit within which one must file a complaint. It was argued that the events had occurred decades ago and as such criminal prescription applied. The lawyers of the disappeared argued however that the crime committed was permanent kidnapping, as opposed to homicide. Since the bodies had not been found, the crime had to be considered as still being committed. Another principle invoked and argued was universal jurisdiction in crimes against humanity, versus the principle of territoriality. Finally, in March 1999, the House of Lords ruled that Pinochet was not immune from acts of torture committed while he was head of state, and that he could be extradited, but only for crimes alleged to have been committed after December 8, 1988, when the Convention Against Torture came into force in the UK. The extradition hearing was scheduled for September 1999.

The conclusion of the process of extradition was as abrupt and unexpected as its beginning. In October, during the extradition hearings, the Chilean government requested Pinochet undergo medical tests, and after reviewing the medical report, UK Home Secretary Jack Straw decided to end the extradition hearing and authorize Pinochet to return to Chile in consideration of his poor health. The former dictator had been detained in London for 503 days. While Pinochet returned to Chile on March 3, 2000, likely feeling triumphant, he would find much had changed. He lost his parliamentary immunity in August, and could now be tried; dozens of separate cases of human rights abuse had been filed against him (Evans, 2006: 241). The notorious Augusto Pinochet was no longer untouchable.

After his return to Chile, judicial proceedings against Pinochet began in earnest. According to Cath Collins, the Chilean Judge Guzmán's investigations into Pinochet's involvement in a number of different incidents, including the Villa Grimaldi torture center, the Caravan of Death, and Operation Condor, became a "roller coaster ride": each case had to be investigated separately because his parliamentary immunity had to be suspended for each set of charges, and his supposed medical unfitness had to be proven (2010a: 20–21). In January 2001, expert medical reports were made. The defense presented Pinochet's doctor Sergio Ferrer's report, and the Legal Medical Service presented an expert opinion that drew the same conclusions: Pinochet had moderate dementia. The complainants presented an alternate report by Dr. Luis Fornazzari, professor of neurology and psychiatry at the University of Toronto, who concluded that Pinochet had a mild senile dementia, and could therefore be tried.

In 2004 the case was nearly closed, but a televised interview Pinochet had given that year was aired in which it was evident he did not have advanced dementia. A few days later, the Supreme Court ruled against Pinochet, declaring he could stand trial. That same month, the Riggs' bank scandal broke: investigations in the United States revealed that Pinochet had 15 million dollars in bank accounts in the Riggs Bank, and criminal complaints were brought against him for tax evasion and fraud as well. After seven years of legal battles, Pinochet died in 2006.

While he was never convicted of human rights violations, his detention had a huge impact on Chilean society and triggered a justice cascade (Sikkink, 2011), a growing trend of holding political leaders criminally accountable. Pinochet's detention created a greater sense of agency, hope, and confidence in the possibility of accountability for many people in Chilean society. Over the years, the authoritarian enclaves that prevented justice were gradually dissolved. The judicial reforms implemented during the Frei administration had a particularly important impact in opening the justice system to change. As the number of cases increased, the Supreme Court appointed 60 judges to preferentially or exclusively investigate cases of human rights violations.[1] Together, the combination of the catalyzing

[1] For further information on judicial decisions on human rights cases, visit expedientesdelarepresion.cl.

force of Pinochet's detention and the judicial reforms has led to a significant increase in the number of human rights cases being brought to the courts, as well as an increase in convictions.

6.4 Key Human Rights Cases in Chile

Both during and after the dictatorship, one of the most important and persistent obstructions to justice in Chile was the 1978 Amnesty Act, which to this day has not been overturned. Thanks to a number of significant inter-American and national court rulings, however, this law is no longer applied in practice. There have been several key human rights cases since the detention of Pinochet which have had lasting impacts on judicial proceedings in Chile, particularly in terms of ending the application of the Amnesty Act in cases of disappearances. Some early cases which ruled the Amnesty law inadmissible were the *Llaulén and Cheuquepán Case* (1993), and the *Uribe and Van Yurick Case* (1994), which concerned the disappearances of José Llaulén and Juan Cheuquepán in 1974, and the disappearance of married couple Edwin Van Yurick and Bárbara Uribe, as well as Edwin's brother Cristián Van Yurick also in 1974. The outcomes of these judicial proceedings had an important impact in eroding the application of the Amnesty law and allowed many cases to be investigated or reopened based on the inadmissibility of the said law.

The ruling against the application of criminal prescription—also known as the statute of limitations—was one of the important successes of the *Llaulén and Cheuquepán Case*. This principle requires plaintiffs to come forward with their case within a certain timeframe or lose the right to take their cause to court. It was frequently invoked to close human rights cases. The *Llaulén and Cheuquepán* ruling effectively established that neither criminal prescription nor the Amnesty law were applicable in the case of prolonged kidnapping, as disappearance is a permanent, ongoing crime until the whereabouts of the individual in question are known. The *Uribe and Van Yurick Case* in 1994 was another important case in rejecting the application of the amnesty law. In this case, it was ruled that Chile's obligations under international treaties such as the Geneva Convention made the Amnesty law inadmissible. The treaty had come into force before the Amnesty law was passed, and thus it took precedence as international treaties are higher than domestic law within Chile's legal hierarchy.

These earlier cases set the stage for the *Poblete Córdoba Case*, in 1998, which used many of the same arguments to rule the Amnesty law inadmissible. Pedro Poblete Córdoba was a union leader and militant with MIR who was detained and then disappeared in 1974. In his case, it was ruled that the Amnesty law did not apply as the state's obligations under the Geneva Convention took precedence, and because disappearance, or kidnapping, is an ongoing crime. While this was not the first time the Amnesty law had been interpreted differently, it had a broader impact in terms of setting a precedent for alternate interpretations than some of the earlier cases had had, and the Amnesty law was essentially deemed inadmissible in all cases of disappearances going forward.

Ultimately, it was the *Almonacid Arellano* et al. *v. Chile Case* in 2006 which resulted in a definitive end to the application of the Amnesty Law. The family of Luis Almonacid, a school teacher and Communist Party activist executed during the dictatorship, brought their case to the Inter-American Court of Human Rights when the State closed Almonacid's case. They argued that Chile had failed to fulfill its obligations to ensure the right to a fair trial and the right to judicial protection under the American Convention of Human Rights, as the Supreme Court had closed their case, declaring that due to the Amnesty Act and criminal prescription Almonacid's case was time barred. In 2006, the Inter-American Court of Human Rights ruled that neither amnesty nor criminal prescription can be invoked in crimes against humanity, and that domestic law cannot be invoked to exonerate crimes that are illegal under an international treaty or convention to which a state is party. In other words, Chile could not use amnesty, criminal prescription, or conflicts between domestic and international law to avoid taking responsibility, as their obligations under the American Convention of Human Rights and other international treaties took priority.

Collectively, these cases dissolved and eroded the Amnesty Act and cemented the recognition and hierarchy of international human rights treaties within the Chilean legal system. Since 1998, major advancements have been made in the pursuit of justice; there have been more convictions of dictatorship-era authorities and higher-ups in the chain of command, for instance, important *pinochetista* General Sergio Arellano Stark in 2008. The number of cases overall has increased as well. In the first 25 years of the transition, 1373 state agents were investigated and prosecuted for crimes under the dictatorship, and 117 were serving custodial sentences in the Punta Peuco prison complex, located north of Santiago. Authoritarian tendencies continue to be dissolved, for instance, since 2016, cases about crimes against humanity cannot be heard by the military justice system. They are dealt with by the ordinary justice system, which is a significant move toward greater accountability.

There have been important achievements in terms of accountability and justice in the past 20 years; however, further progress is still necessary. Pending issues include overly lenient sentencing and more state engagement in holding perpetrators accountable, as justice processes have been largely led by victims and their families (Collins, 2010a: 30). Families of the victims and human rights organizations have also raised concerns and frustrations about "biological impunity"; in the context of a long and drawn-out justice process, many perpetrators die before they can be tried or convicted (Londres 38, 2014). This is an especially compelling argument for a more deliberate approach to state engagement with unresolved human rights and accountability issues. Another important pending issue is the recognition of sexual violence in cases of human rights violations. Sexual violence against women detainees and political prisoners was rampant throughout the dictatorship, but the first important victory on this front was achieved only in 2018. For the first time, the Supreme Court established that the state must compensate a woman who was detained and who survived torture, including rape, as a crime against humanity (*Lara Case*).

6.5 Lessons from the Chilean Experience of Justice

The pursuit of justice in Chile has been a long and complex process, extending far into the transition. It has several key characteristics, which have had an important influence on the course of justice after the return to democracy. The first important characteristic is the existence of detailed and expansive human rights archives and registers. The work of human rights organizations, in particular the *Vicaría de la Solidaridad*, has had a lasting positive impact in supporting the victims and their families in their pursuit of justice, as it has provided a valuable bank of evidence for judicial proceedings.

The second key characteristic of the Chilean pursuit of justice is the interplay between international and domestic pressures. International pressure and international treaties and conventions proved important in providing domestic actors with opportunities to create a more favorable environment for accountability. International treaties were important tools in fighting against the application of the Amnesty law in court, and international pressure, particularly in the case of Pinochet's detention in London, created circumstances which both governments and civil society actors took advantage of to make important advancements in the pursuit of justice. It's clear that the existence of international pressure and involvement of international actors alone is not sufficient to create significant change in accountability processes at the domestic level, as can be seen in the case of El Salvador, where international intervention and involvement played a strong role in the process of creating institutional judicial changes, but where progress toward accountability has been slow (Collins, 2010a, 2010b: 213–217). The strong use of legal strategies by Chilean human rights organizations and activists from quite early on in their response and resistance during the dictatorship created a strong demand for accountability, which allowed domestic actors to act swiftly when international pressure created opportunities for progress.

The third characteristic is the prolonged, long-term nature of judicial investigations into human rights abuses in Chile. Even now, 30 years after the dictatorship ended, there are still active cases, and a strong demand for justice persists. Interestingly, the course of time has not diluted demands for justice; it appears to have strengthened them. The Chilean case is an example of how unresolved human rights violations must be addressed, or else they will simply bubble under the surface and reemerge when events such as Pinochet's detention trigger "irruptions of memory," bringing the injustices of the past back into the spotlight (Wilde, 1999).

The question of pursuing justice after human rights abuses returned in force due to the widespread police brutality during the demonstrations and social unrest that began in October 2019. The response to the human rights violations perpetrated during the protest movement highlights interesting similarities and difference in comparison to Chile's past experiences seeking justice. For instance, the National Institute of Human Rights (INDH) has played a significant role in documenting the abuses committed by police and military personnel during the state of emergency declared in October 2019, and throughout the course of the demonstrations. Their work has paralleled the role played by the *Vicaría de la Solidaridad* during the dictatorship compiling evidence and filing criminal complaints on behalf of victims. Just as during the dictatorship victims and their families desperately knocked on the doors of the *Vicaría de la Solidaridad*, at the end of 2019, victims of state repression knocked on doors of civil society but also public institutions, and especially the National

Institute of Human Rights. As of March 2020, the National Institute of Human Rights had presented 1465 judicial actions on behalf of victims. The reaction of the international community allows for another interesting comparison. Three different international organizations quickly brought forward reports condemning the actions of the police and military during the Fall 2019 demonstrations: the Office of the UN High Commissioner for Human Rights, Amnesty International, and Human Rights Watch. The government has accepted two out of the three reports, rejecting the findings of Amnesty International, thus already accepting, even if only to a limited extent, some responsibility for the crimes committed.

It is too soon yet to tell how the courts will respond this time around in terms of holding perpetrators and authorities accountable for the recent abuses, but there have been some early indications that there is not only a significant demand for accountability but a willingness to hold not only the immediate perpetrators but also political authorities accountable. The political contexts of the dictatorship and today's democracy in crisis are very different, but it is worth noting that while it took decades for any attempt at political impeachment processes or criminal complaints against Pinochet, a "constitutional accusation" was presented against Minister of Interior and Public Security Andrés Chadwick as early as October 30, 2019, for his political responsibility in the crimes and human rights abuses committed by state agents during the protests. The minister was impeached on December 11, 2019. This is not a judgment of judicial responsibility, but rather of political responsibility. Even more recently, an accusation was filed by human rights groups in Chile against President Sebastian Piñera at the International Criminal Court (ICC) for his alleged involvement in the human rights abuses during the 2019 protest movement. It is significant that accountability processes of any nature were initiated as soon as the serious nature of the human rights violations was known. The full repercussions of the 2019 social unrest on Chile's ongoing search for justice remain to be seen.

Bibliography

Amnesty International. (2008). *Chronology of the Case of Augusto Pinochet*, available at https://www.amnesty.org/download/Documents/52000/amr220032008en.pdf

Amnesty International. (2013). *How General Pinochet's Detention Changed the Meaning of Justice*, available at https://www.amnesty.org/en/latest/news/2013/10/how-general-pinochets-detention-changed-meaning-justice/

Bernasconi, O., Gárate, M., Suárez, R., & Mansilla, R. (2019). How to Sustain a Human Rights Organisation Under State Violence. In O. Bernasconi (Ed.), *Political Violence Resistance in Latin America: Documenting Atrocity* (pp. 41–78). Palgrave Macmillan.

Byers, M. (2000). The Law and Politics of the Pinochet Case. *Duke Journal of Comparative & International Law, 10*(2), 415–442.

Collins, C. (2010a). Human Rights Trials in Chile During and After the Pinochet Years. *International Journal of Transitional Justice, 4*(1), 67–86.

Collins, C. (2010b). *Post-transitional Justice: Human Rights Trials in Chile and El Salvador*. Penn State University Press.

Collins, C., Garcia-Godos, J., & Skaar, E. (Eds.). (2016). *Transitional Justice in Latin America: The Uneven Road from Impunity Towards Accountability*. Routledge.

Comisión Nacional de Verdad y Reconciliación. (1991). *Informe Rettig*. Gobierno de Chile.

Del Villar, M. S., Hau, B., Johansson, M. T., & Guerrero, M. (2019). Professions and Profiles: Epistemic Communities and the Registration of Human Rights Violations. In O. Bernasconi (Ed.), *Political Violence Resistance in Latin America: Documenting Atrocity* (Vol. 2019, pp. 79–115). Palgrave Macmillan.

Dorfman, A. (2003). *Exorcising Terror: The Incredible Unending Trial of General Augusto Pinochet*. Pluto Press.

Evans, R. (2006). Pinochet in London: Pinochet in Chile: International and Domestic Politics in Human Rights Policy. *Human Rights Quarterly, 28*(1), 207–244.

Ferrara, A. (2015). *Assessing the Long-term Impact of Truth Commissions: The Chilean Truth and Reconciliation Commission in Historical Perspective*. Routledge.

Hau, B., Lessa, F., & Rojas, H. (2019). Registration of State Violence as Judicial Evidence in Human Rights Trials. In O. Bernasconi (Ed.), *Political Violence Resistance in Latin America: Documenting Atrocity* (pp. 197–228). Palgrave Macmillan.

Hilbink, L. (2014). *Jueces y política en democracia y dictadura: Lecciones desde Chile*. Facultad Lationamericana de Ciencias Sociales, sede México.

Johnstone, G. (2013). *A Restorative Justice Reader*. Routledge.

Laplante, L. J. (2009). Outlawing Amnesty: The Return of Criminal Justice in Transitional Justice Schemes. *Virginia Journal of International Law, 49*, 916–944.

Londres 38. (2014). *Es Necesario Impedir la "Impunidad Biologica" en Crímenes de Lesa Humanidad*, available at https://www.londres38.cl/1937/w3-article-95526.html

Pigrau Solé, A. (2000). The Pinochet Case in Spain. *ILSA Journal of International & Comparative Law, 6*(3), 653–683.

Sikkink, K. (2011). *The Justice Cascade: How Human Rights Prosecutions Are Changing World Politics.* W.W. Norton & Co.

Spooner, M. H. (2011). *The General's Slow Retreat: Chile After Pinochet.* University of California Press.

Stern, S., & Winn, P. (2014). El Tortuoso Camino Chileno a la Memorialización. In P. Winn, S. Stern, F. Lorenz, & A. Marchesi (Eds.), *No hay mañana sin ayer: Batallas por la memoria histórica en el Cono Sur* (pp. 205–326). Lom ediciones.

Wilde, A. (1999). Irruptions of Memory: Expressive Politics in Chile's Transition to Democracy. *Journal of Latin American Studies, 31*(2), 473–500.

Woodhouse, D. (2003). The Progress of Pinochet Through the UK Extradition Procedure: An Analysis of the Legal Challenges and Judicial Decisions. In M. Davis (Ed.), *The Pinochet Case: Origins, Progress and Implications* (pp. 87–106). Institute of Latin American Studies.

CHAPTER 7

"Never Again" and Guarantees of Non-repetition

As we have outlined throughout the previous chapters, in the first 30 years of transitional justice in Chile, notable progress has been made in terms of searching for the truth, memorializing and commemorating, investigating and condemning the perpetrators, and creating reparations for victims. In announcing the First National Human Rights Plan (2017), President Michelle Bachelet effectively described the advancements made during the transition when she declared, "the path taken by the various governments since the return to democracy has allowed progress in areas that would have been impossible to imagine a few years ago." While many may have thought that the sum of all this progress would have been a sufficient guarantee that the agents of the state would not again commit abuses and atrocities, the Chilean experience of transitional justice should not be exaggerated, nor overly optimistic.

The truth is that despite being an oft-praised, classic case study in transitional justice, the Chilean case does not constitute a model to be followed closely by other countries. This has become especially evident since the unrest, now commonly referred to as the *estallido social* (social explosion) of October 2019, and the massive violation of protestors' human rights that followed. The widespread nature of state repression, and in particular the abuses committed by the police, demand a critical review of the progress made in the last three decades, and why it has not been enough to prevent new abuses in turbulent times. This chapter will

H. Rojas, M. Shaftoe, *Human Rights and Transitional Justice in Chile*, Memory Politics and Transitional Justice,
https://doi.org/10.1007/978-3-030-81182-2_7

analyze the main advances in the fifth element of transitional justice: the guarantee of non-repetition. It is argued that, beyond the achievements made, there are still deficits that need to be corrected, especially at the institutional and cultural levels.

Non-repetition differs from the previous transitional justice elements we have discussed, as it focuses more on the future than on the facts of the past, and concentrates on society as a whole rather than focusing primarily on victims. Initiatives of non-repetition not only seek to prevent future human rights violations, but also contribute to strengthening the rule of law, and creating a more democratic and peaceful future. The multiple types of non-repetition measures can be grouped into three major pillars: institutional reform, vetting, and demobilization and disbandment of armed groups (Roht-Arriaza, 2019). In this chapter, we will examine institutional reform from an expanded perspective, by analyzing not only the strengthening of public institutions over the course of the Chilean transition, but also the lack of reform of the economic model and the idea of the welfare state. The lack of discussion around the dismantling of armed groups and the process of vetting in public institutions will also be discussed. This chapter will show that beyond these three concepts, the guarantee of respect of human rights depends on an essential condition: citizens must value, adhere to, and incorporate democratic principles and fundamental rights into their culture. Without a pervasive culture of human rights in all aspects of society, abuses will continue to be perpetrated and justified by some sectors and actors.

7.1 Strengthening of Public Institutions

The World Justice Project is an international organization dedicated to monitoring the rule of law around the world and developing tools to help improve it. For this organization, the rule of law is conceived as a durable system of laws, institutions, norms, and community engagement based on four pillars: accountability, just laws, open government, and accessible justice (WJP, 2020). Its periodic measurements include the review of 44 indicators in 128 countries. In its report published in 2020, Chile places 26th in the ranking, with similar scores to those obtained by Slovenia, Costa Rica, Italy, and Poland (WJP, 2020. 16). During the transition, Chile carried out important institutional reforms, modernizing its courts and creating and consolidating public institutions for the protection of human rights, among other initiatives. It is largely because of these reforms, which we will explore in more depth throughout the chapter, that Chile is currently situated within the top quarter of the World Justice Project ranking. However, the indicators in which Chile continues to score poorly highlight some of the areas in which progress has been slower: police violence, prison system, police investigation, corruption of parliamentarians and politicians, and slow justice in civil matters (WJP, 2020: 57). In order to progress in the ranking and also rebuild citizens' trust in government after the most recent outbreak of state violence, it is essential that these issues be reviewed and addressed.

The justice system is one area in which important progress has been made since the end of the dictatorship. As outlined in Chap. 6, in the second half of the 1990s, reforms were implemented to modernize the administration of criminal justice. During those years, the Judicial Branch was subject to various criticisms: slowness of criminal investigations and trials (Blanco et al., 2004: 263), citizen dissatisfaction with the performance of judges, rising crime, passivity of the courts in the face of human rights violations committed during the dictatorship, corruption, and secrecy in the judicial system (Matus, 1999). With the return to democracy, it was essential to adapt Chilean legislation to international standards of due process (Duce, 2008: 69). After several years of negotiations between the Executive and the Congress, plus the approval of a set of legal bodies, on December 16, 2000, the new Criminal Procedure Code began to govern in two regions of the country, and then extended to the other regions. In this way, a transition was made from an inquisitorial to an adversarial model of justice, and the results have been very positive. Chile now has a more transparent, rational, and effective criminal justice system. In general terms, the human rights violations that have been committed in the last 20 years have been investigated and punished in a timely manner in this new criminal system. The criminal justice system is being put to the test with the 2019 state crackdown, and hopefully it will be able to process the large volume of complaints and investigations underway. The process of modernization of criminal justice has gradually expanded to other types of legal disputes: in 2005, family courts began operating, and in 2008 the new labor justice system was implemented in the country. However, the long-desired but delayed reform of civil justice remains to be implemented, and access to justice for vulnerable sectors needs to be increased.

Public institutions for the protection of human rights have been gradually and slowly consolidated. In order to prosecute the human rights violations of the dictatorship, the Human Rights Programme was created in

1997 in the Ministry of the Interior (Supreme Decree No. 1005). Lawyers in the program worked to uncover the truth and prosecute perpetrators by filing criminal complaints related to serious human rights violations. It was also through this program that much of the state support granted for the recovery of memory sites was channeled, working together with victims' groups and their families. In 2001, the Presidential Advisory Commission for the Protection of People's Rights was created to coordinate and respond to citizens' frustrations and demands in the face of the lack of response from the public administration (Supreme Decree No. 65). This commission may have been the first step toward the creation of the Ombudsman in Chile (Mascareño & Mereminskaya, 2005). In spite of the effort of the professionals who worked in such entities, these institutions faced a significant problem of lack of independence from the government authorities.

This issue proved a major hindrance in the work of governmental human rights institutions until the creation of the National Institute of Human Rights (INDH). After four years of parliamentary discussion, this important institution was constituted in Chile in 2010. It is an autonomous and pluralistic public body in charge of promoting, protecting, and monitoring compliance with legislation and international standards in the field of human rights. Until that time, Chile had not had an institution of this kind, so its creation was a major milestone, through which the country finally embraced the UN Paris Principles on National Human Rights Institutions. The creation of this body, whose board is composed of 11 human rights experts, is a significant step forward in guaranteeing non-repetition. Among the various powers established in Law No. 20,405 (2009), the institute is empowered to bring legal actions in cases of human rights violations (Article 3.5). In addition, it is the body entrusted by law with the task of consolidating a culture of respect for human rights in the country (Article 3.9). According to Law No. 21,154 (2019), the Committee for the Prevention of Torture, initially housed in the National Institute of Human Rights, started working in 2020. The INDH has been instrumental in recording and raising awareness about the human rights abuses of the 2019 *estallido social*, educating the population and protesters about what their rights are and what to do if they are not respected, and helping individuals pursue legal action if they have experienced a violation of their rights. The work done by this institution is essential to Chile's efforts to guarantee non-repetition, and to ensuring that citizens understand how to pursue justice is if their human rights are not respected.

In Chap. 5, we discussed the Museum of Memory and Human Rights, a private foundation that receives public funding, and some of the difficulties in its creation and the criticism it has received from different sectors. Despite these criticisms, the Museum has become a very significant institution in terms of human rights education and promotion. Along with providing valuable information to its visitors about the brutalities of the past, it is an artistic and cultural center used by social movements and academic communities (V. Infante, 2015). Its auditorium and *Plaza de la Memoria* are a permanent amphitheater for commemorative activities. It is also a center for the training and formation of school teachers, providing the tools they need to teach their students about Chile's contemporary history, and its documentation center contributes to the research of Chilean and foreign university students, journalists, and researchers. Therefore, the learning experience of visitors to the Museum has the enormous potential to contribute to the construction and application of a culture of human rights and the narrative of non-repetition of atrocities.

In 2016, the Human Rights Programme was transferred from the Ministry of the Interior to the new Under-Secretariat for Human Rights that had been created under the Ministry of Justice and Human Rights (Law No. 20,885). The Legal Department of the Human Rights Programme works to bring legal proceedings forward for crimes committed during the dictatorship. The Programme also continues to support the recovery and management of sites of memory and symbolic reparation works, among other activities. From an institutional standpoint, the creation of this new Under-Secretariat has strengthened the coordination and systematization of numerous human rights initiatives scattered throughout various public bodies. This was intended to facilitate better coordination of public policies on human rights, in dialogue with the National Human Rights Institute, as well as the various branches of government and international organizations. However, the "social explosion" of 2019 tested the technical and operational capacity of the Under-Secretariat of Human Rights, revealing its lack of leadership in very complex circumstances. Hopefully this experience will provide lessons for the future, so that the Under-Secretariat is more prepared to assume a leading role in the promotion, protection, and defense of citizens' human rights.

Institutional reform within the armed forces and the police is an incredibly important aspect of any transition in which state forces were actively involved in perpetrating human rights abuses. As we have seen throughout this book, the armed forces and the police in Chile were the most significant perpetrators of human rights violations and participated actively in state repression during the dictatorship. Some reforms have been implemented, particularly within the Investigative Police to strengthen the respect of human rights. For almost 30 years, the investigative police have been carrying out the procedures ordered by the courts of justice in order to shed light on human rights violations. The documentary archive it has built up over the course of decades worth of research was recently declared a national historic monument, attesting to the importance of human rights archives (Decree No. 79, Ministry of Education, 2018). In 2004, it created the Human Rights Crimes Investigation Brigade, a highly specialized team that dedicates most of its time to investigating the crimes of the dictatorship (Bonnefoy, 2018). With the reform of criminal procedures, the Investigative Police has been modernized, has better trained professionals, and its budget has increased considerably. It has also raised the standards and controls of the procedures it carries out. Its strategic plan now recognizes that human rights are a cross-cutting value that should guide the work of its detectives and officials.

Despite the passage of three decades, these reforms have evidently not been wide-ranging and expansive enough, and further institutional innovations are urgently required. The excessive level of force deployed by the army and *Carabineros* during the massive demonstrations in the last quarter of 2019 confirms the urgency of introducing substantive reforms in the training processes of the military and police (Human Rights Watch, 2020). It is clear that what has been done until now was not enough to ensure that atrocities were not re-committed. The excessive use of force by the military and the police has worsened a crisis of legitimacy of these institutions in the eyes of the public. To move forward from here, an unflinching look at the problems plaguing these institutions and a commitment to transformative reforms is imperative.

An important aspect of any reform is human rights education, so as to ensure that those who enter the armed, order, and security forces understand and condemn the horrors of the past. There is no room in state institutions for officials who do not have a genuine commitment to the defense of democracy and human rights. The Subsecretariat for Human Rights is responsible for designing and coordinating training and human rights promotion programs in the armed forces and police, but beyond simply providing training programs, human rights education must be a core aspect of all levels of schooling, including primary and secondary school, which any individual seeking to enter the police and armed forces completes. Reforms in terms of institutional regulations around use of force and an independent investigative body to review cases of police abuses are also important aspects to consider.

To move the promotion of human rights forward in a comprehensive way, in 2017, the First National Human Rights Plan was approved. In this plan, the State of Chile has committed itself to adopting concrete measures to respect, protect, and guarantee human rights over a four-year period. The first objective of the plan is "to promote access to the truth, the investigation and punishment of all cases of massive and systematic human rights violations committed under the dictatorship, to ensure reparation for all victims of these crimes, and to preserve historical memory." The state has committed itself to safeguarding the historical heritage of the sites of memory, and promoting a bill and public policies which would improve the currently quite complicated and inconsistent landscape of memorialization. The plan details how the government intends to contribute to community ownership of sites of memory, for example, through the "Routes of Memory" project, which would work to connect and promote various important sites of memory throughout the country and within particular regions.

The second objective of the plan is to "promote and guarantee awareness, education and training in human rights in order to develop a culture of human rights that contributes to the prevention of their violation." The goals are ambitious in the area of education and include curricular reforms to promote the mainstreaming of human rights at all levels of training. The rest of the objectives of the plan refer to other issues not specifically related to transitional justice but which are important for the enforcement of the fundamental rights of migrants and refugees, sexual minorities, indigenous peoples, children and adolescents, etc. The plan includes goals related to police training and improvement of police services to marginalized groups, who experience greater levels of insecurity and violence, under the broader umbrella of police education. In the context of the recent unrest and police brutality, when the plan comes to an end in 2021 and faces an evaluation of its successes and failures, it will be worth spending extra time looking into how to improve the culture of respect of human rights within the police, and why their approach did not prevent widespread abuses, in order for the Second National Human Rights Plan to be more successful.

When contemplating how to further strengthen state institutions in light of the recent unrest, a commitment to creating culture of human rights in all state bodies will require human rights education, but must also be followed up with significant reforms in order to restore the public's confidence in the armed forces and the police and ensure accountability.

7.2 Reform of the Economic Model and the "Subsidiary State"

Naomi Roht-Arriaza argues that to be truly transformative and preventative, guarantees of non-repetition require "getting at root causes, especially economic and social rights violations, and requires a bottom-up analysis of what those root causes are" (2019: 125). In the past, considerations of underlying causes have sometimes been included in the recommendations of truth commission reports, for instance, the recommendations of the South African TRC emphasized economic development and distributive justice. More recently, the 2011 Victims' Law defines guarantees of non-repetition in Colombia and directly included aspects related to addressing underlying causes, explicitly including calls on the state to dismantle the economic and political structures that have led to and support the existence of armed groups (Roht-Arriaza, 2019: 128–129).

In this vein, there is another important institutional reform to consider when thinking about guarantees of non-repetition in Chile, and that is the idea of the "Subsidiary State" which has come about through political discourse and judicial interpretations of Pinochet's 1980 Constitution. "It's not 30 pesos, it's 30 years" is a popular slogan that emerged during the social explosion in October 2019. This slogan referred to the fact that while the protests initially erupted due to an increase in the subway fare by 30 pesos, the protesters' grievances were actually directed at the economic injustices and inequalities that have been left largely unaddressed since the transition to democracy 30 years ago. The key demands of Chileans who took to the streets throughout the last months of 2019 were related to a lack of public spending on social services (E. Sepúlveda, 2020). From the public education system, to public healthcare, to the private pension system, to inadequate minimum wage, protesters have been denouncing the inequalities and injustices generated by the neoliberal economic system imposed during the dictatorship through the principle of the "Subsidiary State," which none of the seven transitional governments took strong, sustained initiative to change over the course of the 30 years of transition (Pizarro Hofer, 2020: 352).

The principle of subsidiarity of the state is not expressly enshrined in the articles of the Constitution (García & Verdugo, 2015); however, the Declaration of Principles of the Military Junta (1974) explains the concept in detail and clearly demonstrates the role of the 1980 Constitution as the culmination of the re-founding mission that the armed forces took upon themselves after the coup of 1973 (Trumper, 2016: 163). Unlike many other countries, whose constitutions establish a social and democratic state, the Chilean Constitution gives the state a subsidiary role (Moyano, 2020: 284): meaning the state does not have the mission to provide or guarantee social services such as health, education, or pensions, instead prioritizing a system in which these services are offered by the private sector in the different markets. The state thus takes on a "subsidiary role" and only intervenes in the markets to resolve social demands when the private sector is unable or unwilling to step in (Allard et al., 2016). As such, the neoliberal model is partially protected within the 1980 Constitution, through its strong protection of property rights and restrictions on how and when the state can create state-owned companies.

Inequality and economic injustice were at the heart of Salvador Allende's controversial election in 1970, and at the heart of the political polarization that ultimately led to the 1973 military coup, but these issues were not addressed or included in transitional justice measures. The imposition of the neoliberal market under the dictatorship led to further economic injustice for many sectors of the population, and the fall of the dictatorship was ultimately precipitated by protests instigated by the economic crisis in 1982. The issue of inequality in Chile therefore has deep roots in the social conflict and turmoil that led to the dictatorship and persisted throughout the 17 years of Pinochet's rule. The institutions imposed by the military regime, in particular the economic model and the 1980 Constitution, have been a source of frustration for many sectors of Chilean society for a long time, and the lack of action on behalf of the *Concertación* and other democratic governments in addressing this issue has led to citizen disillusionment with government: since 1990, voter turnout has plummeted from 86 percent to well below 50 percent in the present (E. Sepúlveda, 2020).

A forward-looking conception of guarantees of non-repetition must consider that the dictatorship's institutional legacy of economic inequality has caused widespread harm to individuals by depriving them of adequate healthcare and education, and maintaining a large segment of the population in economic precarity and relative poverty. This persistent inequality has undermined citizens' faith in government and democracy. The current social movement and the constitutional process that it instigated have created an opportunity for some of the most persistent institutional legacies of the dictatorship finally be put to an end. In response to protesters' calls for a new constitution and better-quality social services, political parties and the government called a referendum on the replacing of the constitution, and on October 25, 2020, the Chilean people voted to replace the constitution through the process of a constituent assembly composed of 155 representatives who will spend a year drafting the new constitution. The elections of its members took place on May 15 and 16, 2021. The recent results confirm the criticism of the traditional parties that have governed during the transition, and citizen distrust of the political class. It is interesting to see the emergence of new social leadership in left and independent sectors, more connected to the real needs of society, and the interest of the majority of voters in moving toward a new, more inclusive and egalitarian social pact.

7.3 Dismantling of Armed Groups

Once democracy was recovered in Chile, the vast majority of the population began to reintegrate themselves into political life and political debate. The 1989 constitutional reform of Article 8 of the Constitution allowed Marxist sectors to participate politically and to run for office. However, during the first years of the transition, some extremist left-wing groups continued to commit terrorist attacks and serious crimes. As Juan Cristóbal Peña states in *Jóvenes Pistoleros: Violencia Política en la Transición*, they continued to "operate armed groups that fought against the dictatorship, just as the security services of the dictatorship, entrenched in the army, continued to operate from the shadows" (2019: 138). In 1987, the Communist Party broke with its armed group, the Manuel Rodríguez Patriotic Front (FPMR), giving rise to the Manuel Rodríguez Patriotic Front-Autonomous (FPMR-A), which continued to pursue the armed way well into the transition. Other groups that committed terrorist acts during those years were the MAPU-Lautaro and the MIR, also extremist left-wing armed groups. Between January 1, 1990, and September 30, 1992, 1775 terrorist or violent acts were committed, an average of 53.8 per month (Coordinating Council for Public Security, 1993: 45).

The acts that caused the greatest public commotion were the assassination of the senator from Santiago, Jaime Guzmán, as he was leaving the constitutional law class he taught at the Catholic University of Chile, and the kidnapping of Cristián Edwards, the son of the owner of *El Mercurio*, who was released after 145 days following a ransom payment of one million dollars. After these events, there was enormous pressure on the Concertación governments from both the right-wing parties and public opinion, for greater citizen security. Carabineros and the Investigative Police were ordered to disband the terrorist groups. The Coordinating Council for Public Security, known as "La Oficina," was created under President Aylwin's government and was charged with intelligence and infiltration work through informants to dismantle the armed groups. Thus, in the 1990s, the police carried out investigations that placed the FPMR-A and Mapu-Lautaro under judicial siege.

When it came to disbanding and dismantling the state's terror groups, however, the situation was far more complicated. The secret police (CNI) was dissolved in 1990, but many of its agents were immediately reincorporated into their respective branches of the armed forces or were hired by them as civil servants. The Aylwin government demanded that Pinochet withdraw a thousand former CNI agents (Cavallo, 1998: 230) from positions in government and the Army, but the former dictator continued to hold a lot of power, and his ongoing influence strained civil-military relations until his arrest in London. The military continued to operate in the shadows, with a worrying degree of autonomy for much of the early transition. This became apparent through a phone tapping scandal in 1993, when the public became aware of systematic telephone tapping carried out by the Army Telecommunications Regiment on the country's political leaders. Captain Fernando Diez took responsibility and the military justice system found him guilty of the crime of non-compliance with military duties. The controversy surrounding the incident shattered the presidential aspirations of the right-wing candidates, Sebastián Piñera and Evelyn Matthei, whose involvement in the scandal delegitimized their candidacies (Otano, 2006 [1995]: 272). This case exemplifies how, in the early years of the transition, "relations between civilian authorities and the military were dysfunctional and undemocratic" (Weeks, 2014: 109). Even as the country was moving toward democracy, former DINA and CNI agents, and some members of the military, continued to commit crimes in secret and with impunity, which was seriously destabilizing for Chile's newly reestablished democratic government.

Over the past decades of the transition, there has actually been very little public discussion about how to reintegrate those who were part of armed and violent groups into society. The result of this has been that in most cases where social reintegration has been possible, it has been done in a silent manner, by hiding past actions to avoid questioning. From time to time, controversy erupts when the past of significant or aspiring political leaders or influential individuals is brought to light. Sometimes "*funas*," public demonstrations to denounce leaders or groups involved in criminal actions, are held against the perpetrators of human rights violations during the dictatorship, especially former army officers who assumed leading roles in the DINA or CNI and who have evaded justice.

The lack of discussion and action surrounding the dismantling of both state and non-state armed extremist groups resulted in a haphazard approach to demobilizing and disbanding these violent entities. The silent reintegration of extremist actors into society without deeper questioning as to how best to do so in a manner that would contribute to social reconstruction and healing has contributed to a culture of polarization and silence around discussing past human rights abuses, because many people fear having their past discovered and therefore prefer not to talk about it. As a result, some former collaborators with the dictatorship, and even perpetrators of human rights abuses, have ended up in positions of influence in important public and private institutions. Combined with the slow course of justice in the early transition, this has amplified a general public sentiment of impunity and lack of justice.

7.4 Vetting

In part due to the lack of discussion about the reintegration of those who were involved in violent groups, the integrity and suitability of public officials continue to be a sensitive issue in Chile. The electoral support that Pinochet received in the 1988 plebiscite plus the authoritarian enclaves in the Constitution created significant restrictions in the early transition. The Concertación governments had to choose between social mobilization and political conflict with the Pinochet movement or seeking consensus with the right-wing parties. In the end, the *Concertación's* strategy was to negotiate with the right and thus gradually advance toward the consolidation of democracy. There is no doubt that the Pinochet movement played an important role in the political debate, at least until Pinochet's death in 2006. In the years of transition, beyond ideological differences and heated political discussions, Chilean politicians had to learn to live together. Supporters and opponents of Pinochet not only sat in the same rooms of the National Congress but also in television studios, public organizations, university classrooms, professional associations, and most social organizations. In Chilean universities, the political leanings of professors and researchers cover the entire ideological spectrum, from the extreme right to the extreme left. It is true that the vast majority of university professors are Democrats, but there are still some who are nostalgic for Pinochet and a few of the Patriotic Front. From time to time, stories from the past come to light and ignite public discussion and controversies surrounding people who adhered both to Pinochet and to the armed path favored by the most radical groups of the Chilean left, particularly when they occupy positions of influence.

Even when individuals are publicly known to have been involved in human rights abuses, and even when action is taken to limit their access to positions of power, they often continue to be employed within the spheres of the armed forces or the police. The list of perpetrators, accomplices, and collaborators who continued to work in state agencies during the transition is enormous. Unfortunately, to this day it has not been possible to remove all public officials who do not believe in and support the promotion of democracy and human rights. In 1998, Miguel Krasnoff, a former brigadier in the armed forces, who is currently one of the individuals holding the most convictions for human rights violations in Chile, was informed that he would not be promoted to General, as the army was seeking to remove some of the most well-known *pinochetistas* from its ranks. Krasnoff retired from the institution but he was later hired as manager of the Military Hotel. He was not convicted for any of the abuses he perpetrated until 2006. More recently, in 2019, 11 former members of the Army were sentenced for the widely publicized "Burnt Case," including Julio Castañer, the young lieutenant who in 1986 lit protesters and activists Rodrigo Rojas de Negri and Carmen Gloria Quintana on fire in the street. Colonel Castañer remained linked to the Army until 2016, and at the time of his arrest he was working as an operations advisor to the Army Division's General Staff. These examples show the reluctance within the armed forces to take conclusive action against perpetrators of human rights violations.

This is an especially relevant issue in the context of the recent unrest and state violence, as the lack of a strong culture of respect for human rights within the armed forces and the police creates an atmosphere of impunity where officers have no sense that they will be held accountable for abusive actions against civilians. Silence pacts and protection networks still persist to a great extent in armed institutions. As long as civil servants who are not committed to fundamental rights continue to work in those institutions, it will continue to be very difficult to make the necessary changes to prevent the continued pattern of repression against citizens, particularly during demonstrations and protests.

In recent years, there has been discussion about the possibility of imposing criminal sanctions against those who deny the atrocities of the dictatorship. A bill was proposed in 2017 to impose criminal sanctions on those who incite violence (Bulletin No. 11424-17). During the parliamentary debate, well-known human rights lawyer and deputy Carmen Hertz put forward a suggestion that denial of crimes against humanity should be included in the bill, and that those who justify, approve, or deny the human rights violations committed during the dictatorship and outlined in the country's various truth commissions should face criminal charges or fines. In January 2020, the Chamber of Deputies generally approved the bill.

In December 2019, a similar bill was submitted to the Senate, seeking to incorporate the crime of denial (*negacionismo*) into the Penal Code (Bulletin No. 13105-06). It remains to be seen whether such an initiative will prosper, although everything suggests that if it is approved by the National Congress, those who oppose it will appeal to the Constitutional Court to have it declared unconstitutional, arguing that it would be a violation of the constitutional guarantee of freedom of expression. Regardless of whether this particular bill is ultimately passed, the widespread state violence in late 2019 makes it abundantly clear that more action must be taken to ensure that political leaders and state officials are committed to human rights protection, and changes must be made to ensure a culture of accountability.

7.5 Toward a Culture of Respect of Human Rights

Chileans' perceptions of the human rights violations committed under the dictatorship are very varied, as the following public opinion polls and surveys will show. The responses to five questions in the Bicentennial Survey of the Pontifical Catholic University of Chile (2013) show just how divided Chilean society is on these topics: for one section of the population, it is important to support initiatives in memory, truth, reparation,

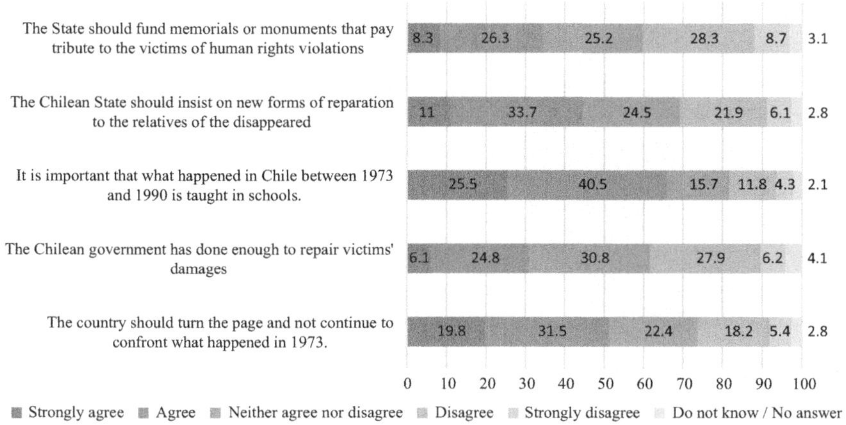

Graph 7.1 Questions on human rights in the 2013 Bicentennial Survey (*N*: 2014. Source: Rojas (2017), based on the Bicentennial Survey)

and justice, while another section considers that these issues are irrelevant and should be overcome. It is also necessary to note that there is a significant section, consistently near a quarter of respondents, which is expressly indifferent or prefers not to give its opinion, as shown in the green segment of the following graph (Graph 7.1).

In the survey *Audit to Democracy*, conducted by UNDP et al. (2010), the majority of respondents confirmed their belief in the importance of truth and justice as a means to deal with the pending issue of human rights in Chile. However, 21 percent were of the opinion that the "problem of human rights" should be overcome, and an additional 8 percent did not know or did not answer the question, "There are different views on how to solve the problem of human rights violations. Of the following positions presented in this card, which one is closer to what you think it would be best for the country?" (Graph 7.2).

In its Public Opinion survey from April to May 1999, the Center for Public Studies (CEP) surveyed whether respondents agreed or not to the idea of "justice to the extent possible," as raised by President Aylwin. When asked if they agreed or not with the idea of doing justice to the extent possible, that is, trying to reconcile justice and peace, 50 percent agreed or strongly agreed, while 15 percent disagreed or strongly

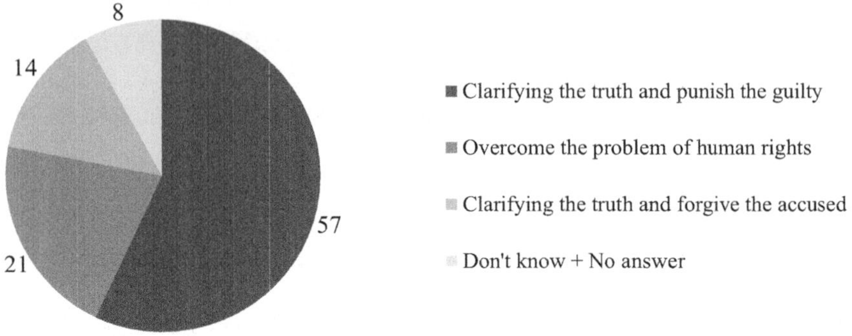

Graph 7.2 How to deal with the problem of Human Rights in Chile (%) (Source: Rojas (2011), based on UNDP et al. 2010)

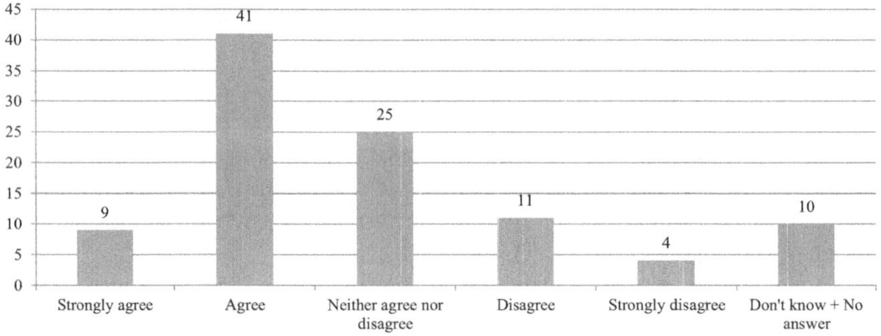

Graph 7.3 Justice to the extent possible (%). (Source: CEP 1999)

disagreed with that statement, but 25 percent answered neither agree nor disagree, and 10 percent did not answer (Graph 7.3).

A few years ago, an important percentage of Chileans estimated that, depending on the circumstances, an authoritarian government could be preferable to a democratic one. Although, in the study *Audit to Democracy* (UNDP et al., 2010), 58 percent of the respondents said that democracy was preferable to any other form of government, the fact that 20 percent of respondents consider that in some circumstances an authoritarian government is preferable is a significant cause for concern. At the time of answering how democratic Chile has been, is, and will be, on a scale of 1

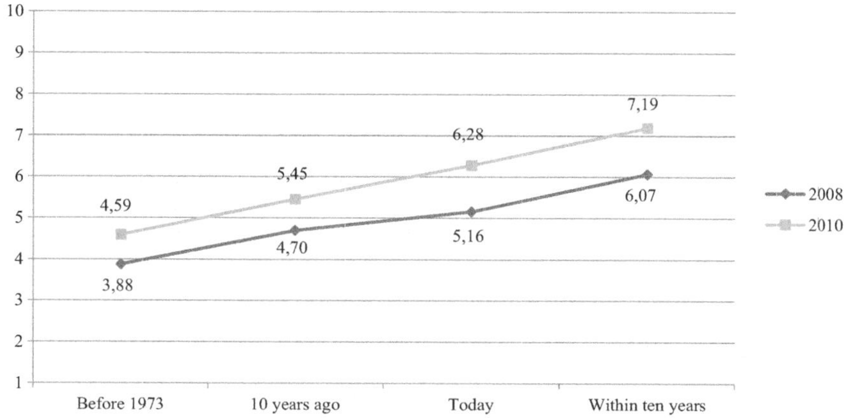

Graph 7.4 How democratic is Chile? (on a scale from 1 to 10) (Source: Rojas (2011), based on the UNDP, et al., 2008 and 2010 surveys)

to 10, with 1 being "not at all democratic" and 10 being "very democratic," the results carried out in 2010 are slightly more optimistic than the ones made in the 2008 survey (Graph 7.4).

These surveys show that some sectors of Chilean society are not sufficiently convinced of the importance of human rights. In some cases, this is due to ideological reasons (extreme right-wing, politically apathetic and indifferent groups), but it is also due to ignorance and lack of knowledge of Chile's recent history. The recent unrest and police brutality show how connected the past is to the present: institutions like the police and the military continue to struggle with overcoming their legacy of repression, which has repercussions on present-day experiences of human rights violations and police brutality. Unfortunately, the latest National Human Rights Survey by the National Institute of Human Rights (2018) missed the opportunity to include questions on human rights violations committed under the dictatorship. All the questions in that survey referred rather to perceptions of the current human rights situation in the country. Hopefully, future versions of this survey will incorporate questions to ascertain the opinions of Chileans regarding past events, as the past and present are very closely connected.

The various surveys and data presented above fit within the pattern that has prevailed throughout the years of transition: human rights violations remain an uncomfortable subject for a sector of the population. This means that improving creating a more open space for discussion around human rights issues is crucial to ensuring that human rights abuses are never perpetrated again.

When seeking to ensure that this time around, the guarantee of non-repetition of human rights violations truly lives up to its slogan "Never Again," government officials, politicians, and human rights activists must work to ensure not only that the remaining institutional legacy of the dictatorship is taken apart, but also that that a special focus is placed on developing a culture of human rights across all levels of Chilean society. Education around the truth about the past and memorialization initiatives are key, as is having an unflinching national conversation about the connections between past and current human rights abuses. It is initiatives which increase the presence, depth, and acceptance of a culture of understanding and promotion of human rights within the Chilean population, alongside strong state institutions, which will ultimately ensure that abuses on such a large scale never occur again.

Bibliography

Allard, R., Hennig, M. C., & Galdámez, L. (2016). El derecho a la salud y su (des) protección en el estado subsidiario. *Estudios Constitucionales, 14*(1), 95–138.

Blanco, R., Hutt, R., & Rojas, H. (2004). Reform to the Criminal Justice System in Chile: Evaluation and Challenges. *Loyola University Chicago International Law Journal, 2*(2), 253–269.

Bonnefoy, P. (2018). *Cazar al cazador. Detectives tras criminales de lesa humanidad.* Debate.

Cavallo, A. (1998). *La Historia Oculta de la Transición.* Grijalbo.

Centro de Estudios Públicos. (1999). Encuesta de Opinión Pública (abril-mayo).

Consejo Coordinador de Seguridad Pública. (1993). *Evaluación de la situación actual del terrorismo en Chile.* Gobierno de Chile.

Duce, M. (2008). La Reforma Procesal Penal en Chile: Logros y Desafíos Período 2000–2007. *URVIO, Revista Latinoamericana de Seguridad Ciudadana, 3*, 67–84.

García, J. F., & Verdugo, S. (2015). Subsidiariedad. Mitos y Realidades en torno a su Teoría y Práctica Constitucional. In P. Ortúzar (Ed.), *Subsidiariedad. Más allá del Estado y del Mercado* (pp. 205–225). Instituto de Estudios para la Sociedad.

Human Rights Watch. (2020). *World Report 2020*, "Chile Events of 2019", available at https://www.hrw.org/world-report/2020/country-chapters/chile.cl

Infante, V. (2015). *Memory Performances at a Memorial Heritage Site: The Case of the Guided Tours at the Museum of Memory and Human Rights in Chile* M.A. thesis in Cultural Heritage Studies, University College London.

Junta Militar. (1974). Declaración de Principios del Gobierno de Chile. *Gobierno de Chile*, available at http://www.elpaisonline.cl/biblioteca/documentos/519-declaracion-de-principios-del-gobierno-de-chile-1973

Mascareño, A., & Mereminskaya, E. (2005). Hacia la Consolidación de la Equidad: Un Defensor del Pueblo para Chile, *Colección de Investigaciones Jurídicas*, Universidad Alberto Hurtado, 7.

Matus, A. (1999). *El Libro Negro de la Justicia Chilena*. Planeta.

Moyano, C. (2020). Los intelectuales de oposición en dictadura: corolario para una reflexión. In C. Moyano & M. Garcés (Eds.), *ONG en dictadura: Conocimiento social, intelectuales y oposición política en el Chile de los ochenta* (pp. 283–291). Ediciones Universidad Alberto Hurtado.

Otano, R. (2006 [1995]). *Nueva crónica de la transición* (2nd ed.). Lom ediciones.

Peña, J. C. (2019). *Jóvenes Pistoleros: Violencia Política en la Transición*. Debate.

Pizarro Hofer, R. (2020). Chile: rebelión contra el Estado subsidiario. *El Trimestre Económico, 87*(346), 333–365.

Roht-Arriaza, N. (2019). Measures of Non-Repetition in Transitional Justice: The Missing Link? In P. Gready & S. Robins (Eds.), *From Transitional to Transformative Justice* (pp. 105–130). Cambridge University Press.

Rojas, H. (2011). *Analysis of the Perceptions of Chileans on Human Rights*. Presentation at The Social and Political Foundations of Constitutions Programme, Foundation for Law, Justice and Society & University of Oxford, Oxford, 8–9 December.

Rojas, H. (2017). *Indifference to Past Human Rights Violations: The Impact of Transitional Justice Success*. Doctoral thesis, University of Oxford.

Sepúlveda, E. (2020). Inequality's Offspring: Why Chile Woke Up. *The Monitor*, available at https://www.policyalternatives.ca/publications/monitor/inequalitys-offspring.

Trumper, C. (2016). *Ephemeral Histories: Public Art, Politics, and the Struggle for the Streets in Chile*. University of California Press.

United Nations Development Programme (UNDP) et al. (2008). *Encuesta Nacional de Auditoría a la Democracia 2008*, available at https://www.estudiospnud.cl/bases-de-datos/encuesta-nacional-de-auditoria-a-la-democracia-2008/

United Nations Development Programme (UNDP) et al. (2010). *Auditoría a la Democracia - Estudio Nacional de Opinión Pública (Sept.-Oct.)*, available at https://www.cepchile.cl/cep/site/docs/20160304/20160304095351/enc_Auditoria-a-la-Democracia_2010.pdf

Weeks, G. (2014). Los militares y los veinte años de la Concertación. In K. Sehnbruch & P. M. Siavelis (Eds.), *El Balance: Política y políticas de la Concertación 1990–2010* (pp. 107–120). Catalonia.

World Justice Project. (2020). *The World Justice Project Rule of Law Index 2020*, available at http://www.worldjusticeproject.org

Final Remarks

The Chilean experience of transitional justice has been one of the best studied cases in the field and is often cited as an example of a successful transition to democracy. The events of October 2019 have demanded a pause and a reevaluation of this perception. Significant progress has been made in Chile over the years, and the recent protests cannot be compared to the systematic policies of state terrorism during the dictatorship; however, the resurgence of state repression has made it clear that repressive tendencies persist in state institutions. This book has sought to outline both the successes and the outstanding gaps of the Chilean transitional justice process in addressing the long-lasting legacy of the dictatorship, in the hopes of providing an opportunity for reflection in Chile and the transitional justice community about the challenges of democratic transitions, and the path forward.

An analysis of the Chilean experience of transitional justice requires an understanding of the historical political processes Chile has gone through from 1964 to date: the "revolution in liberty," "the Chilean road to socialism," and the context in which Chilean society found itself prior to the break from its long democratic tradition. In 1973 the high command of the armed forces and police, urged on by the business elite, conservative political sectors, and the government of the United States, suspended civil and political rights and fiercely repressed the militants and sympathizers of

H. Rojas, M. Shaftoe, *Human Rights and Transitional Justice in Chile*, Memory Politics and Transitional Justice,
https://doi.org/10.1007/978-3-030-81182-2

the left and center-left parties and movements. The Military Junta set out to rebuild the very political foundations of the country, imposing new institutional and economic models without the possibility of citizen deliberation: the 1980 Constitution, the so-called modernization of employment and union laws, regulation of universities, social security, health, privatization of public enterprises, and deregulation of markets, among others. In order to ensure that this neoliberal regulatory framework would endure, the dictatorship's legal and political teams established constitutional obstacles to reform that would be difficult to circumvent once democracy was recovered. Supra-majority quorums were established to approve legal reforms in Congress on matters of utmost social importance, and electoral rules were established that benefited the right-wing and more conservative sectors, which ultimately stalled and quashed many reforms in the post-dictatorship transition.

What has happened in Chile in the 30 years since the transition to democracy has been a complex and unavoidable coexistence between political actors of very different persuasions. The Chilean political scene hosts simultaneously former *pinochetistas* and Pinochet nostalgics, fanatics of neoliberal economic theories, moderate and prudent Social Christians, Social Democrats who yearn for a welfare state and social safety net such as those in many European countries, left-wing revolutionaries (including some obsessed with the Cuban, Venezuelan, or Bolivian experiences), and anarchists. The complexity is increased by the fact that in recent years the percentage of Chileans who are politically apathetic or declare themselves to be politically indifferent has been gradually increasing. The current dispersion of political positions and political-ideological fragmentation makes it very difficult to govern the country. Unless major agreements and cross-cutting alliances between different sectors are reached to promote substantive reforms, Chilean governance structures face a kind of institutional blockage. The lack of broad majorities and consensus slows down or postpones over time the possibilities of introducing the regulatory changes desired by public opinion.

The complicated and fragmented coexistence that emerged and persisted in these 30 years of transition allows us to understand why it has been so difficult to advance not only the agenda of transitional justice but also that of social welfare. The "social eruption" of 2019 must be understood as the explosion of a pressure cooker that had been heating up for the past three decades. A large sector of Chileans simply could not take it anymore and took to the streets to protest against the political-economic model inherited from the dictatorship.

These are Chileans who cannot access the benefits of economic development and growth, and who are deeply in debt and no longer have funds to cover quality education and university payments, and health and housing expenses, or who receive a miserable pension. They are Chileans tired of the abuses of big business, of economic segregation, and of the alarming levels of economic inequality and concentration of wealth. For several weeks, these Chileans protested on the streets in a spontaneous and unorganized expression of anger and discontent, which in some cases manifested itself in vandalism and destruction of public and private property. As if the lessons of the past had not been fully learned and assimilated, the iron fist of state repression reappeared.

In this book, we have shown how the stubborn persistence of the legacy of the dictatorship has left traces which continue to cause important difficulties in Chilean society. We have had to select the information that we consider most relevant to understand the political processes involved. It is impossible to analyze half a century without providing some explanation of the particularities of the transitional justice process in Chile. The examples that we have incorporated in our analysis contribute to the general balance of the progress made and the pending challenges in the search for truth, justice, memory, reparation, and non-repetition in Chile. We offer this account not to focus on the past over the present, but rather with the deep conviction that the future depends largely on a process of collective learning from that stormy past. The levels of social unrest and state repression of 2019 have demonstrated the fragility of democracy and the rule of law in Chile, the consolidation of which can only be achieved when all sectors have engaged in an unwavering commitment to the promotion, protection, and defense of human rights.

Any discussion about how to move forward after systemic human rights violations starts with an honest confrontation of the past. The state-led disinformation and censorship during the 17 years of dictatorship meant that Chileans had limited access to information about much of what had happened during Pinochet's rule. The two official truth commissions, the Rettig Report and the Valech Report, form the main body of official truth-telling initiatives. The Rettig commission's report presented some hard-hitting conclusions, naming state institutions which had been active and complicit in the repression, as well as declaring that there had been no internal war or large-scale armed insurgency and, therefore, that state repression had been illegitimate. The Valech commission's report released over a decade later finally addressed the widespread use of torture during the dictatorship, which had been willfully ignored for years. In many ways, this commission completed the process of official truth-telling, and the conclusions were significant: beyond the Rettig Report's condemnation of state repression as unjustified, the Valech Report declared torture had been a systemic policy of the dictatorship, effectively condemning it as intentional and deliberate violence and not simply isolated excesses by a few rogue officers. These mechanisms, alongside civil society initiatives like academic and journalistic investigations, have greatly contributed to the search for the truth in Chile. However, several significant elements are still pending. The location of many of the disappeared has yet to be established, an issue which is gaining increasing urgency as both family members and perpetrators are aging.

The search for the truth in Chile has been closely tied to its reparations policy, as state-led efforts to redress crimes through reparations were closely linked to the recommendations of the official truth commissions. The Chilean system of reparations has been quite broad, encompassing many different groups of victims, and offering different types of benefits. Hundreds of thousands of victims have benefited from some kind of reparations program, be it the Office for Returning Exiles, monthly pensions, or educational benefits for children, or health benefits through the PRAIS program. The state has most certainly sought to provide reparations for the harms caused, mainly through comprehensive health services and financial support, efforts which have reached many victims. However, there have been some important limitations to reparations policy as well. The lack of follow-through in terms of locating the bodies of the disappeared, which was a part of the government's very first reparations framework, the lack of meaningful reparations for the Mapuche and for rural communities affected by the reversal of land reform, and the lack of significant assessment by the state of the effectiveness of the programs for victims have been some of the main pending issues of Chilean reparations policy. Material reparations and benefits programs make a tangible difference in the everyday lives of victims, but symbolic reparations such as memorials and commemorative initiatives are also essential to wider social recognition of past atrocities.

Due to the lack of a cohesive, collective narrative about human rights violations during the dictatorship, memorializing and commemorating the past continue to be a highly polarizing issue. Over the 30 years of the transition, major progress has been made in creating sites of memory such as the Villa Grimaldi Park for Peace and the Museum of Memory and

Human Rights. Media and culture have also created an important space for memorializing the past and transmitting it to younger generations through films, television series, books, and music. Despite this progress, the difficulties for certain controversial sites to become protected, such as the former torture center Venda Sexy, and the existence of pro-dictatorship memorial sites such as the Jaime Guzmán Memorial, illustrate that conflicting narratives about the past continue to make it complicated for strong legislation regulating sites of memory to be passed. One of the most significant issues with regard to memorialization in Chile is in education andpedagogy. The polarization around discussing human rights violations and the lack of cohesive and collective narrative about the history of the dictatorship have led to a curriculum that is neither effective in supporting teachers in educating students about human rights nor sufficient in terms of conveying the truth about the past to future generations and establishing a culture of respect and promotion of human rights. Improving human rights education and creating a shared memory about the past and its significance are essential to further advancing the discussion around human rights in Chile and advancing their protection.

Unresolved human rights violations do not simply disappear when they go unaddressed, and this is evident in the Chilean experience of the pursuit of justice. Seeking justice has been a long and complex process in Chile. The persistent application of the Amnesty law even many years into the democratic transition protected perpetrators and former agents of the dictatorship from prosecution, and many pro-Pinochet judges remained in the courts. A combination of reforms to the justice system under President Frei, extensive records of human rights violations compiled by civil society organizations during the dictatorship, and the momentum created by Pinochet's arrest in London in 1998 have led to a significant increase in the number of convictions of perpetrators in recent years. There are still pending issues such as the lack of state engagement in holding perpetrators accountable, leaving the onus on victims and their families to advance the pursuit of justice. The necessity for more meaningful state engagement in the search for justice is increased by both the fact that the window for justice is closing as perpetrators and victims are now aging and the recent recurrence of state repression. An important test of the justice system and how well the reforms implemented during the transition have worked will depend on how it handles the large number of cases of police brutality and abuse stemming from the 2019 social unrest.

The progress made in the realms of truth, memory, justice, and reparations has been significant, but it was not enough to prevent human rights violations and state repression from being repeated in October 2019. As part of the guarantee of non-repetition, the Chilean state sought to make changes which would promote a future marked by the protection and respect of human rights by all members of society. Institutional changes were made to the justice system, as well as to incorporate human rights into state agencies, the armed forces and the police. Efforts to reform the police and armed forces may have been stifled by the fact that for a long time little was done to dismantle state related armed groups such as the secret police (DINA and CNI), or remove members who were known perpetrators of human rights abuses from positions of influence, thus perpetuating a culture of state repression within these organizations. In addition, two significant institutional legacies of the dictatorship, the 1980 Constitution and the neoliberal economic system, were left essentially untouched for many years. These institutions have been at the core of the recent unrest. Ultimately, along with the roadblocks in the 1980 Constitution, an aspect that has made institutional change difficult for political leaders has been the lack of a strong culture of human rights in all sectors of Chilean society.

The gaps in the Chilean transitional justice process have highlighted the importance of prioritizing victims' voices and include broad societal participation about what the collective future should look like. Civil society in Chile, particularly victims and their families, have been vocal throughout the transition about their needs and demands and have been the driving force for progress in every element of the transition that we have discussed above. As the country looks to dismantle the remaining legacies of the past, all victims must be centered in a way that prioritizes restoring their dignity, and with it their ability to live fulfilling lives. Chile must seek to create and reform institutions in a way that will guarantee a better future for all members of society, and above all, it is crucial that all sectors of Chilean society work together to develop a culture of human rights to ensure that respect for human rights is guaranteed for future generations.

The events of October 2019 have shown how important it is to understand and address the violent past, as its legacy extends to the present and is long lasting and complex. It is with an eye on both the unresolved problems of the past and a vision for a just future that Chile will continue to move forward. Through the recent results of the October 2020 plebiscite and the May 2021 elections for the Constitutional convention, Chilean society has begun the process of dismantling the two main social structures imposed by the dictatorship and then administered by the governments of the transition: the 1980 Constitution and the neoliberal economic model. It is to be hoped that the discussion in the Constitutional Convention takes place in a peaceful and democratic manner, and that the next Constitution will better represent the vast majority of Chileans. There is still much to be said and heard in Chilean society about the political violence it has experienced in previous decades and more recent times. For example, regarding the work of the Constitutional Convention, nearly 300 hearings were held in August 2021 before the Subcommittee on Historical Truth, Integral Reparation and Guarantees of Non-Repetition of the Human Rights Committee. All these public statements are currently being systematized and analyzed with the support of numerous volunteers, but they need to be socialized in order to provoke larger collective reflections. With the expected approval of a new Constitution—written with gender parity and 17 seats reserved for representatives of indigenous peoples—not only will the transition to democracy come to an end, but the Republic of Chile is likely to be rebuilt from the ground up.

Bibliography

Abrão, P., & Torelly, M. (2011). The Reparations Program as the Lynchpin of Transitional Justice in Brazil. In F. Réategui (Ed.), *Transitional Justice Handbook for Latin America* (pp. 443–485). Brazilian Amnesty Commission, Ministry of Justice/International Center for Transitional Justice.

Aciru, M., Parmentier, S., Saeed, H., & Rauschenbach, M. (2016). Human Rights in Situations of Transitional Justice. In E. Fishwick, M. Marmo, & L. Weber (Eds.), *The Routledge International Handbook of Criminology and Human Rights* (pp. 261–272). Routledge.

Acuña, N. (2018). Prólogo: Por el camino de las series. In J. Mateos-Pérez & G. Ochoa (Eds.), *Chile en las series de televisión: Los 80, Los archivos del Cardenal y El reemplazante* (pp. 9–14). RIL editores.

Agnic, O. (2006). *Pinochet S.A. La base de la fortuna*. RIL editores.

Agüero, I. (2008). *El Diario de Agustín*. Documentary, 80 m.

Ahumada, J. (1958). *En vez de la miseria*. Editorial del Pacífico.

Akhavan, P. (1998). Justice in the Hague, Peace in the Former Yugoslavia? A Commentary on the United Nations War Crimes Tribunal. *Human Rights Quarterly, 20*(4), 737–816.

Albertus, M., & Menaldo, V. (2018). *Authoritarianism and the Elite Origins of Democracy*. Cambridge University Press.

Allard, R., Hennig, M. C., & Galdámez, L. (2016). El derecho a la salud y su (des) protección en el estado subsidiario. *Estudios Constitucionales, 14*(1), 95–138.

H. Rojas, M. Shaftoe, *Human Rights and Transitional Justice in Chile*, Memory Politics and Transitional Justice,
https://doi.org/10.1007/978-3-030-81182-2

Amnesty International. (2008). *Chronology of the Case of Augusto Pinochet*, available at https://www.amnesty.org/download/Documents/52000/amr2200 32008en.pdf

Amnesty International. (2013). *How General Pinochet's Detention Changed the Meaning of Justice*, available at https://www.amnesty.org/en/latest/news/2013/10/how-general-pinochets-detention-changed-meaning-justice/

Amorós, M. (2019). *Pinochet. Biografía militar y política*. Ediciones B.

Ancalao Gavilán, D. (2018). *Violación a los derechos humanos de la nación Mapuche en Chile*. Fundación Instituto de Desarrollo y Liderazgo Indígena, available at https://media.elmostrador.cl/2018/05/392175.pdf

Angell, A. (1971, February). Chile: From Christian Democracy to Marxism? *Current History*: 84–89.

Angell, A. (2009). Chile desde 1958. In L. Bethel (Ed.), *Chile desde la Independencia* (pp. 167–255). Ediciones Universidad Católica Silva Henríquez.

Aranda, G. (2004). *Vicaría de la Solidaridad: Una experiencia sin fronteras*. Ediciones ChileAmérica – CESOC.

Arnoso, M., Cárdenas, M., & Páez, D. (2012). Diferencias intergeneracionales en la mirada hacia el pasado represivo chileno. *Psicología Política, 45*, 7–26.

Atria, F., Larraín, G., Benavente, J. M., Couso, J., & Joignant, A. (2013). *El otro modelo: Del orden neoliberal al regimen de lo público*. Debate.

Aylwin, J. (2000). Los conflictos en el territorio Mapuche: Antecedentes y perspectivas. *Perspectivas, 3*(2), 277–300.

Balasco, L. M. (2017). Reparative Development: Re-Conceptualising Reparations in Transitional Justice Processes. *Conflict, Security & Development, 17*(1), 1–20.

Barahona de Brito, A., González-Enríquez, C., & Aguilar, P. (2001). *The Politics of Memory: Transitional Justice in Democratizing Societies*. Oxford University Press.

Barraza, V. (2018). *El Cine en Chile (2005–2015): Políticas y poéticas del nuevo siglo*. Editorial Cuarto Propio.

Bastías, M. (2013). *Sociedad civil en dictadura: relaciones transnacionales, organizaciones y socialización política en Chile*. Ediciones Universidad Alberto Hurtado.

Becker, N. (2011). *Una mujer en Villa Grimaldi*. Pehuén.

Bellisario, A. (2006). The Chilean Agrarian Transformation: The Pre-Agrarian Reform Period (1955–1965). *Journal of Agrarian Change, 6*(2), 167–204.

Bellisario, A. (2007). The Chilean Agrarian Transformation: Agrarian Reform and Capitalist 'Partial' Counter-Agrarian Reform, 1964–1980. Part 1: Reformism, Socialism and Free-Market Neoliberalism. *Journal of Agrarian Change, 7*(1), 1–34

Bengoa, J. (1988). *Historia Social de la Agricultura Chilena, Vol. I El Poder y la Subordinación*. Ediciones Sur.

Bengoa, J. (2004). *La Memoria Olvidada. Historia de los Pueblos Indígenas de Chile*. Publicaciones del Bicentenario.

Benhabib, S. (2004). *The Rights of Others: Aliens, Residents, and Citizens.* Cambridge University Press.

Bernasconi, O., Gárate, M., Suárez, R., & Mansilla, R. (2019). How to Sustain a Human Rights Organisation Under State Violence. In O. Bernasconi (Ed.), *Political Violence Resistance in Latin America: Documenting Atrocity* (pp. 41–78). Palgrave Macmillan.

Blanco, F. (2010). *Desmemoria y perversión: privatizar lo público, mediatizar lo íntimo, administrar lo privado.* Editorial Cuarto Propio.

Blanco, R., Hutt, R., & Rojas, H. (2004). Reform to the Criminal Justice System in Chile: Evaluation and Challenges. *Loyola University Chicago International Law Journal, 2*(2), 253–269.

Boeninger, E. (2007). *Políticas Públicas en Democracia. Institucionalidad y experiencia chilena, 1990–2006.* Uqbar editores.

Bonnefoy, P. (2018). *Cazar al cazador. Detectives tras criminales de lesa humanidad.* Debate.

Borzutzky, S. (2017). *Human Rights in Chile: The Unfinished Struggle for Truth and Justice.* Palgrave Macmillan.

Brunner, J. J. (1986). De la universidad vigilada a la universidad empresa. La educación superior en Chile. *Nueva Sociedad, 84,* 140–146.

Bucciferro, C. (2012). *For-Get: Identity, Media, and Democracy in Chile.* University Press of America.

Buckley-Zistel, S., & Stanley, R. (2011). *Gender in Transitional Justice.* Palgrave Macmillan.

Byers, M. (2000). The Law and Politics of the Pinochet Case. *Duke Journal of Comparative & International Law, 10*(2), 415–442.

Cardoch, N. (2014, September 11). *Entrevista a Ricardo Brodsky: La importancia de la memoria histórica en educación en Chile.* Facultad de Filosofía y Humanidades de la Universidad de Chile, available at http://www.filosofia.uchile.cl/noticias/105211/la-importancia-de-la-memoria-historica-en-educacion-en-chile

Carlin, R. E. (2006). The Decline of Citizen Participation in Electoral Politics in Post-Authoritarian Chile. *Democratization, 13*(4), 632–651.

Casals, M. (2014). "Chile en la Encrucijada". Anticomunismo y propaganda en la campaña del terror de las elecciones presidenciales 1964. In T. Harmer & A. Riquelme (Eds.), *Chile y la guerra fría global* (pp. 89–111). RIL editores.

Casassus, J. (2013). *Camino en la oscuridad.* Debate.

Case 1254-2011. 34th Criminal Court of Santiago, Judge Mireya López Miranda (*Ministra en Visita de la Corte de Apelaciones de Santiago*).

Cassidy, S. (2002 [1977]). *Audacity to Believe.* Darton, Longman and Todd Ltd.

Castro Valdebenito, H. (2019). *Memoria, Patrimonio y Ciudadanías.* Editorial América en Movimiento.

Cavallo, A. (1998). *La Historia Oculta de la Transición.* Grijalbo.

Centre for Justice and Reconciliation. (2020). *Tutorial: Introduction to Transitional Justice*, available at http://restorativejustice.org/restorative-justice/about-restorative-justice/tutorial-intro-to-restorative-justice/#sthash.p3iSpxiI.3wPsNLdk.dpbs

Centro de Estudios Públicos. (1999). Encuesta de Opinión Pública (abril-mayo).

Colectivo Mujeres Sobrevivientes Siempre Resistentes. (2016). *Comunicado Colectivo Mujeres Sobrevivientes Siempre Resistentes*, available at http://www.laizquierdadiario.cl/Comunicado-Colectivo-de-Mujeres-Sobrevivientes-Siempre-Resistentes-a-la-Opinion-Publica-Nacional-e

Collins, C. (2010a). Human Rights Trials in Chile During and After the Pinochet Years. *International Journal of Transitional Justice, 4*(1), 67–86.

Collins, C. (2010b). *Post-transitional Justice: Human Rights Trials in Chile and El Salvador*. Penn State University Press.

Collins, C. (2013). La política de la justicia: Chile más allá del caso Pinochet. In C. Collins, K. Hite, & A. Joignant (Eds.), *Las Políticas de la Memoria en Chile: Desde Pinochet a Bachelet* (pp. 85–115). Ediciones Universidad Diego Portales.

Collins, C. (2014). Los Derechos Humanos durante la Concertación. In K. Sehnbruch & P. M. Siavelis (Eds.), *El Balance: Política y Políticas de la Concertación 1990–2010* (pp. 143–166). Catalonia.

Collins, C. (2017). Truth-Justice-Reparations Interaction Effects in Transitional Justice Practice: The Case of the 'Valech Commission' in Chile. *Journal of Latin American Studies, 49*(1), 55–82.

Collins, C., Garcia-Godos, J., & Skaar, E. (Eds.). (2016). *Transitional Justice in Latin America: The Uneven Road from Impunity Towards Accountability*. Routledge.

Collins, C., & Hite, K. (2009). Memorial Fragments, Monumental Silences and Reawakenings in 21st-Century Chile. *Millennium, 38*(2), 379–400.

Collins, C., Hite, K., & Joignant, A. (2013). Introduction. In C. Collins, K. Hite, & A. Joignant (Eds.), *Las Políticas de la Memoria en Chile: Desde Pinochet a Bachelet* (pp. 25–54). Ediciones Universidad Diego Portales.

Comisión Nacional de Verdad y Reconciliación. (1991). *Informe Rettig*. Gobierno de Chile.

Comisión Nacional sobre Prisión Política y Tortura. (2005). *Informe de la Comisión Nacional sobre Prisión Política y Tortura*, available at https://bibliotecadigital.indh.cl/handle/123456789/455

Consejo Coordinador de Seguridad Pública. (1993). *Evaluación de la situación actual del terrorismo en Chile*. Gobierno de Chile.

Contraloría General de la República (CGR). (2013). Informe final sobre examen de cuentas relativo a los pagos de pensiones no contributivas a Exonerados Políticos del sector civil efectuados a través del Instituto de Previsión Social, IPS (Informe No. 81-2012).

Contreras, D., & Ffrench-Davis, R. (2012). *Policy Regimes, Inequality, Poverty and Growth: The Chilean Experience, 1973–2010* (WIDER Working Paper No.

4), available at https://www.econstor.eu/dspace/bitstream/10419/81078/1/682723371.pdf

Contreras, G., & Navia, P. (2013). Diferencias generacionales en la participación electoral en Chile, 1988–2010. *Revista de Ciencia Política, 33*(2), 419–441.

Cortés Terzi, A. (2000). *El circuito extrainstitucional del poder*. Ediciones Chileamérica-CESOC.

Crispi, J. (1982). El agro chileno después de 1973: expansión capitalista y campesinización pauperizante. *Revista Mexicana de Sociología, 44*(2), 481–514.

De Greiff, P. (Ed.). (2006). *The Handbook of Reparations*. Oxford University Press.

De Grieff, P., & Duthie, R. (Eds.). (2009). *Transitional Justice and Development: Making Connections*. Social Science Research Council.

de la Parra, M. A. (1997). *La mala memoria*. Planeta.

Del Villar, M. S., Hau, B., Johansson, M. T., & Guerrero, M. (2019). Professions and Profiles: Epistemic Communities and the Registration of Human Rights Violations. In O. Bernasconi (Ed.), *Political Violence Resistance in Latin America: Documenting Atrocity* (pp. 79–115). Palgrave Macmillan.

Delamaza, G. (2016). Sociedad Civil, Ciudadanía y Movimientos Sociales en el Chile de Hoy. In M. A. Garretón (Ed.), *La Gran Ruptura: Institucionalidad política y actores sociales en el Chile del siglo XXI* (pp. 109–131). LOM ediciones.

Dhawan, N. (2011). Transitions to Justice. In S. Buckley-Zistel & R. Stanley (Eds.), *Gender in Transitional Justice* (pp. 264–282). Palgrave Macmillan.

Di Giminiani, P. (2018). *Sentient Lands: Indigeneity, Property, and Political Imagination in Neoliberal Chile*. University of Arizona Press.

Domaradzki, S., Khvostova, M., & Pupovac, D. (2019). Karel Vasak's Generations of Rights and the Contemporary Human Rights Discourse. *Human Rights Review, 20*(4), 423–443.

Donoso, S. (2013). Dynamics of Change in Chile: Explaining the Emergence of the *Pingüino* Movement. *Journal of Latin American Studies, 45*(1), 1–29.

Donoso, S. (2017). "Outsider" and "Insider" Strategies: Chile's Student Movement, 1990–2014. In S. Donoso & M. von Bülow (Eds.), *Social Movements in Chile* (pp. 65–97). Palgrave Macmillan.

Dorfman, A. (2003). *Exorcising Terror: The Incredible Unending Trial of General Augusto Pinochet*. Pluto Press.

Drake, P. W. (2004). Foreword. In P. Winn (Ed.), *Victims of the Chilean Miracle. Workers and Neoliberalism in the Pinochet Era, 1973–2002* (pp. ix–xiii). Duke University Press.

Duce, M. (2008). La Reforma Procesal Penal en Chile: Logros y Desafíos Período 2000–2007. *URVIO, Revista Latinoamericana de Seguridad Ciudadana, 3*, 67–84.

Dugard, J. (1991). The Role of International Law in the Struggle for Liberation in South Africa. *Social Justice, 18*(1/2), 83–94.

Durán, T. et al. (2000). *Muerte y Desaparición Forzada en La Araucanía: Una Aproximación Étnica*, available at http://www.derechos.org/koaga/x/mapuches/

Echeverría, M. (2008). *Krassnoff.* Catalonia.

Elster, J. (2004). *Closing the Books: Transitional Justice in Historical Perspective.* Cambridge University Press (Spanish trans. Elster, J. (2006). *Rendición de cuentas: la justicia transicional en perspectiva histórica.* Katz).

Engel, E., & Navia, P. (2006). *Que gane "el más mejor": Mérito y competencia en el Chile de hoy.* Debate.

Escáriz Oñate, M. (2020). *Regulación de los Sitios de Memoria en el Cono Sur: Análisis Crítico y Propuestas para Chile.* Law thesis, Alberto Hurtado University.

Escudero, M. (2018). Congreso Nacional: Organización y funciones. In C. Huneeus & O. Avendaño (Eds.), *El Sistema Político de Chile* (pp. 119–151). LOM Ediciones.

European Court of Human Rights (ECHR). (2012). *Case of El-Masri v. The Former Yugoslav Republic of Macedonia*, Judgment of December 13, 2012.

European Court of Human Rights (ECHR). (2013). *Case of Janowiec and Others v. Russia*, Judgment of October 21, 2013.

European Court of Human Rights (ECHR). (2014). *O'Keeffe v. Ireland*, Judgment of January 28, 2014.

Evans, R. (2006). Pinochet in London: Pinochet in Chile: International and Domestic Politics in Human Rights Policy. *Human Rights Quarterly, 28*(1), 207–244.

Fermandois, J. (2013). *La revolución inconclusa. La izquierda chilena y el gobierno de la Unidad Popular.* Centro de Estudios Públicos.

Ferrara, A. (2015). *Assessing the Long-term Impact of Truth Commissions: The Chilean Truth and Reconciliation Commission in Historical Perspective.* Routledge.

Ferrara, A. (2017). El Largo Camino a la Verdad en Chile. Una Perspectiva Histórica. In R. Jimeno (Ed.), *Justicia Transicional: Historia y Actualidad* (pp. 213–239). Thomson Reuters Aranzadi.

Ferro, M. (1988). *Cinema and History.* Wayne State University Press.

Foxley, A. (1982). Experimentos Neoliberales en América Latina. *Colección Estudios CIEPLAN*, 7.

Friedman, J., & Hofman, A. (2013). *Inequality and the Top of the Income Distribution in Chile 1990–2012: Questioning the Consensus*, available at https://doi.org/10.2139/ssrn.2242259

Fuentes, C. (2012). *El Pacto: Poder, Constitución y Prácticas Políticas en Chile (1990–2010).* Ediciones Universidad Diego Portales.

Fuentes, C. (2013). *El Fraude.* Hueders.

Gárate, M. (2013). *La Revolución Capitalista de Chile 1973–2003.* Ediciones Universidad Alberto Hurtado.

García, A. (2011). *La muerte lenta de los desaparecidos en Chile.* Editorial Cuarto Propio.

García, J. F., & Verdugo, S. (2015). Subsidiariedad. Mitos y Realidades en torno a su Teoría y Práctica Constitucional. In P. Ortúzar (Ed.), *Subsidiariedad. Más allá del Estado y del Mercado* (pp. 205–225). Instituto de Estudios para la Sociedad.

Garretón, M.A. (1989). La Posibilidad Democrática en Chile. *Cuadernos de Difusión*, FLACSO-Chile.

Gazmuri, R. (2013). *La construcción ideológica del curriculum chileno en historia y ciencias sociales.* Doctoral thesis, Universidad Autónoma de Barcelona.

Gill, L. (2005). *Escuela de las Américas: Entrenamiento militar, violencia política e impunidad en las Américas.* Lom ediciones.

Gobierno de Chile. (2017). *Primer Plan Nacional de Derechos Humanos*, available at https://planderechoshumanos.gob.cl

Goicovic Donoso, I. (2015). Campos conceptuales, perspectivas de análisis y ciclos históricos en el estudio del movimiento Mapuche. In J. Pinto (Ed.), *Conflictos étnicos, sociales y económicos: Araucanía 1900–2014* (pp. 19–44). Pehuén.

Gómez, F. (2006). El derecho de las víctimas a la reparación por violaciones graves y sistemáticas de los derechos humanos. In F. Gómez (Ed.), *El derecho a la memoria* (pp. 23–75). Instituto de Derechos Humanos Pedro Arrupe de la Universidad de Deusto.

Gómez-Barris, M. (2009). *Where Memory Dwells: Culture and State Violence in Chile.* University of California Press.

Gómez-Barris, M. (2010). Witness Citizenship: The Place of Villa Grimaldi in Chilean Memory. *Sociological Forum, 25*(1), 27–46.

Gómez-Barris, M. (2015). Mapuche Mnemonics: Beyond Modernity's Violence. *Memory Studies, 8*(1), 75–85.

Góngora, M. (1988). *Ensayo histórico sobre la noción de estado en Chile en los siglos XIX y XX.* Editorial Universitaria.

González, M. (2013). *La Conjura: Los mil y un días del golpe* (2nd ed.). Catalonia.

Gready, P., & Robins, S. (Eds.). (2019). *From Transitional to Transformative Justice.* Cambridge University Press.

Grupo de Investigaciones Agrarias de la Academia de Humanismo Cristiano. (1979). Tenencia de la tierra en Chile. *Cuadernillo de Información Agraria*, 1.

Guembe, J. (2006). Economic Reparations for Grave Human Rights Violations. In P. De Greiff (Ed.), *The Handbook of Reparations* (pp. 22–51). Oxford University Press.

Gustafson, K. (2007). *Hostile Intent: U.S. Covert Operations in Chile, 1964–1974.* Potomac Books Inc.

Guzmán, J. (2005). *En el Borde del Mundo: Memorias del Juez que Procesó a Pinochet.* Editorial Anagrama.

Guzmán, N. (2014). *Ingrid Olderock, La mujer de los perros.* Ceibo Ediciones.

Halbwachs, M. (1950). *La mémoire collective*. Presses Universitaires de France.
Halbwachs, M. (1994 [1925]). *Les cadres sociaux de la mémoire*. Albin Michel.
Harmer, T. (2013). *El gobierno de Allende y la Guerra Fría interamericana*. Ediciones Universidad Diego Portales.
Harvey, D. (2007). *A Brief History of Neoliberalism*. Oxford University Press.
Haslam, J. (2005). *The Nixon Administration and the Death of Allende's Chile*. Verso.
Hau, B., Lessa, F., & Rojas, H. (2019). Registration of State Violence as Judicial Evidence in Human Rights Trials. In O. Bernasconi (Ed.), *Political Violence Resistance in Latin America: Documenting Atrocity* (pp. 197–228). Palgrave Macmillan.
Hayner, P. (2011). *Unspeakable Truths: Transitional Justice and the Challenge of Truth Commissions* (2nd ed.). Routledge.
Hidalgo, P. (2011). *El Ciclo Político de la Concertación (1990–2010)*. Uqbar editores.
Hilbink, L. (2014). *Jueces y política en democracia y dictadura: Lecciones desde Chile*. Facultad Lationamericana de Ciencias Sociales, sede México.
Hite, K. (2000). *When the Romance Ended: Leaders of the Chilean Left, 1968–1998*. Columbia University Press.
Hite, K. (2013). *Política y arte de la conmemoración. Memoriales en América Latina y España*. Mandrágora Ediciones.
Hite, K., & Collins, C. (2009). Memorial Fragments, Monumental Silences and Reawakenings in 21st-Century Chile. *Millennium: Journal of International Studies, 38*(2), 379–400.
Hojman, D. E. (1996). Poverty and Inequality in Chile: Are Democratic Politics and Neoliberal Economics Good for You? *Journal of Interamerican Studies and World Affairs, 38*(2/3), 73–96.
Human Rights Watch. (2020). *World Report 2020*, "Chile Events of 2019", available at https://www.hrw.org/world-report/2020/country-chapters/chile.cl
Huneeus, C. (2000). *El Régimen de Pinochet*. Editorial Sudamericana.
Huneeus, C. (2003). *Chile, Un País Dividido. La Actualidad del Pasado*. Catalonia.
Huneeus, C. (2014). *La democracia semisoberana. Chile después de Pinochet*. Taurus.
Infante, S. (2015). *Del discurso al aula: recontextualización de textos escolares en materia de Dictadura militar y derechos humanos para sexto año básico en Chile*. Museo de la Memoria y los Derechos Humanos.
Infante, V. (2015). *Memory Performances at a Memorial Heritage Site: The Case of the Guided Tours at the Museum of Memory and Human Rights in Chile*. M.A. thesis in Cultural Heritage Studies, University College London.
Instituto de Políticas Públicas en Derechos Humanos del Mercosur (IPPDH). (2012). *Principios fundamentales para las políticas públicas en materia de sitios de memoria*, available at https://www.ippdh.mercosur.int/principios-fundamentales-para-las-politicas-publicas-en-materia-de-sitios-de-memoria

Instituto de Previsión Social (2021). *Leyes de reparación*, available at https://nuevo.ips.gob.cl/servlet/internet/inicio/beneficios-y-pensiones/leyes-de-reparacion

Instituto Nacional de Derechos Humanos (INDH). (2018). *Encuesta Nacional de Derechos Humanos*, available at http:www.indh.cl

Instituto Nacional de Derechos Humanos (INDH). (2020). *Acciones Judiciales Reporte 19 de marzo de 2020*, available at https://www.indh.cl/archivo-de-reportes-de-estadisticas/

Inter-American Commission on Human Rights (IACHR). (2014). *The Right to the Truth in the Americas*, available at https://www.oas.org/en/iachr/reports/pdfs/Right-to-Truth-en.pdf

Inter-American Court of Human Rights (IACtHR). (1997). *Case Loayza Tamayo v. Peru*, Judgment of September 17, 1997.

Inter-American Court of Human Rights (IACtHR). (2001). *Case Barrios Altos v. Peru*. Merits, Judgment of March 14, 2001.

Inter-American Court of Human Rights (IACtHR). (2003). *Case of Bulacio v. Argentina*. Judgment of September 18, 2003.

Inter-American Court of Human Rights (IACtHR). (2004). *Case of Plan de Sánchez Massacre v. Guatemala*.

Inter-American Court of Human Rights (IACtHR). (2006a). *Case of Almonacid Arellano et al. v. Chile*, Judgment of September 26, 2006.

Inter-American Court of Human Rights (IACtHR). (2006b). *Case of La Cantuta v. Peru*. Merits, Reparation and Costs. Judgment of November 29, 2006.

Inter-American Court of Human Rights (IACtHR). (2006c). *Case Claude Reyes et al. v. Chile*. Merits, Reparations and Costs, Judgment of September 19, 2006.

Inter-American Court of Human Rights (IACtHR). (2009). *Case of the "Las Dos Erres" Massacre v. Guatemala*. Preliminary Objection, Merits, Reparations, and Costs, Judgment of November 24, 2009.

International Center for Transitional Justice (ICTJ). (2018). *What Is Transitional Justice?* available at https://www.ictj.org/about/transitional-justice

International Committee of the Red Cross (ICRC). (1977), *Protocol Additional to the Geneva Conventions of 12 August 1949, and relating to the Protection of Victims of International Armed Conflicts (Protocol I)*, 8 June 1977, 1125 UNTS 3, available at https://www.refworld.org/docid/3ae6b36b4.html

Jadresic, E., & Zahler, R. (2000). *Chile's Rapid Growth in the 1990s-Good Policies, Good Luck, or Political Change?*. IMF Working Paper No. 00/153. Available at: https://www.imf.org/en/Publications/WP/Issues/2016/12/30/Chile-s-Rapid-Growth-in-the-1990-s-Good-Policies-Good-Luck-or-Political-Change-3789

Jara, D. (2013). *The Aftermath of Political Violence: The Opposition's Second Generation in the Post-Coup Chile and Its Familial Memory*. Ph.D. thesis in Sociology, University of London – Goldsmiths.

Jara, D., Badilla, M., Figueiredo, A., Cornejo, M., & Riveros, V. (2018). Tracing Mapuche Exclusion from Post-Dictatorial Truth Commissions in Chile: Official and Grassroots Initiatives. *International Journal of Transitional Justice, 12*(3), 479–498.

Jelin, E. (2002). *Los Trabajos de la Memoria*. Siglo XXI.

Jocelyn-Holt, A. (1998). *El Chile Perplejo: Del avanzar sin transar al transar sin parar*. Planeta.

Johnstone, G. (2013). *A Restorative Justice Reader*. Routledge.

Joignant, A. (2002). La democracia de la indiferencia. Despolitización, desencanto y malestar en el gobierno de Eduardo Frei Ruiz-Tagle. In O. Muñoz & C. Stefoni (Eds.), *El Periodo del Presidente Frei Ruiz-Tagle* (pp. 83–106). FLACSO-Chile & Editorial Universitaria.

Joinet, L. (1997). *The Administration of Justice and the Human Rights of Detainees. Question of the Impunity of Perpetrators of Human Rights Violations (Civil and Political)*. Commission on Human Rights, Sub-Commission on Prevention of Discrimination and Protection of Minorities, 49th Session, available at https://undocs.org/E/CN.4/Sub.2/1997/20/Rev.1

Junta Militar. (1974). Declaración de Principios del Gobierno de Chile. *Gobierno de Chile*, available at http://www.elpaisonline.cl/biblioteca/documentos/519-declaracion-de-principios-del-gobierno-de-chile-1973

Kay, C. (2000). Latin America's Agrarian Transformation: Peasantization and Proletarianization. In D. Bryceson, C. Kay, & J. Mooij (Eds.), *Disappearing Peasantries? Rural Labour in Africa, Asia and Latin America* (pp. 123–138). Intermediate Technology Publications.

Kim, H. J., & Sikkink, K. (2012–2013). How Do Human Rights Prosecutions Improve Human Rights After Transition? *Interdisciplinary Journal of Human Rights Law, 7*(1), 69–90.

Koh, H. (1999). How Is International Human Rights Law Enforced? *Indiana Law Journal, 74*(4), 1397–1418.

Kornbluh, P. (2003). *Los EEUU y el Derrocamiento de Allende. Una historia desclasificada*. Ediciones B.

Kornbluh, P. (2004). *Pinochet. Los archivos secretos*. Ed. Crítica.

Kritz, N. (1995). *Transitional Justice: How Emerging Democracies Reckon with Former Regimes*. United States Institute of Peace.

Kunstmann, W., & Torres, V. (Eds.). (2008). *Cien Voces Rompen el Silencio: Testimonios de Ex-Presos Politicos de la Dictadura Militar en Chile 1973–1990*. Dirección de Bibliotecas, Archivos y Museos.

Kurth, J. (2005). Humanitarian Intervention After the War in Iraq: Legal Ideals Vs Military Realities. *Orbis, 50*, 87–101.

Lagos, R. (1961). *La concentración del poder económico*. Editorial del Pacífico.

Lagos, R. (2012). *The Southern Tiger: Chile's Fight for a Democracy and a Prosperous Future*. Palgrave Macmillan.

Lagos, R. (2013). *Mi vida. De la infancia a la lucha contra la dictadura*. Debate.
Laplante, L. J. (2009). Outlawing Amnesty: The Return of Criminal Justice in Transitional Justice Schemes. *Virginia Journal of International Law, 49*, 916–944.
Larrañaga, O., & Rodríguez, M. E. (2014). Desigualdad de Ingresos y Pobreza en Chile 1990 a 2013. *Documento de Trabajo*, UNDP – Chile, available at http://www.cl.undp.org/content/dam/chile/docs/pobreza/undp_cl_pobreza_cap_7_desiguypob.pdf
Lavín, J. (1987). *Chile: Revolución silenciosa*. Zig-Zag.
Lazzara, M. J. (2006). *Chile in Transition. The Poetics and Politics of Memory*. University of Press of Florida.
Lechner, N. (1998). Modernización y Democratización: Un dilema del desarrollo chileno. *Estudios Públicos, 70*, 231–242.
Lessa, F. (2013). *Memory and Transitional Justice in Argentina and Uruguay: Against Impunity*. Palgrave Macmillan.
Lessa, F. (2019). Operation Condor on Trial: Justice for Transnational Human Rights Crimes in South America. *Journal of Latin American Studies, 51*(2), 409–439.
Lie, T., Binningsbø, H., & Gates, S. (2007). *Post-Conflict Justice and Sustainable Peace* (Policy Research Working Paper No. 4191). World Bank.
Lira, E. (2005). Mesa de Diálogo de Derechos Humanos. In E. Lira & G. Morales (Eds.), *Derechos humanos y reparación: una discusión pendiente* (pp. 152–164). Lom ediciones.
Lira, E. (2006). The Reparations Policy for Human Rights Violations in Chile. In P. de Greiff (Ed.), *The Handbook of Reparations* (pp. 55–99). Oxford University Press.
Lira, E. (2010). Trauma, duelo, reparación y memoria. *Revista de Estudios Sociales, 36*, 14–28.
Lira, E. (2016). Reflections on Rehabilitation as a Form of Reparation in Chile after Pinochet's Dictatorship. *International Human Rights Law Review, 5*(2), 194–216.
Lira, E., & Castillo, M. I. (1991). *Psicología de la amenaza política y del miedo*. Instituto Latinoamericano de Salud Mental y Derechos Humanos.
Lira, E., & Loveman, B. (2013). Torture as Public Policy. In C. Collins, K. Hite, & A. Joignant (Eds.), *The Politics of Memory in Chile from Pinochet to Bachelet* (pp. 91–132). First Forum Press.
Lira, E., & Loveman, B. (2014). *Poder Judicial y Conflictos Políticos (Chile: 1925–1958)*. Lom ediciones.
Lira, E., & Rojas, H. (Eds.). (2009). *Libertad Sindical y Derechos Humanos: Análisis de los Informes del Comité de Libertad Sindical de la OIT (1973–1990)*. Lom ediciones.

Londres 38. (2014). *Es Necesario Impedir la "Impunidad Biologica" en Crímenes de Lesa Humanidad*, available at https://www.londres38.cl/1937/w3-article-95526.html

López, L. (2018). *"A mí no me pasó". Memorias del miedo en personas que no fueron víctimas de violaciones a los derechos humanos en la dictadura cívico-militar chilena (1973–1990)*. Ph.D. thesis in Social Sciences, University of Chile.

López, L., & Hevia, E. (2016). Archivo oral de Villa Grimaldi: experiencia y reflexiones. In M. G. Acuña et al. (Eds.), *Archivos y memoria de la represión en América Latina (1973–1990)* (pp. 107–129). Lom Ediciones.

Loveman, B., & Lira, E. (2000). *Las ardientes cenizas del olvido: Vía chilena de Reconciliación Política 1932–1994.* Lom Ediciones.

Loveman, B., & Lira, E. (2021). *Los campesinos "exonerados de la tierra". Leyes y políticas de reparación y clientelismo político en Chile.* Der Ediciones.

Macdonald, M. (1947). Natural Rights. *Proceedings of the Aristotelian Society, 47*, 225–250.

Macdonald, A. (2013). *Local Understandings and Experiences of Transitional Justice: A Review of the Evidence* (JSRP Paper No. 6). The Justice and Security Research Programme, London School of Economics, available at http://eprints.lse.ac.uk/56354/1/JSRP_Paper6_Local_understandings_and_experiences_of_transitional_justice_Macdonald_2013.pdf

Maddison, S., & Shepherd, L. (2014). Peacebuilding and the Postcolonial Politics of Transitional Justice. *Peacebuilding, 2*(3), 253–269.

Madikida, C., Segal, L., & van den Berg, C. (2008). The Reconstruction of Memory at Constitution Hill. *The Public Historian, 30*(1), 17–25.

Magasich, J. (2020a). *Historia de la Unidad Popular* (Tiempos de preparación: de los orígenes al 3 de septiembre de 1970) (Vol. 1). Lom ediciones.

Magasich, J. (2020b). *Historia de la Unidad Popular* (De la elección a la asunción: los álgidos 60 días del 4 de septiembre al 3 de noviembre de 1970) (Vol. 2). Lom ediciones.

Magendzo, A., & Toledo, M. I. (2009). Educación en Derechos Humanos: Curriculum Historia y Ciencias Sociales del 2° Año de Enseñanza Media. Subunidad "Régimen Militar y Transición a la Democracia". *Estudios Pedagógicos, 35*(1), 139–154.

Mascareño, A., & Mereminskaya, E. (2005). Hacia la Consolidación de la Equidad: Un Defensor del Pueblo para Chile, *Colección de Investigaciones Jurídicas*, Universidad Alberto Hurtado, 7.

Matamala, D. (2015). *Poderoso caballero: El peso del dinero en la política chilena.* Catalonia.

Mateos-Pérez, J., & Ochoa, G. (2018). *Chile en las series de televisión. Los 80, Los Archivos del Cardenal y El Reemplazante.* RIL Editores.

Matus, A. (1999). *El Libro Negro de la Justicia Chilena.* Planeta.

Matus, J. (2020, July 18). Fiscalía cifra en 8.827 las víctimas de violencia institucional en la crisis. *La Tercera*, p. 19.

Mayol, A. (2012). *El Derrumbe del Modelo. La crisis de la economía de mercado en el Chile contemporáneo*. Lom ediciones.

McAdams, A. (2011). Transitional Justice: The Issue that Won't Go Away. *International Journal of Transitional Justice, 5*(2), 304–312.

Mendelof, D. (2004). Truth-Seeking, Truth-Telling, and Postconflict Peacebuilding: Curb the Enthusiasm? *International Studies Review, 6*(3), 355–380.

Mendieta, E. (2007). *Global Fragments: Latinamericanisms, Globalizations, and Critical Theory*. State University of New York Press.

Miller, Z. (2008). Effects of Invisibility: In Search of the 'Economic' in Transitional Justice. *The International Journal of Transitional Justice, 2*, 266–291.

Ministerio de Desarrollo Social. (2013). *CASEN 2013. Encuesta de Caracterización Socioeconómica Nacional*, available at http://observatorio.ministeriodesarrollosocial.gob.cl/casen-multidimensional/casen/casen_2013.php

Montealegre, J. (2003). *Frazadas del Estadio Nacional*. Lom ediciones.

Moulian, T. (2002 [1997]). *Chile Actual: Anatomía de un Mito* (3rd ed.). Lom Ediciones.

Moyano, C. (2020). Los intelectuales de oposición en dictadura: corolario para una reflexión. In C. Moyano & M. Garcés (Eds.), *ONG en dictadura: Conocimiento social, intelectuales y oposición política en el Chile de los ochenta* (pp. 283–291). Ediciones Universidad Alberto Hurtado.

Moyn, S. (2010). *The Last Utopia: Human Rights in History*. Belknap Press of Harvard University Press.

Moyn, S. (2018). *Not Enough: Human Rights in an Unequal World*. Available at ProQuest Ebook Central, https://ebookcentral.proquest.com

Museo de la Memoria y los Derechos Humanos. (2014). *Memoria Anual del Museo de la Memoria y los Derechos Humanos*, available at https://ww3.museodelamemoria.cl/wp-content/files_mf/1460129457MEMORIA2014.pdf

Mutua, M. (2001). Savages, Victims, and Saviors: The Metaphor of Human Rights. *Harvard International Law Journal, 42*(1), 201–245.

Nagy, R. (2008). Transitional Justice as Global Project: Critical Reflections. *Third World Quarterly, 29*(2), 275–289.

Nash, K. (2015). *Political Sociology of Human Rights*. Cambridge University Press.

Navia, P. (2004). Participación electoral en Chile, 1988–2001. *Revista de Ciencia Política, 24*(1), 81–103.

Nino, C. (1996). *Radical Evil on Trial*. Yale University Press.

Nora, P. (Ed.). (1996). *Realms of Memory. The Construction of the French Past* (Conflicts and Divisions) (Vol. I). Columbia University Press.

Novoa, E. (1992). *Los Resquicios Legales*. Ediciones Bat.

O'Shaughnessy, H. (2000). *Pinochet: The Politics of Torture*. New York University Press.

Ochoa, G., & Maillard, C. (2011). *La Persistencia de la Memoria: Londres 38, un espacio de memorias en construcción*. Londres 38, espacio de memorias.

OECD. (2014). *Society at a Glance 2014: OECD Social Indicators*, available at https://doi.org/10.1787/soc_glance-2014-en

OECD. (2017). *How's Life? 2017: Measuring Well-Being*. OECD Publishing, available at https://doi.org.proxy.bib.uottawa.ca/10.1787/how_life-2017-en

Office of the High Commissioner of Human Rights, OHCHR. (2015). *International Human Rights Law*, available at www.ohchr.org/en/professionalinterest/pages/internationallaw.aspx

Office of the High Commissioner of Human Rights, OHCHR. (2019). *Informe sobre la Misión a Chile, 30 de octubre – 22 de noviembre de 2019*, available at https://www.ohchr.org/Documents/Countries/CL/Report_Chile_2019_SP.pdf

Olsen, T., Payne, L., & Reiter, A. (2010a). *Transitional Justice in Balance: Comparing Processes, Weighing Efficacy*. United States Institute of Peace.

Olsen, T., Payne, L., & Reiter, A. (2010b). The Justice Balance: When Transitional Justice Improves Human Rights and Democracy. *Human Rights Quarterly, 32*(4), 980–1007.

Olsen, T., Payne, L., & Reiter, A. (2010c). Transitional Justice in the World, 1970–2007: Insights from a New Dataset. *Journal of Peace Research, 47*(6), 803–809.

Orellana, M. E. (2002). *Allende. Alma en Pena*. Editorial Cuatro Vientos.

Orentlicher, D. F. (1991). *Report of the Independent Expert to Update the Set of Principles to Combat Impunity*. UN Economic and Social Council.

Otano, R. (2006 [1995]). *Nueva crónica de la transición* (2nd ed.). Lom ediciones.

Oteíza, T. (2009). De "la conspiración de silencio" al reconocimiento de voces alternativas. Las violaciones a los derechos humanos en Chile según el Informe Valech (2003). *Revista Latinoamericana de Estudios del Discurso, 9*(1), 87–111.

Park, G. (2010). Truth as Justice: Legal and Extralegal Development of the Right to Truth. *Harvard International Review, 31*(4), 24–27.

Passmore, L. (2017). *The Wars Inside Chile's Barracks: Remembering Military Service Under Pinochet*. University of Wisconsin Press.

Payne, L. (2008). *Unsettling Accounts: Neither Truth nor Reconciliation in Confessions of State Violence*. Duke University Press.

Peña, J. C. (2007). *Los Fusileros: Crónica secreta de una guerrilla en Chile*. Debate.

Peña, J. C. (2019). *Jóvenes Pistoleros: Violencia Política en la Transición*. Debate.

Peñaloza, C. (2015). *El Camino de la Memoria. De la Represión a la Justicia en Chile, 1973–2013*. Editorial Cuarto Propio.

Peris Blanes, J. (2005). *La imposible voz: Memoria y representación de los campos de concentración en Chile: la posición del testigo*. Cuarto Propio.

Pigrau Solé, A. (2000). The Pinochet Case in Spain. *ILSA Journal of International & Comparative Law, 6*(3), 653–683.

Pino-Ojeda, W. (2011). *Noche y niebla: neoliberalismo, memoria y trauma en el Chile postautoritario*. Editorial Cuarto Propio.

Piper, I. (2005). *Obstinaciones de la Memoria: La dictadura militar chilena en las tramas del recuerdo*. Ph.D. thesis, Universitat Autònoma de Barcelona.

Pizarro Hofer, R. (2020). Chile: rebelión contra el Estado subsidiario. *El Trimestre Económico, 87*(346), 333–365.

Policzer, P. (2009). *The Rise and Fall of Repression in Chile*. University of Notre Dame Press.

Pontificia Universidad Católica de Chile & Adimark-GfK. (2013). *Encuesta Nacional Bicentenario 2013*, available at http://encuestabicentenario.uc.cl/resultados/

Presidential Advisory Commission for the Qualification of Disappeared Detainees, Political Executed, and Victims of Political Imprisonment and Torture. (2011). *Final Report*. Santiago (in Spanish).

Ramji-Nogales, J. (2010). Designing Bespoke Transitional Justice: A Pluralist Process Approach. *Michigan Journal of International Law, 32*(1), 1–72.

Rensmann, L. (2017). Critical Theory of Human Rights. In M. Thompson (Ed.), *The Palgrave Handbook of Critical Theory* (Political Philosophy and Public Purpose) (pp. 631–653). Palgrave Macmillan.

Richards, P. (2016). *Racismo: el modelo chileno y el multiculturalismo neoliberal bajo la Concertación, 1990–2010*. Pehuén.

Riquelme, A. (2014). La Guerra Fría en Chile: Los intricados nexos entre lo nacional y lo global. In T. Harmer & A. Riquelme (Eds.), *Chile y la guerra fría global* (pp. 11–43). RIL editores.

Roht-Arriaza, N. (1990). State Responsibility to Investigate and Prosecute Grave Human Rights Violations in International Law. *California Law Review, 78*(2), 449–513.

Roht-Arriaza, N. (2019). Measures of Non-Repetition in Transitional Justice: The Missing Link? In P. Gready & S. Robins (Eds.), *From Transitional to Transformative Justice* (pp. 105–130). Cambridge University Press.

Rojas Baeza, P. (2004). Romper el silencio. In P. Verdugo (Ed.), *De la tortura no se habla: Agüero versus Meneses* (pp. 161–180). Catalonia.

Rojas, F. (2001). La Detención del General Pinochet: Notas para su interpretación y evaluación del impacto en el sistema político chileno. In F. Rojas & C. Stefoni (Eds.), *El "caso Pinochet": Visiones hemisféricas de su detención en Londres* (pp. 21–39). FLACSO-Chile.

Rojas, H. (2011). *Analysis of the Perceptions of Chileans on Human Rights*. Presentation at The Social and Political Foundations of Constitutions Programme, Foundation for Law, Justice and Society & University of Oxford, 8–9 December.

Rojas, H. (2012). Torture in Chile (1973–1990): Analysis of One Hundred Survivors' Testimonies. *California Western International Law Journal, 42*, 353–392.

Rojas, H. (2015). Biopolitics and Homo Sacer in a Torture Center in Chile. *Revista Direito GV São Paulo, 11*(1), 257–276.

Rojas, H. (2017). *Indifference to Past Human Rights Violations: The Impact of Transitional Justice Success*. Doctoral thesis, University of Oxford.

Rojas, H. (2019). Chile despertó. *Revista Mensaje, 685*, 14–17.

Rojas, H., & Pascual, T. (2019). El tránsito de la justicia transicional. In L. de Vivanco & M. T. Johansson (Eds.), *Pasados Contemporáneos. Acercamientos interdisciplinarios a los Derechos Humanos y las Memorias en Perú y América Latina* (pp. 75–93). Editorial Iberoamericana/Vervuert.

Rojas, H., & Suárez, R. (2019, September 12). *Registros de detenidas/os desaparecidas/os y su incorporación en expedientes judiciales sobre violaciones a los derechos humanos en Chile*. Presentation at "Encuentro Internacional sobre Procesos de Documentación de Desaparición y Desaparición Forzada de Personas. Perspectivas Comparadas: México, Chile y Colombia". Universidad Iberoamericana de México.

Rubio, G. (2013). *Memoria, Política y Pedagogía: Los caminos hacia la enseñanza del pasado reciente en Chile*. Lom ediciones.

Ruderer, S. (2010). La política del pasado en Chile 1990–2006: ¿Un modelo chileno? *Revista Universum, 25*(2), 161–177.

Ruiz-Tagle, J. (1973). Huelga en El Teniente: Un conflicto mal planteado. *Revista Mensaje, 219*, 216–218.

Salazar, M. (2011). *Las letras del horror: La DINA*. Lom ediciones.

Salazar, M. (2012). *Las letras del horror: La CNI*. Lom ediciones.

Sanabria, H. (2007). *The Anthropology of Latin America and the Caribbean*. Pearson Allyn and Bacon.

Sands, D. R. (1982). Chile Under Frei: The Alliance for Progress. *The Fletcher Forum*, 33–60.

Sanhueza, G. (1999). La Crisis Financiera de los Años 80 en Chile: Análisis de sus Soluciones y su Costo. *Economía Chilena, 2*(1), 43–68.

Schlotterbeck, M. (2018). *Beyond the Vanguard: Everyday Revolutionaries in Allende's Chile*. University of California Press.

Sen, A. (1997). Human Rights and Asian Values: What Kee Kuan Yew and Le Peng Don't Understand About Asia. *The New Republic, 217*(2–3), 33–40.

Sepúlveda, A. (2020). *La Unidad Popular. Los mil días de Salvador Allende y la vía chilena al socialismo*. Sudamericana.

Sepúlveda, E. (2020). Inequality's Offspring: Why Chile Woke Up. *The Monitor*, available at https://www.policyalternatives.ca/publications/monitor/inequalitys-offspring.

Sierra, L. (2005). Reabrir y Cicatrizar: Notas sobre el *Informe Valech* y sus Reacciones. *Anuario de Derechos Humanos* (pp. 157–166). Universidad de Chile.

Sikkink, K. (2011). *The Justice Cascade: How Human Rights Prosecutions Are Changing World Politics*. W.W. Norton & Co.

Sikkink, K. (2017). *Evidence for Hope: Making Human Rights Work in the 21st Century*. Princeton University Press.

Silva, P. (1991). Technocrats and Politics in Chile – From the Chicago Boys to the CIEPLAN Monks. *Journal of Latin American Studies, 23*(2), 385–410.

Skaar, E., García-Godos, J., & Collins, C. (Eds.). (2016). *Transitional Justice in Latin America: The Uneven Road from Impunity Towards Accountability*. Routledge.

Skoknic, F. (2013). El rol de Agustín Edwards antes y después del 11 de septiembre de 1973. *CIPER Chile*, available at http://ciperchile.cl/2013/09/10/el-rol-de-agustin-edwards-antes-y-despues-del-11-de-septiembre-de-1973/

Snyder, J., & Vinjamuri, L. (2003). Trials and Errors: Principle and Pragmatism in Strategies of International Justice. *International Security, 28*(3), 5–44.

Solimano, A. (2012). *Chile and the Neoliberal Trap the Post-Pinochet Era*. Cambridge University Press.

Sorensen, K. I. (2011). Chilean Print Media and Human Rights: Mainstream Silence Versus Satirical Subversion. *Peace and Change, 36*(3), 400–426.

Sorensen, K. I. (2015). *Los Medios, La Memoria y los Derechos Humanos en Chile*. RIL Editores.

Spooner, M. H. (2011). *The General's Slow Retreat: Chile After Pinochet*. University of California Press.

SQC. (2012). *Transición en la medida de lo posible: entrevista a Ricardo Lagos*, available at https://www.youtube.com/watch?v=9sME3GcTP94

Squella, A. (2019). *Derechos Humanos*. Editorial UV de la Universidad de Valparaíso.

Stedman, S. (1997). Spoiler Problems in Peace Processes. *International Security, 22*(2), 5–53.

Stern, S. (2006). *Battling for Hearts and Minds: Memory Struggles in Pinochet's Chile, 1973–1988*. Duke University Press.

Stern, S. (2009). *Recordando el Chile de Pinochet: en vísperas de Londres 1998*. Ediciones Universidad Diego Portales.

Stern, S., & Winn, P. (2014). El Tortuoso Camino Chileno a la Memorialización. In P. Winn, S. Stern, F. Lorenz, & A. Marchesi (Eds.), *No hay mañana sin ayer: Batallas por la memoria histórica en el Cono Sur* (pp. 205–326). Lom ediciones.

Subercaseaux, B. (1997). *Chile, ¿un país moderno?* Ediciones B.

Supreme Court of Chile. (1998). *Caso Poblete Córdoba*, Case No. 469-98.

Supreme Court of Chile. (2018). *Caso Lara con Fisco*, Case No. 31.711-2017.

Teitel, R. (2000). *Transitional Justice*. Oxford University Press.

Teitel, R. (2003). Transitional Justice Genealogy. *Harvard Human Rights Journal, 16*, 69–94.

Teitel, R. (2017). Genealogía de la justicia transicional. In R. Jimeno (Ed.), *Justicia Transicional: Historia y Actualidad* (pp. 31–67). Thomson Reuters/ Ed. Aranzadi.

Tironi, E. (2013). *Sin Miedo, Sin Odio, Sin Violencia. Una Historia Personal del No*. Ariel.

Toledo, M. I., Veneros, D., & Magendzo, A. (2009). *Visita a un lugar de memoria: Guía para el trabajo en derechos humanos*. Lom ediciones.

Tricot, T. (2015). *Un Sociólogo en el Frente Patriótico Manuel Rodríguez. Testimonio de un Militante*. Ceibo Ediciones.

Trumper, C. (2016). *Ephemeral Histories: Public Art, Politics, and the Struggle for the Streets in Chile*. University of California Press.

United Nations. (1948). *Universal Declaration of Human Rights*, available at https://www.un.org/en/about-us/universal-declaration-of-human-rights.

United Nations. (2005). *Basic Principles and Guidelines on the Right to a Remedy and Reparation for Victims of Gross Violations of International Human Rights Law and Serious Violations of International Humanitarian Law*, available at https://www.ohchr.org/en/professionalinterest/pages/remedyandreparation.aspx

United Nations. (2010). *Guidance Note of the Secretary General: United Nations Approach to Transitional Justice*, available at https://www.un.org/ruleoflaw/files/TJ_Guidance_Note_March_2010FINAL.pdf

United Nations. (2017). *UN Experts Urge Chile Not to Use Anti-Terrorism Law Against Mapuche Indigenous Peoples*, available at https://www.ohchr.org/en/NewsEvents/Pages/DisplayNews.aspx?NewsID=22209&LangID=E

United Nations. (2021). *What Are Human Rights?* available at https://www.ohchr.org/en/issues/pages/whatarehumanrights.aspx

United Nations Development Programme (UNDP) et al. (2008). *Encuesta Nacional de Auditoría a la Democracia 2008*, available at https://www.estudiospnud.cl/bases-de-datos/encuesta-nacional-de-auditoria-a-la-democracia-2008/

United Nations Development Programme (UNDP) et al. (2010). *Auditoría a la Democracia*, available at https://www.cepchile.cl/cep/site/docs/20160304/20160304095351/enc_Auditoria-a-la-Democracia_2010.pdf

United Nations Security Council. (2004). The Rule of Law and Transitional Justice in Conflict and Post-Conflict Societies. Report of the Secretary-General. UN Doc. S/2004/616.

United States Senate Select Committee to Study Governmental Operations with Respect to Intelligence Activities Report. (1975). *Covert Action in Chile, 1963–1973 (Church Report)*, available at https://fas.org/irp/ops/policy/church-chile.htm

Uprimny, R. (2006). *¿Justicia transicional sin transición?: Verdad, justicia y reparación para Colombia* (p. 1). Centro de Estudios de Derecho, Justicia y Sociedad.

Valdés, H. (1996 [1974]). *Tejas Verdes. Diario de un Campo de Concentración en Chile*. Lom ediciones/Ediciones CESOC.

Valdés, J. G. (1995). *Pinochet's Economists. The Chicago School in Chile*. Cambridge University Press.

Vašák, K. (1977). Human Rights: A Thirty-Year Struggle: The Sustained Efforts to Give Force of Law to the Universal Declaration of Human Rights. *UNESCO Courier, 11*, 29–32.

Waltz, S. (2002). Reclaiming and Rebuilding the History of the Universal Declaration of Human Rights. *Third World Quarterly, 23*(3), 437–448.

Weeks, G. (2014). Los militares y los veinte años de la Concertación. In K. Sehnbruch & P. M. Siavelis (Eds.), *El Balance: Política y políticas de la Concertación 1990–2010* (pp. 107–120). Catalonia.

Weibel, M. (2020, July 15). Balance penal del estallido: Fiscalía investiga a 466 agentes del Estado y gobierno acusa a 3.274 personas de cometer actos violentos. *Ciper Chile*, available at https://ciperchile.cl/2020/07/15/balance-penal-del-estallido-fiscalia-investiga-a-466-agentes-del-estado-y-gobierno-acusa-a-3-274-personas-de-cometer-actos-violentos/?fbclid=IwAR0w8pMGZp3F7AMPtTPdnBli1TPnnj0uQ4sWuE3sQDZ20XPHC3NzAT8sxAI

Westad, O. A. (2018). *La Guerra Fría: Una historia mundial*. Galaxia Gutenberg.

Wilde, A. (1999). Irruptions of Memory: Expressive Politics in Chile's Transition to Democracy. *Journal of Latin American Studies, 31*(2), 473–500.

Winn, P. (2013). *La revolución chilena*. Lom Ediciones.

Woodhouse, D. (2003). The Progress of Pinochet Through the UK Extradition Procedure: An Analysis of the Legal Challenges and Judicial Decisions. In M. Davis (Ed.), *The Pinochet Case: Origins, Progress and Implications* (pp. 87–106). Institute of Latin American Studies.

World Justice Project. (2020). *The World Justice Project Rule of Law Index 2020*, available at http://www.worldjusticeproject.org

Wright, T. C., & Oñate, R. (2007). Chilean Political Exile. *Latin American Perspectives*, 155, *34*(4), 31–47.

Yaikin, B. (2016). Las cifras ocultas del PRAIS: El programa de salud para víctimas de la dictadura con fecha de vencimiento. *El Desconcierto*, available at https://www.eldesconcierto.cl/2016/08/22/las-cifras-ocultas-del-prais-el-programa-de-salud-para-victimas-de-la-dictadura-con-fecha-de-vencimiento/

Yepes, R. U. (2009). Transformative Reparations of Massive Gross Human Rights Violations: Between Corrective and Distributive Justice. *Netherlands Quarterly of Human Rights, 27*(4), 625–647.

Yusuf, H. (2018). Colonialism and the Dilemmas of Transitional Justice in Nigeria. *International Journal on Transitional Justice, 12*, 257–276.

Zalaquett, J. (1990). Confronting Human Rights Violations Committed by Former Governments: Applicable Principles and Political Constraints. *Hamline Law Review, 13*(3), 623–660.

Index[1]

A

Agrarian reform, 31, 34, 34n1, 36, 42, 100, 101, 107

Agrupación de Familiares de Detenidos y Desaparecidos (AFDD), 97

Allende, Salvador, 29, 31–33, 35–39, 100, 114, 115, 125, 144, 163

Alliance for Progress, 33, 35

Amnesty Law, Amnesty Act, 19, 32, 50, 75, 138, 141–145, 148, 149, 151, 179

Aquinas, Thomas of, 3

Archives, 14, 55, 66, 73, 82, 119, 122, 138, 141, 150, 160

Army, armed forces, vi, 21, 23, 29, 31, 38–40, 42–44, 46–52, 49n7, 57, 73–77, 81, 86, 114, 142, 143, 159, 160, 162–167, 175, 180

Authoritarian enclaves, 19, 44, 49, 53, 147, 166

Aylwin, Patricio, 48–50, 49n7, 71, 73, 76, 86, 94, 95, 97, 99, 102, 103, 115, 120, 138, 142, 165, 169

B

Bachelet, Michelle, 48, 54–56, 83, 115, 120, 122, 123, 125, 126, 155

C

Caravan of Death, 68, 147

Cascade of justice, 139

Case of the Burnt (*Caso Quemados*), 46

Catholic Church, 35, 140

Censorship, 46, 47, 66–71, 114, 127, 128, 177

[1] Note: Page numbers followed by 'n' refer to notes.

H. Rojas, M. Shaftoe, *Human Rights and Transitional Justice in Chile*, Memory Politics and Transitional Justice,
https://doi.org/10.1007/978-3-030-81182-2

Central Intelligence Agency (CIA), 33, 37, 38, 114
Chicago Boys, 42, 43
Chile Actual, Anatomia de un Mito, 75, 76
Chilean Road to Socialism, 29, 36, 39, 175
Christian Democratic Party (DC), Christian Democrat, 34–36, 38, 45, 71, 139
Christian Left Party (IC), 40
The Clinic, 127
Collective memory, 17, 55, 71, 111–118, 120, 125, 128, 129, 132, 141
  multiple conflicting collective memories, 113, 126
Committee for the Defense of People's Rights (CODEPU), 94
Communist Party(PC), communist, 35, 40, 67, 143, 149, 164
Concertación, 19, 45–47, 49, 50, 52, 54–56, 102, 115, 121, 125, 142, 143, 163, 165, 166
Conspiracy of consensus, 50, 51
Constitution
  constitutional reform, 7, 23, 32, 36, 47, 49, 49n6, 143, 144, 164
  1980 Constitution, 8, 8n1, 23, 44, 45, 47–49, 53–55, 162, 163, 176, 180, 181
Contreras, Manuel, 41, 75, 142
Conventions, 5–7, 21, 149, 150, 180
Criminal trials, 10, 12–14, 66, 69, 137
Culture of human rights, 23, 156, 159, 161–162, 172, 180

D
Democracy, democratic
  elections, 47, 115
  return to, v, vi, 19, 47, 100, 115, 127, 133, 150, 155, 157
  transition, 12, 33, 44, 47–58, 75, 101, 103, 162, 175, 176, 179, 181
Democratic Alliance (*Alianza Democratica*), 45, 47
Demonstrations, demonstrate, v, 4, 49, 113, 124, 133, 151, 152, 160, 163, 166, 168
De Vitoria, Francisco, 3
Dialogue Roundtable (*Mesa de Dialogo*), 52, 76–77, 86
Dictatorship, v–vii, 1, 7–10, 19, 23, 29, 30, 32, 33, 39–48, 50, 51, 53–57, 66–68, 71, 73–75, 77, 80–82, 85–87, 91, 94, 96–103, 107, 113–116, 119–125, 127–133, 138–141, 143, 144, 148–152, 157, 159–164, 166, 168, 171, 172, 175–181
Division of Social Communication (DINACOS), 67

E
Economic Commission for Latin America and the Caribbean (ECLAC), 31
Economic crisis, 31, 44, 45, 130, 163
Economy, 29–31, 34, 36, 37, 42, 43, 45, 51
Education, vi, 7, 21, 32, 35, 37, 42, 44, 55, 57, 96, 97, 104, 120, 121, 140, 159–163, 172, 177, 179
Elections, 8n1, 29, 33, 35, 36, 38, 45–47, 54, 56, 57, 96, 115, 142, 163, 164, 180
El Mercurio, 38, 49n7, 67, 76, 130, 165
Executions, executed, 14, 41, 48, 71, 73, 86, 93, 96–98, 101, 104, 119, 149
Exile, exiled, 41, 48, 95, 96, 98, 99, 107, 114, 128

F
Families of the victims, 97, 119, 150
Forced disappearances, 15, 96, 97, 124
Frei Montalva, Eduardo, 29, 31–34
Frei Ruiz-Tagle, Eduardo, 48, 51, 115, 120, 143

G
Garces, Joan, 144
Garzon, Baltasar, 78, 83, 144
Grotius, Hugo, 3
Guzman, Jaime, 49, 74, 125, 126, 132, 164, 179
Guzman, Juan, 19, 145, 147

H
Habeas corpus writs (*recursos de amparo*), 40
Hacienda, 30, 31, 36
Human rights
 essentials of, 2–9
 international human rights law, 7, 145
 violations, v–vii, 1, 8–22, 50–53, 58, 65, 69, 71, 72, 74–76, 87, 91, 92, 98, 105, 108, 111, 114, 116–118, 120, 125, 127, 130, 132, 133, 138, 139, 141, 144, 145, 147, 150–152, 157, 158, 160, 161, 166–169, 171, 172, 177–180

I
Impunity, 11, 12, 14, 15, 19–21, 32, 57, 65, 69, 70, 75, 137, 138, 143, 146, 165–167
Indifference, indifferent, 38, 40, 42, 51, 52, 68, 85, 113, 129, 169, 171, 176
Institute of Public Policy on Human Rights (IPPDH), 117
Inter-American Commission of Human Rights, 41
Inter-American Court of Human Rights (IACtHR), 8, 16, 17, 19, 20, 66, 92, 93, 112, 140, 149
International treaties, 5–7, 8n1, 21, 22, 78, 79, 92, 148–150
Ius Naturale, 3

J
Jimenez, Tucapel, 46
Judicial investigation, 19, 53, 138, 142, 151
Judicial reform, 147, 148
Justice
 restorative, 18, 20, 137, 138
 transitional, vi, vii, 1–24, 30, 48, 50, 53, 58, 65, 69, 71, 76, 92, 93, 106, 111, 112, 119, 122, 155, 156, 161, 163, 175–177, 180
Justice to the extent possible, 49n7, 169, 170

L
Lagos, Ricardo, 38, 47, 48, 53, 54, 77, 79, 96, 98, 103, 107, 115, 120, 122
Land owners, 30, 31, 37
Land reform, 30, 34, 95, 100, 107, 178
La Segunda, 67, 130
Las Ultimas Noticias, 67
Locke, John, 3

M
Manuel Rodriguez Patriotic Front (FPMR), 45, 46, 49, 74, 126, 164

Mapuche, 23, 81, 82, 101, 102, 105, 107, 178
Mapu-Lautaro, 45, 164, 165
Marin, Gladys, 143, 146
Marxism, marxist, 35, 41, 44, 114, 164
Media, 39, 44, 46, 66–68, 74, 81, 113, 114, 117, 127–129, 132, 142, 179
Memory, memorialisation, memorialising, 1, 10, 13, 14, 17–18, 21, 23, 52, 55, 58, 65, 75, 76, 83, 92, 106, 108, 111–133, 155, 158, 159, 161, 168, 172, 177–180
  collective memory, 17, 55, 71, 111–118, 120, 125, 126, 128, 129, 132, 141
Military coup, 29, 30, 32, 39, 50, 100, 128, 130, 163
Military junta, 44, 67, 100, 114, 116, 132, 141, 163, 176
Mines, mining, 34–37
Moulian, Tomas, 53, 75, 76, 86
Movement of the Revolutionary Left (MIR), 38n2, 40, 45, 140, 149, 164
Museum of Memory and Human Rights (MMHR), 55, 76, 119, 122, 126, 132, 179

N

National Association of Public Employees (ANEF), 46
National Information Centre, 40
National Institute of Human Rights (INDH), vi, 21, 83, 151, 152, 158, 171
National Intelligence Directorate (DINA), 40, 119, 124, 140, 165, 166, 180
Neoliberalism, neoliberal, v, 6, 23, 31, 39, 42–44, 55, 57, 130, 131, 133, 162, 163, 176, 180, 181
Never Again (*Nunca Mas*), v, vi, 17, 112, 155–172
No Hay Mañana Sin Ayer, 53, 77, 96, 103, 104
Non-repetition, vii, 10, 14, 20–24, 57, 76, 92, 155–172
Nueva Mayoria, 56

O

Operation Condor, 41, 144, 147
Organization for Economic Cooperation and Development (OECD), 56, 57
Orlando Letelier Case, 142

P

Pedagogy, 113, 129–132, 179
Piñera, Sebastian, v, 48, 55–57, 83, 131, 132, 152
Pinochet, Augusto, v, vi, 1, 29, 30, 33, 39–49, 52–54, 57, 68, 69, 73–76, 78, 79, 81–83, 86, 94, 96, 102, 113, 115, 116, 121, 126, 127, 130–132, 138–140, 142–148, 151, 152, 162, 163, 165–167, 176, 177, 179
  detention in London, 53, 83, 94, 151
Plan Z, 40, 67, 68
Police, v, vi, 31, 39, 45, 49, 57, 70, 81, 133, 142, 151, 152, 155, 157, 159–162, 165, 167, 171, 176, 179, 180
Political transition, 1, 10–12, 32, 48, 56, 86, 137
  transitional governments, 137

Program of Reparations and Comprehensive Healthcare for Victims (PRAIS), 95, 96, 98, 99, 103, 106, 107, 178
Promotion of democracy, 9, 167
Protests, protesters, v, vi, 23, 32, 45, 55, 57, 126, 128, 130, 132, 133, 151, 152, 158, 159, 162–164, 167, 168, 175, 176
Pufendorf, Samuel, 3

R

Reconciliation, 9, 11–13, 15, 20, 48, 50, 51, 65, 69, 70, 76, 82, 86, 91, 97, 112, 130, 131, 137, 141
Referendum
  1988 plebiscite, 54, 68, 115, 166
  1988 referendum, 45, 50, 52, 115
  1989 referendum, 7
  No campaign, 45
  2020 referendum, 57
Re-foundation, re-founding, 39, 163
Regime, 1, 2, 4, 9, 12, 16, 29–31, 33, 39–45, 47, 50, 52, 67–69, 73, 80, 86, 100–102, 114, 127, 128, 140, 141, 163
Reparations
  pensions, 95–97, 101, 103, 107
  policy, 5, 16, 76, 84, 92–94, 96, 98, 103–108, 142, 178
Report
  Rettig Report, 71–77, 81, 86, 94, 97, 98, 115, 139, 177, 178
  Valech Report, 79, 82, 83, 86, 104, 123, 177, 178
Restorative justice, 18, 20, 137, 138
Return to democracy, v, vi, 19, 47, 100, 115, 127, 133, 150, 155, 157
Revista
  Análisis, 67, 127
  APSI, 67
  Cauce, 67, 127
  Hoy, 67
  Mensaje, 67
  Solidaridad, 68, 127, 140
Revolution in Liberty, 29, 33–35, 39, 175
Rights
  human rights, v–vii, 1–24, 29–30, 65, 91, 111, 138, 155
  right to memory, 111, 112
Right to justice, 19, 20, 138
Right to the truth, 15, 21, 66

S

Secret police, 39–41, 81, 119, 124, 140, 142, 165, 180
Silva Henríquez, Raúl (Cardinal), 41, 73, 140
Sites of memory, 1, 112, 113, 115–126, 132, 159, 161, 178, 179
Slaughtered case (*Caso Degollados*), 46, 142
Social Aid Foundation of Christian Churches (FASIC), 94, 98
Social construction, socially constructed, 5, 112
Social explosion (*estallido social*), 155, 158, 159, 162
Socialism, socialist, Socialist Party(PS), 29, 33, 36, 37, 40, 45, 67, 80, 139
Social unrest, v, 23, 24, 57, 132, 151, 152, 177, 179
Stark, Sergio Arellano, 68, 149
State-centrism, state-centrist, 31, 37
State of emergency, v, 151
State terrorism, vii, 9, 39, 41, 85, 114, 118, 125, 140, 175
Student protests, 55

T

Torture
  detention centres, 102, 119, 124
  survivors of torture, 5, 16, 66, 72, 78, 83, 84, 86, 93, 96, 104, 105
  UN Convention Against Torture, 77, 92
  victims' testimonies, 41, 78, 80, 83–85
Transitional governments, 44, 75, 76, 137, 162
Transitional justice
  elements, 9–24, 58, 92, 93, 106, 156
  mechanisms, 9, 10, 21, 22
Truth, vii, 5, 8, 10, 12, 14–15, 20–23, 52, 65–87, 91–93, 95, 97, 106, 107, 141, 155, 158, 161, 168, 169, 172, 177–180
Truth commissions
  Rettig Commission, Truth and Reconciliation Commission (TRC), 48, 50, 71–87, 98, 104, 106, 177
  Valech Commission, National Commission on Torture and Political Imprisonment, 77–83, 86, 96, 103, 104, 177

U

Unidad Popular (UP), 35–40, 46, 114, 115, 127, 132
United Nations (UN), 2, 5–7, 9, 12, 56, 69, 70, 92, 102
United Nations Convention Against Torture, 77, 92
United Nations Educational, Scientific and Cultural Organization (UNESCO), 55
Universal Declaration of Human Rights (UDHR), 4–6

V

Veil of silence, 75
Venda Sexy, 80n1, 119, 124–126, 179
Verdugo, Patricia, 68, 78, 86, 127
Vicariate of Solidarity (*Vicaria de Solidaridad*), 41, 67, 79, 94, 98, 127, 128, 140, 141
  Peace Committee (*Comité Pro Paz*), 41
Villa Grimaldi, 115, 119, 122, 123, 126, 132, 147, 178

The manufacturer's authorised representative in the EU is Springer Nature Customer Service Centre GmbH, Europaplatz 3, 69115 Heidelberg, Germany. If you have any concerns regarding our products, please contact ProductSafety@springernature.com

Printed and bound by CPI Group (UK) Ltd, Croydon, CR0 4YY
30/09/2026
02225455-0005